BILINGUAL EDUCATION AND BILINGUALISM 16
Series Editors: Colin Baker and Nancy Hornberger

Multicultural Children in the Early Years

Creative Teaching, Meaningful Learning

Peter Woods, Mari Boyle and Nick Hubbard

MULTILINGUAL MATTERS LTD
Clevedon • Philadelphia • Toronto • Sydney • Johannesburg

Library of Congress Cataloging in Publication Data

Woods, Peter
Multicultural Children in the Early Years: Creative Teaching, Meaningful Learning
Peter Woods, Mari Boyle and Nick Hubbard
Bilingual Education and Bilingualism: 16
Includes bibliographical references and index
I. Boyle, Mari. II. Hubbard, Nick. III. Title. IV. Series
LC3736.G6W66   1999
370.117–dc21   98-33348

British Library Cataloguing in Publication Data

A CIP catalogue record for this book is available from the British Library.

ISBN 1-85359-435-0 (hbk)
ISBN 1-85359-434-2 (pbk)

Multilingual Matters Ltd

UK: Frankfurt Lodge, Clevedon Hall, Victoria Road, Clevedon BS21 7HH.
USA: 325 Chestnut Street, Philadelphia, PA 19106, USA.
Canada: 5201 Dufferin Street, North York, Ontario M3H 5T8, Canada.
Australia: P.O. Box 586, Artamon, NSW, Australia.
South Africa: PO Box 1080, Northcliffe 2115, Johannesburg, South Africa.

Typeset by Bookcraft Ltd, Stroud.
Printed and bound in Great Britain by WBC Book Manufacturers Ltd.

Contents

Acknowledgements

We would like to thank the staff, parents and children of Westside Lower School and Bridge Nursery School for their help and hospitality during our research. We are particularly grateful to Chris, Rosalind, Jenni, Theresa, Kate, Linda and Nadia who were especially generous with their time and co-operation despite their other responsibilities. We would also like to thank Liz Grugeon for her helpful advice on aspects of the Stories chapter and Asha Gulati who carried out translations from Panjabi for the same chapter. For their comments on various drafts of the text we are grateful to Bob Jeffrey, Geoff Troman, Denise Carlyle, Barbara Mayor, Eve Gregory, Geoffrey Walford, Alexander Massey and Andrew Pollard.

Colin Baker and Nancy Hornberger made some useful suggestions at a later stage. We would like to thank Colin also for his kind encouragement throughout the preparation of the book. Aileen Cousins and Jan Giddins have given valuable secretarial aid throughout the project.

We are grateful to the ESRC for funding the research upon which this book is based (project R000235123); and to the Centre for Sociology and Social Research at the Open University for providing further crucial resources during the writing-up period.

Glossary

Attainment Targets (ATs)

These are definable and specified aspects of knowledge, skill and understanding for most subject areas within the National Curriculum which children are expected to achieve. Their numbers have been greatly reduced since the Dearing Report.

Dearing Report (1993)

Sir Ron Dearing was requested in April 1993 to review and 'slim down' the 1988 National Curriculum which had proven unwieldy for teachers and schools to implement effectively. His subsequent recommendations are laid out in the Dearing Report and a revised National Curriculum based on Sir Ron's findings was implemented in September 1995.

Department for Education and Employment (DFEE)

The government department responsible for education policies in England and Wales. Formerly the Department for Education (DFE) and before that the Department of Education and Science (DES), with responsibility for science removed in 1992.

Desirable Outcomes for Children's Learning on entering compulsory education (DLOs)

The DLOs were introduced in 1996 by the School Curriculum and Assessment Authority (SCAA – see below). They were designed as a suggested basis for a pre-statutory curriculum covering six areas of learning: Personal and Social Development; Language and Literacy; Mathematics; Knowledge and Understanding of the World; Physical Development; and Creative Development. It is suggested in the document that children should have attained certain skills in these six areas by the time they leave pre-statutory provision at the age of five. Although the DLOs are not compulsory and remain at the level of recommendations they do form the framework for the Office for Standards in Education (OFSTED) system of inspection of pre-school settings.

Education Reform Act 1988 (ERA)

This was the first major reform of education in England and Wales since 1944. One of the main aspects of the 1988 Act was the introduction of a prescribed National Curriculum.

Her Majesty's Inspectorate (HMI)

Formerly part of the DES, HMI were responsible for inspecting schools and collating information regarding education in England and Wales. The HMI has since been replaced by the 'independent' Office for Standards in Education (OFSTED – see below).

Key Stages (KS)

The National Curriculum programmes of study are organised into four Key Stages and relate to age-groups of pupils:

KS1   5- to 7-year-olds
KS2   7- to 11-year-olds
KS3   11- to 14-year-olds
KS4   14- to 16-year-olds

Local Education Authorities (LEAs)

Local government departments within England and Wales responsible for education services at a local level. Their powers were greatly reduced after the 1988 Education Reform Act and the 1993 Education Act.

Local Management of Schools (LMS)

The ERA removed control of a substantial part of each county school's budget from individual LEAs and placed it directly in the hands of school governing bodies. The latter now have responsibility for school staffing, maintenance of buildings and the purchase of services from LEAs.

National Curriculum (NC)

Introduced in 1988 as part of the ERA, the National Curriculum is the syllabus that children from the ages of 5–16 years in England and Wales should study. It consists of ten foundation subjects (11 in Wales), three of which, English, Mathematics and Science (also Welsh in Wales), are designated 'core' subjects. State-maintained schools are required to teach the ten foundation subjects by law. While religious education is not part of the National Curriculum, it is a statutory requirement.

National Curriculum Council (NCC)

A body established by the ERA in 1988 with responsibility for the National Curriculum in state schools.

Nursery Education

There is a wide range of provision for children between the ages of three and five in England and Wales. This generally includes playgroups, child day-care centres, private nursery schools, LEA-run nursery schools, and nursery units attached to primary schools. Some are run on a voluntary basis, others by qualified teaching staff. There are currently government moves to ensure that all four-year-old children have a place in nurseries or primary schools for the year before they begin official statutory education.

Office for Standards in Education (OFSTED)

An 'independent' body that has responsibility for inspecting state-maintained schools and colleges in England and Wales. OFSTED has the authority to pass or fail a school or college, and more recently has been given the power to assess individual teachers' skills, also with the authority to pass or fail teachers. Additionally OFSTED carries out research and collects information on the standards of education within England and Wales.

Plowden Report

This report (*Children and their Primary Schools*, published by the Central Advisory Council for Education, 1967) resulted from the examination, by a committee chaired by Lady Plowden, of primary education in England and Wales. The report had a powerful influence on subsequent policy and practice in schools due to its emphasis on the importance of child-centred education.

Primary Education

Primary education covers the age-group of 5–11 years and is the beginning of compulsory schooling in England and Wales. Some children do however begin state school at the age of four years in Reception classes or Four-plus units, but they are not required by law to begin study of the National Curriculum until they are five years old. Most children attend primary schools and then transfer at the age of 11 to a secondary school. There are some schools known as lower or first schools, which take children only up to the age of eight or nine years. The children then transfer to middle schools (9–13 years) and finally to upper schools (13–16 years).

Programmes of Study

Detailed statutory content for each of the foundation subjects in the National Curriculum, covering the matters, skills and processes to be taught.

Qualifications and Curriculum Authority

See under SCAA.

School Curriculum and Assessment Authority (SCAA)

Replaced two previously separate government bodies, the National Curriculum Council and the School Examination and Assessment Council, in 1993. SCAA had responsibility for the curriculum and its assessment in schools. It has now been replaced by the Qualifications and Curriculum Authority (QCA).

School Examination and Assessment Council (SEAC)

Established under the 1988 ERA, SEAC had responsibility for the assessment of the National Curriculum in state schools. It has subsequently been replaced, first by the SCAA and now by the QCA.

Section 11 of the Local Government Act 1966

Under Section 11 LEAs can apply for special funding to support the employment of additional staff to work with children from Commonwealth countries who speak a language other than English. The staff are generally known as Section 11 teachers. The funding for Section 11 support has undergone several changes, including cuts which have meant the loss of Section 11 projects in some areas (Gillborn, 1995).

Standard Assessment Tasks (SATs)

Progress through the National Curriculum is assessed through SATs at the end of the first three Key Stages (at 7, 11 and 14 years old) in English and mathematics. Pupils were initially expected to sit tests in science also, but the Dearing Report found this to be too unmanageable for teachers and pupils. Together with teacher summaries of pupils' progress throughout the year, the tests provide an overall judgement of pupils' achievements and progress that is reported to parents.

Introduction

Restructuring

As with many other countries, England and Wales in recent years have seen a radical restructuring of the education system. The Education Reform Act of 1988 introduced a new, prescribed National Curriculum, and a new standardised system of national assessment; set attainment targets in each of its subjects for children to reach at certain ages; appointed special bodies to oversee the implementation and assessment of the curriculum; and required Local Education Authorities (LEAs), school governors and headteachers to ensure that the National Curriculum was taught in all state schools. New management structures increased the powers of the consumers (parents) at the expense of the producers (teachers and teacher trainers); and of the central government and school governors at the expense of the LEAs. In 1992, the Office for Standards in Education (OFSTED) was set up to oversee the inspection of all state schools, initially on a four-yearly cycle. This apparatus was seen as necessary to drive up educational standards that were thought to be too low for modern-day requirements and for national well-being in the world at large. Education, it was felt, had become altogether too cosy in the 1970s and 1980s. The reforms were designed to give it a harder, more competitive edge. The thinking behind these reforms and their immediate effects in schools have been well documented elsewhere (Pollard *et al.*, 1994; Campbell & Neill, 1994a and b; Evans *et al.*, 1994; Woods *et al.*, 1997). For the purposes of this book, three aspects of the reforms are particularly significant.

The first concerns multiculturalism and bilingualism. Implicit in the National Curriculum is the notion of 'entitlement', that is that all children are entitled to be taught certain basic things. However, bilingual learners have received short shrift in the recent legislation. The National Curriculum has little to say about equality of opportunity, and 'effectively marginalises community languages and mother tongues' (Reid, 1992: 18), crowding the timetable with statutory subjects. As currently drafted, therefore, the National Curriculum seems to be of limited relevance to bilingual learners. There is a danger that issues such as equal opportunities will become marginalised. It is feared that this will be exacerbated by the weakening in power and influence of the LEAs, some of which have kept such issues in

1

the forefront of policy (Troyna, 1995). In general, Tomlinson and Craft (1995: 3–4) argue, 'educational policies since 1988 have affected ethnic relations and cultural pluralism in schools in less than positive ways', several initiatives such as 'raising the achievement levels of ethnic minorities' and 'redefining the concept of "being British"' having disappeared. Some argue, therefore, that equality of opportunity needs bringing back on to the agenda. But how do highly aware teachers promote mother-tongue teaching in such circumstances? How can bilingualism be seen and developed as a resource within the context of the National Curriculum? How can the 'entitlement' implicit in the National Curriculum be made a reality for all children?

The second issue is the concomitant attack that came to be made on the child-centred teaching methods that had held sway in nursery and primary education since the Plowden Report of 1967. As long ago as 1975, Sharp and Green (1975: 86) had identified 'powerful and evocative sentiment' in the 'child-centred ideology', and had concluded that 'its implications for curriculum practice are vague, imprecise and therefore problematic'. More recently this conclusion has been endorsed by Alexander (1992), whose research fuelled a highly controversial government paper (Alexander, Rose & Woodhead, 1992). This called for more whole-class teaching, an end to 'dogmas' about 'child-centredness' and acceptance of the subject-based National Curriculum as a *fait accompli*. Its arguments were strongly refuted by early years teachers (David, Curtis & Siraj-Blatchford, 1992), who defended child-centredness with early learners. Where, we wondered, do young bilingual pupils stand in relation to this pedagogical debate?

The third issue concerns the increased pressures on teachers brought on by the reforms. These pressures have lent weight to theories of intensification, de-skilling and deprofessionalisation (Apple, 1986). For teachers, there has been more extensive classroom planning, an increase in administrative and assessment tasks, and in general an increase in prescription and accountability (Campbell & Neill, 1990; Hargreaves, 1994). At the chalkface there is more to do, less time to do it in, less time for re-skilling and for professional interaction, few opportunities for creative work, a diversification of responsibility, and a reduction in quality of service. There are said to be crises of confidence in professional knowledge and in the teacher role. Some fear the loss of work that is most meaningful to them, as well as to children (Lawn & Grace, 1987; Nias, 1989), and that teachers are becoming more like technicians than professionals (Schon, 1983). On the other hand, while most would accept that there certainly has been a measure of intensification, some would dispute whether this inevitably entails de-skilling, and have identified among teachers new-found opportunities in the reforms (Campbell & Neill, 1994b; Evans *et al.*, 1994; Gipps *et al.*, 1995; Osborn, 1995; Cooper & McIntyre, 1996). We were interested, therefore, to see how teachers working among bilingual children were affected by intensification – constraint or opportunity?

Creative Teaching and Learning

With regard to pedagogy, we have found it more useful to think in terms of 'creative' rather than 'child-centred' teaching, since this concept was generated from what primary teachers in English schools actually do. It provides the framework through which we examine the teaching in the schools featuring in this book. We have elaborated and illustrated the concept in a number of studies (Woods, 1990, 1993, 1995; Woods & Jeffrey, 1996). Creative teachers are flexible about how they apply their philosophies and methodologies to the varied and highly complex situations they meet in the classroom. They find inventive 'ways in' to children's learning, and are responsive to opportunities for 'ways in' that arise during teaching (Woods & Jeffrey, 1996: 6). Teachers have ownership of their ideas and practices, not merely fulfilling the requirements of others, and they control the pedagogical processes they practise – they devise, organise, vary, mix whatever teaching methods and strategies they feel will most effectively advance their aims (Jeffrey & Woods, 1997: 15). They are not told how to teach by others.

Most importantly – and especially for the bilingual subjects of this book – creative teaching is applied within a framework of 'relevance' (Jeffrey & Woods, 1997: 16). It is possible to be highly creative, but also highly ineffective. To avoid this, the teacher 'must be culturally attuned to his or her pupils, and to other aspects of the situation, some of which may be beyond the teacher's immediate control' (Woods, 1990: 33–4). Creative teaching thus takes into account situational factors and reflects not only the generally accepted values of the society in which children live, but also their own particular cultures. It is designed to yield 'personal knowledge' (Edwards & Mercer, 1987) and 'child-meaningful learning' distinguished by 'curiosity, originality, initiative, co-operation, perseverance, open-mindedness, self-criticism, responsibility, self-confidence and independence' (Best, 1991: 275). Creative teaching thus promotes creative learning in which similar qualities are observed:

> There is innovation – pupils are changed in some way, often radically ... In this mode, pupils have control over their own learning processes, and ownership of the knowledge produced, which is relevant to their concerns. (Woods, 1995: 2)

It might be argued that creative teaching and learning are of particular significance in early years settings, especially at the present time, and especially with bilingual and bicultural children (see David *et al.*, 1992). It might be thought, too, that there is a great need for this kind of approach generally as changing work patterns and demands call for greater flexibility and adaptational powers among the workforce.

Given the controversy, therefore, clarification on both sides of the debate is urgent. As Alexander (1992: 194) argues, there is a clear need for the application of 'conceptual and empirical tests'. We also need contributions towards 'the development of an archive of case studies of attempts by progressive schools and teachers to sustain their existing priorities in the light of, and despite, the requirements of the Act' (Halpin 1990: 31).

In the research reported in this book, the general aim was to consider creative teaching, and its response ('creative learning'), within a specific context – that of three institutions with a high proportion of bilingual pupils. Combined, these constituted, in methodological terms, a 'critical case', promising a stringent test of some of the previously identified properties of creative teaching and learning, and exploring their bearing on some of the key issues of the day in the areas of bilingualism and multiculturalism. Thus we examine how teachers' approaches are attuned to the child's cultural attitudes towards learning; affective states, such as 'confidence'; skills in 'the art of learning' (Woods, 1993); and existing and potential abilities. We also explore how 'control' and 'ownership' are constituted, and what they actually involve in practice in the teaching of bilingual children. Special attention is paid to 'relevance', since we see this as one of the key properties in multicultural circumstances (see Jeffrey & Woods, 1997).

Specific questions that we address include:

- What kind of access to the National Curriculum is offered to bilingual pupils?

- What principles guide the teaching in the schools, and how do they relate to teachers' practice?

- How do the children experience that practice?

- What factors constrain and/or aid the teachers' practice?

- How do young bilingual children accomplish the transition to institutional life in English society, and how do they adapt to the diverse cultures of their experience?

- What is the relationship between bilingual children's home and school lives?

- What role in their children's education do parents play?

- What are the implications for educational policy and practice?

Bilingualism

We should explain what we mean by 'bilingualism'. Only one child among our samples had very little English, though the rest spoke it with varying proficiency.

The majority of the children spoke languages other than English on a daily basis. For example Imran was born in England and is of Indian origin. He attended the local Sikh temple regularly throughout the week, where he not only learned about his religion and culture, but also how to read and write Panjabi. However, he clearly saw himself as an English speaker. For example, when asked how his mum told him stories, he replied, 'She reads them from a book ... she reads them in my voice [in English]'. At another stage, Imran was sitting reading a dual-text storybook, *Prince Cinders*. Asked if his parents ever told him stories in Panjabi, English or in both, he pointed to the English script in the book and replied 'This', and said that he only spoke English at home. This example highlights how the term 'bilingual' when used to identify children from ethnic minorities can be a misnomer. Not all children from ethnic minority backgrounds are bilingual in that they speak an additional language to, in this instance, English. In fact, what is meant by 'bilingualism' has changed, particularly during this century:

> There has been a movement from viewing biliguality primarily as a linguistic skill to regarding it as a multidimensional phenomenon, from believing it to be a negative hindrance to considering it a positive asset. In parallel, definitions of what is understood by the term 'bilingualism' have changed according to the centre of interest. (Gregory, 1994: 152)

Early studies of the 1920s and 1930s were concerned with linguistic competence, and bilingualism was understood in terms of 'balanced bilingualism'. By the 1950s and 1960s language was viewed more in terms of use than of competence, and a child was considered bilingual 'as soon as he is able to make himself understood within his limited linguistic and social environment' (Rivers, 1969: 35–36). More recent studies have recognised the multidimensional aspects of bilingualism (Halliday, 1975; Skutnabb-Kangas, 1981; Grosjean, 1982; Romaine, 1989); that it cannot be solely attributed to linguistic ability, but that there are psychological, social and cultural issues all linked to identity. If we are to view bilingualism in this way, then Imran might be considered bilingual. In many ways it may however be more appropriate to focus on the social and cultural aspects of many children in Imran's situation. He was most certainly not alone in class in his view of himself in terms of language. Azmat, who strongly identified herself as Iraqi, highlighted similar issues. Asked what schoolwork she practised at home, she replied:

Azmat: [My parents] give me spellings and maths work, and some Arabic work, but I'm not very good at Arabic.

Mari: And would you like to be good at Arabic?

Azmat: Yeah ... I understand people speaking Arabic a bit, but I can't speak Arabic.

Mari: So you want to try and learn more?

Azmat: How to say it.

Certainly for many of the children in this study identity went beyond language ability. In actuality, though many of them spoke Urdu or Panjabi, they often referred to their spoken language as Indian or Pakistani, and talked about themselves in these terms also. Their identity included not only which languages they spoke, but also their country of origin and for many their religious affiliation. Yet as they began school they entered into a very different situation, into another culture, and therefore needed not only to develop proficiency in an additional language, but also to learn to exist in an additional culture. In effect, they became at least developing 'biculturals'. It is in this sense that we employ the term in this book.

Methods

The research took place in three institutions:

- A lower school, which we call Westside Lower School, in a Midlands town.

- The nursery unit of the lower school, which we call Westside Nursery Unit.

- A separate nursery school in the same town, which we call Bridge Nursery School.

At the time of the research the lower school was serving a multi-ethnic community, the main ethnic groups being Pakistani and Indian, with a growing number of families from Bangladesh, and smaller numbers of African-Caribbean, Arab, Italian and white English families. The housing in the area was a mixture of council- and privately-owned homes. The school catered for around 190 pupils aged between three and nine years of age, up to 90% of them from families who originated from the Punjab area of India and Pakistan. There were six full-time class-based teachers, two full-time Section 11 (see Glossary) teachers and one full-time bilingual non-teaching assistant (NTA) in the lower school. The headteacher, Chris, also taught half time in the Reception/Year 1 class. She came to the school in 1990 and this was her first headship. All but two teachers were staff at the school prior to her appointment.

The school itself was relatively modern. The classrooms were spacious and each had its own sink and art area. The school also had a library and a well-equipped technology room. There was an outdoor swimming pool for use during the summer. There was a large playground and playing field, and a wild garden area that the children used for nature studies.

Bridge was a Group 1 nursery school serving a mixed ethnic area with a high proportion of families of Asian origin, mainly from the Indian subcontinent. The area consisted of private housing, mostly owner-occupied. The school was housed in a single-storey Victorian building. The rooms were called Blue Room and Green Room. The children were divided into a registration group for each coloured room but were free to wander from one to another during the session. Attached to Green Room were the kitchen and the staffroom, used also by the mothers' and toddlers' group. The school had a large outdoor area consisting of a grassed section and a concreted area. There was extensive fixed equipment, such as climbing frames and a large sandpit, and moveable apparatus, such as construction blocks and frames as well as trolleys and scooters. There were also flower-borders where the children were encouraged to grow plants with the help of members of staff. At the rear of the outside garden was a large enclosed pond and wildlife area.

The school admitted 80 full-time equivalent children. The largest admission group occurred from September, a high percentage of them three-year-olds. As at December 1996 there were 44 morning, 45 afternoon and 23 full-time children, who remained at the school until the term after they reached the age of five. Since Bridge was a local authority nursery school in its own right it did not have a specific catchment area and was able to feed into a number of local lower schools. At the time of the research the proportion of ethnic minority children, including those with English as an additional language, was approximately 50%. The school's staffing consisted of the headteacher, the deputy headteacher, two further teachers, three nursery nurses and a Section 11 assistant who was a Panjabi speaker. Most of our observations of children and teachers took place in Green Room, in which staffing consisted of the deputy headteacher (Kate), another teacher (Pamela) and a nursery nurse. The Section 11 assistant (Sonia) also worked in the room during sessions each week.

Westside Nursery Unit was housed in a separate modern building next to the main school. The unit consisted of two large classrooms, one of which led into a walled outdoor area. There was an additional small room which was used for a library and had a cassette machine for stories. There was also a kitchen in which children carried out cooking activities with adults and an office that could be used by a group of children and an adult at story-time. The outdoor area was part grassed and part slabbed. Equipment consisted of two large climbing frames, a moveable sand tray and small equipment such as tricycles and scooters.

At December 1996 there were 22 morning, 22 afternoon and 18 full-time children in attendance. New children were admitted at the beginning of the term following their third birthday. As a department of the lower school the unit acted as the main feeder to the school's Reception class, to which children progressed the term after they had reached the age of five. The proportion of ethnic minority children was approximately 90%. Staffing in the unit consisted of a co-ordinating teacher (Jenni), two nursery nurses (Anne and Linda) and a bilingual part-time Section 11 nursery nurse (Nadia) who worked in the unit each afternoon. Throughout the text, we refer to staff collectively at the nurseries as 'teachers'.

Research in the schools took two years (October, 1994 to December, 1996). Peter was the director of the research. Mari studied a group of 18 children and their two teachers in Reception/Year 1 through to Year 2 classes at the lower school. Nick studied 12 children and their parents at the Westside Nursery Unit and at Bridge Nursery School. The parents interviewed at Westside Nursery Unit consisted of seven families, all of whom were Muslims, two originally from Bangladesh and five originally from Pakistan. The remaining five families, interviewed at Bridge Nursery School, consisted of one Muslim family whose country of origin was Pakistan and four Hindu families whose country of origin was India.

Qualitative research was employed, entailing long-term participant observation in the schools. Methods of data collection included unstructured and semi-structured interviews with parents and teachers, including nursery nurses and instructors, and conversations with children; observations, both participant and non-participant, of teachers and children at work; and examination of documentary evidence such as written policy, diaries, and children's work (see Woods, 1986, 1996a). Interviews and conversations were tape-recorded and transcribed. Special approaches were developed to facilitate relating to the young bilingual children (see Boyle, 1999). How one knows what, when and how children have learned is an abiding problem in education. It is a crucial issue in the National Curriculum, and in the pedagogical debate discussed earlier. As Nias (1989: 205) says, 'teachers rely in the last resort for recognition upon their pupils, for no one else knows, or can know, how effectively they have taught' (see also Guba & Lincoln, 1981). We sought, therefore, to develop new ways of assessing pupils based on their own perspectives and constructions of meaning. In this sense, pupils also acted as collaborators. This is even more important with bilingual children, for even where teachers are adopting a declared multicultural policy, their view of reality can still be rooted in their own culture and their own perspectives (Moore, 1993). As well as more usual methods of observing pupil reactions and monitoring the documents they produce, we experimented with discussing with pupils; inviting pupils to discuss among themselves, recording their conversations; conversing with them in different situations, including their homes, with the agreement of their parents. In line with the learning theory, the evaluation embraced more than simply cognitive matters, including affective, aesthetic, and moral development.

Opportunities also arose to explore methods of researching which highlighted previously unexplored areas of study. The use of largely unstructured interviews with parents enabled them to express ideas about themselves and their children, which revealed particularly significant issues of culture, language and familial responsibility as well as tensions in relation to the schools. The conversations with children in school provided a voice for those children and led to the emergence of important issues concerning how bilingual learners view themselves culturally and linguistically, both as children and as pupils.

A feature of the methods was the participation of the researchers in the work of the schools in such a way as to be supportive of the teachers, as well as to advance their own research insights. For example, both researchers were invited to attend the lower school's OFSTED inspection. This not only led to practical support for teachers in the classrooms being researched during the inspection itself, but also enabled an in-depth study to be made of the effects of an inspection on the work and life of the school (see Woods *et al.*, 1997, Chapter 4). Nick also took part in the initial home visits to parents whose children would be entering the nursery for the first time. Again, this provided a practical support for the work of the teachers as well as enabling the researcher to study at first hand the home visiting policy of the unit. Both researchers also took an active part in the work of the classrooms including working with groups of children on a regular basis, for example, reading and telling stories. In this way, participant observation became collaborative teaching and research (Carr & Kemmis, 1986; Woods & Pollard, 1988; Day, 1991; Biott & Nias, 1992).

Westside would be regarded as a 'good' school by many people. Indeed it was identified as such by the full school inspection that took place during the research. However, we found the situation rather more complex. In many ways, the school followed policies and practices which most would applaud. In some areas, however, their young bilingual students were less well served. We aim to bring these out, and to delineate the extent and character of constraint and opportunity for both teachers and children.

Summary and Organisation of the Book

We give below a brief summary of each of the chapters, which, taken together, provides an overview of the whole book. At the end of each chapter in the text, we make some practical suggestions for teachers to consider.

Chapter 1: Teacher perspectives

The first three chapters focus on the teachers' approaches and practices. We begin by considering teachers' beliefs, values and philosophies. Their approach to teaching was characterised by child-centredness, holism, and a strong emphasis on care, within a context of pragmatism. We examine also their views on multiculturalism and bilingualism. While these were written into policy documents, there were nonetheless several areas of the curriculum and of the school's activities which seemed relevant, to which they could have been extended. Teachers tended to prioritise the children's social, as opposed to their cultural, development. Mother-tongue use and development was approved of and tolerated, but not really promoted. We also discuss how teachers' views were reflected in the materials they used to resource their teaching, and how they arranged and decorated their class-rooms. We conclude that the environment at all of our institutions in essence reflected a teachers' rather than a children's culture. It has to be recognised, however, that teachers' work has intensified in recent years, and we end the chapter by looking at how they feel they are coping with the potential constraints involved.

Chapter 2: Teaching the National Curriculum

The National Curriculum has not been particularly kind to bilingual learners. The original document was anglocentric, but even so, a number of multicultural statements have been removed from it as it has been subsequently revised. English is also emphasised as the language of instruction and learning, and this is all endorsed by the assessment system which teachers have to employ. Furthermore, these structures and expectations are increasingly being reflected at earlier stages of the pupil's career – as, to one degree or another, at our nurseries. But the National Curriculum is not all constraint. In Chapter 2 we look at various areas of the curriculum that have key significance for bilingual children. By examining some actual examples of teaching, we show that it is a mixture of limitations and opportunities, and that there is scope for teachers to work creatively rather than simply following prescribed patterns.

Chapter 3: The relevance of creative teaching

We develop the theme of opportunity further in the next two chapters. In previous research on creative teaching, we have identified the critical factors of ownership of knowledge, control of pedagogical processes, innovation of material and activity, and relevance of values and context. The latter, we suggest, is especially significant in the teaching of bilingual children, especially when the first three are under pressure as a result of recent educational developments in England and Wales. In Chapter 3 we explore the theme of relevance and its educational significance, noting how it is manifested in the encouragement of children's free play; in activities that start from the child; in the development of home–school links; in the practice of revisiting topics and skills; in the teaching that occurs 'in the margins' of programmed activity; and through spontaneous reaction to children's interests.

Chapter 4: The educational significance of stories

The educational benefits of stories among young children are well known. They have even more significance among bilingual children, as we show in Chapter 4. These children use 'personal storying' to create meaning to form bridges between home and school, child and adult, imagination and reality, and thus create holistic, personal knowledge. Stories also provide an excellent means of promoting creative teaching and learning. We illustrate this through an extended analysis of a project based on a story, which involved language and conceptual development, social, emotional and cultural understanding, and the promotion of literacy skills. We consider the opportunities for stories and storying provided for the children, and their cultural relevance, finding that, both at school and at home, these ministered very strongly to the dominant English culture.

Chapter 5: Bilingual children in transition

In the next three chapters we turn to the children's experiences and perspectives. In Chapter 5 we consider the experience of bilingual children on starting at the nurseries, and on transferring from nursery to school. Such transitions have been shown to be key moments in a pupil's career, establishing modes of behaviour, attitudes to learning and social frameworks and relationships for years ahead. They are even more significant for bilingual children. We argue that such children are inducted not only into a general pupil role, as are many pupils, but into one based on an anglicised model which fails to take their own background cultures fully into account. The new identity becomes designated in the ritual of registration, based on English custom, which checks presence, marks pupilhood, reminds continually and establishes formality. A different status is attached to play (a child's activity) and to work (a pupil's activity), a distinction which inhibits bilingual children in particular. The children in our survey quickly learned the rules attached to dressing and undressing, but pride in mastering the new pupil skills was mixed with shame emanating from their own cultural experiences. Older children from the same ethnic groups were used to acquaint the new recruits with school rules involving movement and behaviour. The school did incorporate many of the cultural differences of the children into everyday aspects, but all within a basically anglicised framework. This was particularly the case with regard to language, where teachers permitted children to converse in their mother tongue in class, but did not actively promote it, nor otherwise use the children's bilingualism to their mutual advantage. Many different cultural strands make up these children's identities. We argue that the latter will be the stronger and the richer where the former is given equivalent status and recognition.

Chapter 6: The children's perspective

In this chapter we consider how our bilingual children found ways, at times, of making their learning relevant to their prior knowledge, and in certain instances were able to gain control over their learning, so coming to 'own' the knowledge and skills they acquired. Their learning, on occasions, was also innovative, leading to new and alternative ways of establishing their knowledge, and new directions for their enquiries that were unforeseen at the outset. For this 'creative learning' to occur, the children need 'opportunities', and we consider the provision that ministered to this form of learning. Where knowledge taught was relevant to the children, the potential for personal ownership and control of that learning was increased. However, such knowledge had to be understood – it could be relevant, but abstruse, especially if unconnected with the children's prior knowledge. Free play provided the best opportunities for creative learning. In the lower school because of the more formal demands made on teachers by the National Curriculum, there were limitations imposed by the need for 'getting done'. Nevertheless opportunities did arise for children to pursue their own interests, and it was significant that their control over their learning increased on these occasions.

Chapter 7: The children's identities

We broaden the focus here to look at the whole of the children's social worlds, and how identities are produced from the various forms of relationships developed. Identity formation is a complex business, and is an ongoing process, subject to shifts and changes and consisting of many strands, sometimes contradictory. At school, we saw how ability at schoolwork was a key defining feature. Age was another, encouraged here by the differentiation required by the National Curriculum. Gender was also a significant divider, the children resolutely rejecting teachers' attempts to mix girls and boys together, but also in part promoted by other aspects of teachers' organisation and approach. In general, teachers reinforced children's identities in these respects. Ethnic and religious identities were, however, not strengthened at school in the same way, the anglicised model predominating. These identities were reinforced more through home and the local community. We go on to consider the interplay between identity and peer relationships, and to investigate the nature and meaning of friendship among our bilingual children. While such factors were important for the children's cultural identities, these were mainly supported outside school in community activities, as at the mosque or temple, and by parents, as we describe in Chapter 8.

Chapter 8: The parents' perspective

Parents also underwent transitions when their children began and changed school. They developed as educators, forging new identities for themselves. But they also suffered some loss of influence and status. Parents articulated the tensions they felt over their children's increasing use of English and conformity to English cultural norms, and their diminishing use of their own languages and culture. They recognised the market value of English, but were strongly supportive of their own community languages and cultural identities. The school's emphasis on the former created a cultural divide between home and school. Teachers' relationships with the parents, though caring, fell short of embracing them in partnership, an arrangement accepted by parents, who felt that school was the province of the teachers, and that on the whole the teachers were promoting multiculturalism reasonably well. We suggest that one way to tackle the problems revealed in this chapter – and elsewhere in the book – is to develop the school as a 'learning community'.

Chapter 1

Teachers' Perspectives

We begin with the teachers' approaches and philosophies, and how they resourced their teaching. In Chapters 2–4 we shall consider how they put their ideas into practice. David *et al.* (1992) claim that most early years' teachers are child-centred in their approach and that they support active, as opposed to transmissional learning. They are pragmatic, as opposed to dogmatic; and are persuaded by 'fitness for purpose' considerations with regard to teaching method (Mortimore, 1992). Our teachers would certainly subscribe to this in broad terms. Whilst all our teachers placed the child at the centre of the educational process, their own role in this process was expressed at times in a very specific way, and at others more generally. We have identified three main elements of our teachers' approach – holism, child-centredness, and care. We illustrate each of these from among our teachers, then go on to consider their views on multiculturalism and bilingualism, and how they resourced their teaching within a cultural context. We conclude with a note on how our teachers see themselves coping with intensification.

Teaching Approach

Holism

The teachers believed that knowledge was integral and related in all its parts. They also saw education as more than simply teaching children the content of the National Curriculum or satisfying the suggestions contained in the Desirable Outcomes for Children's Learning (DLOs). They saw it as concerned with 'person-making' (Brehony, 1992). For example, at Westside Jenni believed that children were 'lamps to be lit, not vessels to be filled'. The idea of empowering the whole child was also emphasised at Bridge, whose policy document stated:

> The aim of the school is to provide a broad, balanced and relevant curriculum which allows for and meets children's individual needs, giving them access to learning and ultimately working towards children taking control of their own learning, because they are articulate, literate, numerate and motivated.

The policy in the nursery at Westside stressed the importance of encouraging the children to reach their 'full potential' by making the 'fullest use of the opportunities, experiences and responsibilities that our curriculum offers'.

Both the nurseries and the lower school sought to integrate much of their curriculum around topics, despite having policy documents that divided the curriculum into separate subject areas to reflect the organisation of the National Curriculum. Woods and Jeffrey (1996: 122) comment that dividing the curriculum into specific subject areas 'constructs distinct boundaries around subjects and insulates them both from each other, and from the teacher, reducing the power of the teacher over what they transmit'. By making the choice to organise the actual implementation of the curriculum through topic work the teachers are asserting their ownership of the curriculum and re-establishing a sense of power. In discussing her work in a previous school prior to the introduction of the National Curriculum Chris indicated how this approach worked:

> They were children who needed lots of activities to develop concentration. There were all sorts of things, phones, and clocks, and old radios. We were looking at electricity and circuits, so they took it all apart, and put it back together again and actually got the radio working. They were very skilled ... so we channelled the curriculum through that kind of thing.

The tendency at the lower school was to identify a major overall theme, for instance 'movement', and then to identify aspects of the National Curriculum which would apply to this topic. Examples would be science work exploring forces, geography focused on map-making and direction, and technology centred on making things that move. Yet it was clear that there were limits to developing a complete cross-curricular approach because of the requirements in the National Curriculum by which teachers are obliged to cover certain content (see Chapter 2). Subsequently, within the topic of 'movement' cited above, a mini-topic in history was also covered relating to the Romans (History Attainment Target 1, pre-Dearing, *story, myths and legends*).

A philosophy of holism was also applied to the way the teachers viewed the purpose of education, as Chris illustrated: 'I do still very much believe in child-centred education and that you educate for a whole person and that you educate through all kinds of activities.' She believed that the education system should be led by the needs and the rights of the child:

> I'm a great believer in children having the right to achieve, having the right to learn, and the right to focused, quality teaching. Lots of the way we're working now is very much setting targets for achievement, but targets about the children not targets just plucked out for somebody else. They're not machines, and it's all got to be meaningful and relevant and useful and make sense to them ... Learning is for life.

Chris's belief that education has an impact on 'person-making' extended to her own children who had all become high achievers:

They are very nice, caring, kind, supportive people, which has always mattered more than their sense of achievement through school. It has been something that makes me feel that life will be reasonably kind to them because they know how to take pleasure in how they spend their time.

One way in which Chris believed that children could develop their learning beyond the confines of the National Curriculum was through the relationships that teachers create with their pupils:

I'm interested in [the children's] reaction to what I say, I'm interested in their reaction to what other children say, because that is all part of the learning development. You don't have to like what they say, but you need to be able to gain their understanding, their views about things, how far they enjoy it, what they can achieve, that they can do that, that learning is about all sorts of things, not just topic work, but it is also about them as people.

Developing positive views of self amongst their pupils was an integral part of all our teachers' philosophies. Chris said:

The way that they know how to learn in school, they know they *need* to learn, and in order to get the best results they have to try, they have to be aware of what education can give them. It's again involved with this whole process of what makes a good relationship with anybody, or with anything ... but their attitude to learning, their attitude to themselves, their attitude to really learning, that there are challenges, and how they approach things, how they take on new things.

This aspect of person-making and belief in the rights and needs of the child is closely linked to a philosophy of child-centredness and care.

Child-centredness

The Early Years Curriculum Group (1989: 2) suggests that young children should be provided with 'a broad and stimulating environment which reflects the cultural backgrounds and interests of the children'.

Each child starts school with a unique set of experiences gained at home and in his or her community. A learning environment should respond to each child's need for something familiar, something new and challenging, and something which enables him or her to pursue a current interest. An environment and daily programme which offers maximum choice to individual children in terms of access to equipment and space, use of time, and opportunities for collaboration with others is most appropriate.

This approach embodies Rosalind's view that 'the nursery exists for the benefit of the children it serves and without the children we wouldn't be there'. She described her own pedagogy as 'implicit subtle teaching', whereby the educator rather than acting as a direct imparter of knowledge becomes a facilitator, sensitive to the children's particular interests:

> I see that the essence of nursery teaching is the essence of good teaching: getting the children involved, not teaching too directly in an isolated way but binding it up in lots of other contexts and being meaningful. If you structure the nursery too much, the children don't bring their own interests so you can't develop the real, important learning experiences.

Jenni echoed this idea when she justified the approach taken in the nursery at Westside:

> I think it's probably more spontaneous than teaching is in a lower school. Do you remember when we had the Irish dancers and the little girls came back and put the record in? That's what I like about it because we can do that, you can just follow on, it's spontaneous. You can say, 'Well let's do it', or, 'Let's go and paint because the paint's out already' and you haven't got to set it all up and plan it.

Learning is considered best achieved through active rather than passive involvement of the child in the learning process. Children become the agents of their own learning, and are given the opportunity to make discoveries for themselves (Edwards & Mercer, 1987). Thus within the nurseries there were two main approaches to learning. 'Unstructured play activities' allowed the children to select activities and explore for themselves, and provided them with pre-school skills. For example, painting and drawing were an introduction to writing; tracing and puzzles became aids to fine motor control; and sand, water, the outside area and construction activities formed an introduction to science.

These were not entirely self-operated activities (Bruner, 1980), as Jenni explains:

> Children aren't naturally going to know how to investigate things on their own ... We were exploring bubbles this morning in science and [Anne and Linda] said, 'What about bubble follow-up activities?' and we said, 'Well, bubble painting'. Now children wouldn't think of doing that on their own, they wouldn't say, 'Well let's put some paint in bottles and put paper on the bottom and blow bubbles on them'. We actually have to show them.

Whilst teachers in the lower school felt more constrained by the National Curriculum than those in the nurseries (see Chapter 2), they too sought ways of involving children in their own learning and reacting to the children, as Chris indicated:

> Every aspect of the curriculum is covered, but there are lots of ways you can take things on, and most of the time it does work, but you must take the time to react to the needs of the children. You must remember these are people you're

dealing with. They are not going to sit there quietly waiting for an input. It is there, and we do follow it, but we also take on the interests of the children.

As we shall see in later chapters, Chris often abandoned planned lessons in responding to the children's interests.

Theresa sought to utilise children's individual skills and interests in different areas of the curriculum through the use of 'fluid grouping', whereby she would group children in different ways in order to develop a sense of whole-class feeling, but additionally to encourage the children to learn from each other:

> I don't like to keep children all in the same group because I like them to be a class so that they do have opportunities with other children. I don't like having ability groups because I think children have different things to offer. Some of the children aren't perhaps very able, like Sadyia, who actually can be very good at the artwork or practical work and she's often got quite a lot to offer. I like to give them opportunities to work with other children and make new friends and to use their skills, whatever they are, with a different group.

Theresa recognised the importance of social learning to the child in the lower school:

> Number one is them being happy in the class and their social skills and their self-confidence, that they can do things, and that they've got points of view. I do like them to settle down and feel that they can say things and express their views and their feelings. It doesn't always work out in practice – things are so busy that you just have to decide, but that's the theory. And particularly with difficult children, I do try and spend more time on listening to them, find out why they're not happy ... because invariably the ones that aren't getting on are children that are having social problems. Once they're in friendship groups with the other children, they learn just as much really from the other children as they do from you.

Teachers were pragmatic, rather than dogmatic, in their approach. Jenni, for example, rejected more traditional styles of teaching partly because 'I have never found anybody who could explain it to me ... I couldn't see the reason behind it ... I couldn't make it work for me.' However, she did believe in a more directly interventionist role for the teacher in certain circumstances (Bruner, 1986) because this did 'work'. This was outlined in policy documents as including 'carefully planned activities providing for conceptual development and mathematical language' in Mathematics Experience, structured as well as unstructured activities in Music, and working freely or 'with direction' in Creative Arts and Physical Education.

Jenni stressed the value of 'what worked'. She saw her job as 'exploring and developing personality and understanding and creativity and imagination rather than cramming them full of facts', but there was no one route to achieving this:

> You use things you've learned because I've never felt that one idea was always right … what works for one child won't work for another … It's changed a lot since I've been here, we've brought things in and said, 'No, that doesn't work and we'll try this', and it's been a flexible, 'what does everyone think?' process really. You've got to work with something that works with you, haven't you?

This echoes Alexander's (1997: 270) 'fitness-for-purpose' concept:

> The stance is pluralist: there are many versions of good practice, not just one or a few, and these are defined not away from the classroom but within it, since they arise directly from the decisions of teachers as they seek to match professional practice with educational purpose, and from the unique contexts and dynamics which have influenced these decisions.

Thus, whilst the initial focus of a lesson might be determined by the National Curriculum and a teacher-directed framework, teachers do see opportunities within sessions for children to support each other, and to take some control of their own learning. They use a number of methods to help achieve this. However, despite their concerns for children as people, and with their interests, none of the teachers referred specifically to how their views related to teaching children of ethnic minorities. Their beliefs seem culture-free in the sense that the child of 'child-centred' education is a 'universal child', and that regardless of colour, creed or class all children have certain needs and rights.

Care

Care is often considered a central aspect of primary teaching (Acker, 1995; Hargreaves & Tucker, 1991). As the majority of early years teachers are women, it has also been suggested that the teaching of young children is merely an extension of such teachers' natural 'mothering' instinct, the development of the 'mother made conscious' (Steedman, 1988). We have documented elsewhere Chris's strongly caring nature (see Boyle & Woods, 1996; Woods *et al.*, 1997), and indicated how, as for Nias's (1989: 41) teachers, 'caring was not a soft option': 'it's very, very important but it isn't enough, we actually are responsible for developing children's lives.' Neither was their caring limited to social aspects of the children's lives, but extended to issues such as health: 'They have a right to a sound, good, education but that is wider than literacy and numeracy … They also have the right to the wider side of education, the medical side, physiotherapists, and all agencies that are around.'

Theresa also indicated how important it was to understand individual children's circumstances both inside and outside school, and the direct relationship that has on their learning. She had built up extensive pictures of individual children that included both their academic progress and relevant information about their home lives:

> Riad was learning almost nothing when he first came in, and really up until the OFSTED he was learning very little because he was so wrapped up in all his problems that there was no room for anything else. With him it's not so much what he's got down on paper, it's his response ... his whole behaviour ... He's not been particularly good this week. He wasn't very well over the weekend – they went away for the weekend and his dad didn't give him his medicine, so he had a wheezy attack – and he can't sleep and it makes him a bit tense.

Caring in this way is not merely a matter of 'motherly concern', but has a practical value. It enables the teacher to understand the individual child, providing them with knowledge that can help them to develop ways of helping children who are perhaps experiencing difficulties or causing problems in the classroom. However, while the teachers' caring attitude resulted in many benefits for pupils, it was in essence constructed on a deficit model of the children's backgrounds. Both Theresa and Chris, for example, talked about the social problems that many of the children had in their lives, and Chris believed that the school itself was able to offer 'the children a great deal of things that they may not get elsewhere'. Theresa was concerned that many of the children were living in a certain amount of deprivation and had unsettled family lives that would impact on their school experiences. However, teachers' anxiety to compensate for what they saw as deficiencies in the children's backgrounds seemed to leave out of account the strengths and advantages that lay in those backgrounds, and ran the danger of marginalising cultural and linguistic relevance.

Multiculturalism

Said (1994) notes that in our modern world no one is of one particular culture; that, though we might label groups on the basis of a country of origin, religious views or colour, these are merely starting points. The children of our research reflected this multicultural development. We could label them in general terms as being of South Asian origin, whilst at the same time the majority were British Asians, having been born in Britain. They could be identified more particularly by their country of origin, Pakistani, Indian, Bangaldeshi, or by their religious beliefs, Muslim (Pakistani and Bangaldeshi children), Sikh (Panjabi Indian), Hindu (Indian). Culture is not an inert state. Whilst there may be traditions which have been part of a particular culture for hundreds or even thousands of years, there are constantly new practices which become absorbed into that culture. Siraj-Blatchford (1994: 28–29) points out:

> Culture, like language, is dynamic and ever changing. Our parents pass on their culture to their children but they do it through vehicles such as language, play,

art and literature. Schools and other educational institutions extend our learning in this way through the humanities, science, the arts etc. Our culture also determines what clothes we wear, our diet, religious beliefs and relationships. Culture is much more than this, but the important point is that it is learned and that it is all around us.

Bridge Nursery School's multicultural policy recognised that 'we live in a multi-ethnic society and that opportunities should be equal for all children regardless of their race and culture'. There was also a recognition of the 'value of religious and other festivals', in order to 'give all our children the opportunity to experience and appreciate the richness and diversity of cultures other than their own'. The nursery needed to make all areas reflect 'the multicultural society in which we live', and suggested that books, tapes and other equipment should relate to 'those different cultures'. Similarly Westside Nursery Unit encouraged their children to 'be aware of, and have pride in their rich cultural heritage'. 'We learn of and discuss this heritage through festivals and family celebrations. Whenever possible we encourage an awareness of the immediate community between home and school.' Linda, one of the nursery nurses in the unit, felt that 'If you have just traditionally English things it's like everything else, it makes you very narrow-minded. It's nice to have bits from everything, all different cultures. I think they should have lots of things like that in strictly English schools.'

The potential existed for the development of these ideas in other policy documents. For example, mention of the need for cultural diversity was not included in policies dealing with National Curriculum subjects such as Mathematical Experience, Science, Information and Design Technology, Music and Creative Arts. Generally in all units, the practice, too, as we shall see in later chapters, fell somewhat short of the policy. The lower school's multicultural policy acknowledged some of the problems inherent within the curriculum:

> The ethos of the school is what gives it its character. Concerned with it are the attitudes, norms and values and beliefs transmitted through the 'hidden' or 'overt' curriculum. Central to this is the promotion of a positive attitude to our multicultural and multi-ethnic society. This includes creating an atmosphere in which the children and parents can discuss problems and concerns in an atmosphere of trust.

In seeking to counter any possible tensions that might occur within the school, there was an additional antiracist policy that was developed separately 'to enhance its importance'. In this, there was recognition that racism can occur via the curriculum and that teachers and pupils should be provided with opportunities to 'recognise and respond to biased opinion'. One of the main strategies for combating racism was 'to find ways to enhance tolerance and respect of other cultures rather than drawing attention to differences', reflecting the strong ethos of 'care' discussed earlier. As we shall see in Chapter 8, parents of children in the lower school were very encouraging in their views of the school's approach to multiculturalism and their combating of racism. Yet Chris recognised that the school still faced difficulties, particularly in trying to place multiculturalism at the centre of the curriculum:

> I think we try very hard to the level of resources that we use and certainly in terms of geography, yes that's fine, stories and literature ... but it's very hard and we've got a curriculum that is very prescriptive. The science is very hard, the history really is very difficult to get through without making comparisons and without making children feel their culture is [inferior] ... the R.E. is fine, the art we do, I mean those things that are really practical. So perhaps it's not as bad, but you're so aware of trying to move on, and you're so aware of looking at what you're not hitting, you sometimes do forget.

Chris's comments indicate some of the pressures that face teachers in trying to develop a multicultural curriculum through a prescriptive National Curriculum (see Chapter 2), where target setting and levels of achievement can prevail over other aims of education as described earlier by our teachers.

Bilingualism

Siraj-Blatchford (1994: 46), comments: 'In British education and care systems, being bilingual is still too often perceived as an aberration, or worse, as something children should grow out of'. Yet research has shown that supporting a child's first language aids both educational development and second language learning (Cummins, 1984; Pinsent, 1992). The written policies at both nurseries and the lower school acknowledge this view. Bridge, for example, recognised:

> ... that the use of community languages in school enriches the experience of all children. Children acquiring the main language of the school as a second language and children whose first language it is, broaden their experience and advance their learning by hearing other languages.

Rosalind echoed this:

> It's very important that we do value the home language, the Bengali language and the Panjabi language as much as any other languages. That would be encouraged in school because my understanding of language development is that the more skilled in your mother tongue, the more skilled you'd be in other languages. It means that our British children are hearing a rich variety of languages that can only add to their knowledge of language.

At Westside Nursery Unit there was a general description in the written policy of the importance of language acquisition. The role of the adult was viewed as providing 'opportunities for the children to listen and communicate ideas and use their linguistic skills to socialise with peers and adults'. The importance of the encouragement of community languages was described in a specific section on Mother Tongue. The policy emphasised that the 'children's own language' be respected and that the children should be encouraged to develop linguistic skills in their mother tongue. Examples of how this was to be achieved were not given, but it was emphasised that adults should try to learn words and phrases which would help them to 'communicate effectively with the children and their families', and that the children's abilities to translate be used to 'encourage the skill of bilingual translation'. Jenni, the co-ordinator of the unit, similarly believed in the benefits of children being fluent in their mother tongue:

> I've always thought that if you're fluent in one language, you're more quickly fluent in this language and if you're having problems with one, you'll have problems with the other. So really you shouldn't inhibit them using the language they're not having problems with.

Once the children had begun at the lower school the teachers by law had to deliver the National Curriculum and, as their 'Speaking and Listening' policy states, 'The aim under the National Curriculum English Guidelines is for children to develop English'. Yet within the policy there is an expressed belief that 'One path towards this is to support the children's Mother Tongue. For children to feel confident about themselves as learners, support for Mother Tongue is vital.' Examples of how this is to be achieved are: 'Showing value for first language(s) in providing dual language and multilingual texts'; and 'Making explicit to children the purpose of an activity and what they are being asked to do with explanations from other bilingual children or support teachers who share the same Mother Tongue.' Additional support is given through the use of Section 11 support, whereby special teachers work with individuals or groups within the classrooms, with specific objectives:

- 'To give the children greater access to literacy skills and therefore to a literate curriculum. We do see this as curriculum access, as the remainder of the class are working on developing phonic/spelling skills.'

- 'To help children develop an understanding of the mechanics of language which they can relate to their own Mother Tongue.'

Chris was very enthusiastic regarding the need to support children's mother tongues: 'It's something we would want to be doing all the time, it's very important.' But she also acknowledged that there were problems in implementing the policy fully, such as the teachers' own limited awareness and knowledge of other languages, the over-riding view that English is synonymous with the concept of the successful learner, and the reluctance of bilingual support staff and teachers to use mother tongue in more varied situations, rather than only where direct translation may be needed. Thus, though teachers appeared happy to *allow* pupils to talk in their home languages at school, it was not specifically *encouraged*, nor were teachers heard to use any words of the children's own languages. It was also observed that none of the bilingual support staff was asked to work with children in mother tongue by class teachers, nor was there any specific school-formulated policy at any of the institutions relating directly to the bilingual support staff's use of mother tongue in the classroom.

Perhaps the reason for this was that mother-tongue maintenance and/or developing a multicultural framework were not seen as the most important factors affecting child development. As noted earlier, the teachers prioritised the children's social development. Similarly when Theresa was asked about the language needs of the children in her class, she considered them as something which pervaded all aspects of school life. They were therefore constantly attended to within the general context of learning, and 'we almost don't think of it as a problem, we actually teach the language with everything that we do' (see Chapter 3).

The policy of cultural and linguistic diversity, therefore, had not been altogether successfully translated into practice. The emphasis on language had been to extend children's learning of English at the expense of their mother tongue. The cultural framework of the institutions similarly reflected the teachers' culture, rather than the children's. A comment in one of the policies reflected the recognition of diversity, but hinted at the channelling into one culture:

> Many of our children are from a different culture and will arrive in our nursery with different skills, experiences and values. All children will need to be introduced to *our curriculum* with care and understanding. [Our italic.]

Resourcing Teaching

The circumstances in which people work – the building, architecture, the rooms, how they are arranged, furniture, decorations, equipment etc. – have been shown to be of crucial importance to the nature and productivity of an exercise (see Woods, 1983). How were our schools resourced in these respects?

Teaching materials

The materials teachers used influenced children's ability to make sense of new knowledge. At Bridge, the play curriculum included activities involving books, home corner, cookery, music, clay, painting, writing, sand, water, wooden bricks (large and small), and in the outdoor area wheeled toys, climbing equipment and gardening. It was stressed that these activities were provided at all times, although they might change 'depending upon children's observed interests'. Rosalind thought they should 'allow continuity and progression so that ... so you could come in and do a piece of woodwork at your level, even though you're skilled, you could actually go to the woodwork bench and select appropriate materials and do something yourself.'

Naturalism and holism were emphasised in the provision of apparatus made from natural materials. As a result, constructional equipment whether large or small was generally made from wood, and clay was used rather than play dough or plasticine, although children were able to make dough in collaboration with adults as a normal day-to-day activity. The outdoor area was also viewed as a natural extension of the work of the classroom. For example, a display on minibeasts consisting of pictures and books was prepared by a teacher with a view to encouraging the children's interest in aspects of the outdoor area, and to stimulate them to find some of the animals featured.

These ideas echo the notion of constantly available activities (Nutbrown, 1994: 32) which are in their turn capable of development (Abbott, 1994: 79; David, 1990: 76). They also embrace the idea of free-flow play delineated by Bruce (1991: 4) in which children are able to 'apply their own learning in a voluntary and intrinsically motivated way' (see also David, 1992: 78).

Resourcing at Westside was similarly a high priority throughout the school, not only in terms of materials used in lessons but also of creating a comfortable atmosphere for children and staff to work in, which Chris thought of vital importance (Boyle & Woods, 1996). Chris had spent a considerable amount of the school budget on refurbishing the school and its classrooms. It now boasted an outdoor swimming-pool, a very spacious and well-equipped library, a new technology room, carpeted areas and computers in every classroom.

The teachers also spent a considerable amount of time and effort planning their classrooms. Labels on cupboards and doors were clearly printed or had pictures to go with them so that children could easily find books or materials they needed. The reading areas in both Chris's and Theresa's classrooms were furnished with comfortable chairs and cushions for the children to relax in when they chose to read. Displays on the walls reflected the children's work, rather than the teachers', and because the architecture of the school meant low ceilings, the majority of the displays were at children's eye level.

Physical resources in the two nurseries similarly provided for comfortable areas in which children could play and work. There were areas with soft chairs and cushions where books were displayed for them to share with others or look at themselves. There were carpets on which they were able to sit either with chosen activities or for talking with others. There were also opportunities for them to use a computer, while in the outside areas there were climbing frames and scooters. At

Bridge there were various sets of large construction equipment such as wooden blocks and frames. Displays were a particular feature of the nursery unit at Westside, consisting of two-and three-dimensional pictures and collages reflecting the termly theme. These displays were designed and mounted by teachers and arose generally from the structured activities carried out by the children. At Bridge there were a few displays of children's paintings and models and some table displays prepared by teachers, generally reflecting aspects of the current termly topic. However, children were encouraged to take their paintings and models home if they so wished because it was considered that these belonged to the children who had made them.

The choice of materials to be used during lessons in the lower school was also made on the basis of their appropriateness for the children, rather than simply how well they would fit in with the requirements of the National Curriculum. The teachers spent a great deal of time looking at resourcing, and when on occasions they had used a particular resource in their classrooms which had been particularly successful or inappropriate they would discuss this with their colleagues. As one teacher commented:

> If something has worked and they are really pleased with something, everybody knows about it, just as much as they do when they've had a terrible day, and everything they've done's gone, fallen to bits ... And if somebody does something good, or has a good idea, nobody would dream of keeping it to themselves. It develops at different levels and people take it and make it their own.

The local community was used to heighten relevance. The lower school, for example, invited a local operatic company to spend a week in the school working with some of the older children. After pupils had visited the local library, the librarian was asked to join in a whole-school storytelling session. Frequent trips were made to study the local environment. The shopping area, the park and the local housing were all studied as part of geographical, historical and scientific projects. The local church, the Sikh temple and the mosque were also visited on a frequent basis and linked to the celebration of religious festivals. However, community leaders were rarely invited to the school to share in the festivals celebrated by staff and pupils.

While both the nurseries and the lower school aimed at providing resources which would stimulate children's learning, there was potential for further development of resources relevant to the children's cultures and languages, as we go on to discuss.

The cultural relevance of context

Both nurseries attempted to make the educational context culturally relevant.

The home corners provided the potential for imaginative play related to the children's own familial experiences. 'Dressing up' was closely linked to home play, and both nurseries contained a few Asian materials with which children could make saris. At Bridge there were opportunities for children to make barfi and other Asian foods during the week in which Diwali or Eid were celebrated. At such times at Westside there would be appropriate wall displays based on children's pictures of divas or of mendi patterns. At Bridge, teachers prepared displays connected with topics in which they were encouraging the children to become interested, including temporary table displays consisting of pictures and artefacts connected with the current celebration of Diwali or Eid.

However, there was scope for extending these initiatives in order to develop their relevance for the schools' bilingual children. For example, the home corners contained only the domestic equipment that would be available in standard English homes. They could have included materials with which the children could identify, as well as items such as food dishes with which the children could recreate the diversity of items available at Asian meal times. Similarly the greatest number of clothes provided reflected an English culture, and could have included more of a range. Cooking activities too at both nurseries almost exclusively reflected the same specific culture, whether they consisted of making crispies, dough, biscuits, cakes or chutney. The potential available from widening the cultures represented in, for example, cooking activities was emphasised by the opportunities for learning which were evident in the links children themselves made between home and school through their play. On one occasion Aditya (4 years 2 months) was making cheese scones with Kate and was kneading the dough to mix the flour and margarine. She was observed taking a piece of the dough and working it into a ball. She then put this between her hands and began to flatten it, working it from hand to hand in imitation of the way chapatis are made, a method she had obviously seen her mother using at home. Aditya's imitation of home cooking practices emphasises the opportunities available for making these links even more explicit and relevant, by providing occasions on which food from Asian and other cultures could have been made by the children themselves as a normal part of the curriculum. Generally, the provision of Asian food when festivals such as Diwali or Eid were being celebrated was left to parents and to Nadia, the bilingual assistant at Westside, who would bring food from her home.

At Westside nursery, displays of children's art reflected work that they were carrying out under teacher supervision at that particular time, generally based on the topic for that term. Cultural artefacts or pictures were generally only used in displays when Diwali or Eid were being celebrated. Artefacts and pictures reflecting Asian cultures did not form part of displays at any other times during the year. At Bridge there was only the occasional evidence of community languages displayed for children to see, and for educational reasons there were only a few examples of environmental print in evidence, including labelling of equipment. At Westside there were some labels in community languages, usually associated with displays of work, although these languages were not represented consistently on labelling or environmental print around the unit. While both nurseries had book areas, the overwhelming majority of books were written in English only and generally reflected an anglicised culture rather than a multicultural one. The potential for learning afforded by the diverse perspectives provided by the children's cultural knowledge and experiences (Stevenson, 1992: 36) were therefore by no means fully exploited.

At the lower school there were efforts to provide relevant cultural resources and to find opportunities within the curriculum to develop multicultural themes. Visitors entering the school were greeted by a display that usually reflected one of the main cultures of the children at the school. For example, for one term there was a display of Bengali art work; the term after, a child who had returned from an extended visit to her home country in Africa brought back some material which was used by a member of staff as the central piece to the entrance display. Around the walls of the hall where the children gathered for assemblies Islamic prayers had been written out by some of the pupils and were placed in a display, together with a prayer mat. Other displays in the hall featured festivals celebrated by the main religious groups and a series of life-size drawings of 'people who help us' which included members of the local community such as Pakistani and Indian shopkeepers. In the technology room most labels were written in Panjabi, Urdu, Bengali and English script and there was a dual-language recipe book created by some of the older children in the school. In the Reception class, dressing-up clothes included saris and scarves. There were black dolls for the children to play with, though some of these had distinctly European features (see also Siraj-Blatchford, 1992). Within the classrooms dual-language story tapes were available and, though few in number, were used regularly by the children, often as a free choice. A few dual-language books were also available, though reading books were generally screened for suitability and the school had set aside money to increase the numbers of dual-text language books and story tapes. Music was another area in which the school sought to represent cultural diversity. It was played at the beginning of each assembly and came from a number of different sources, both modern and classical, including traditional music from Ireland, Hungary, Africa, India and other countries. There were also instances when children who attended music lessons at the Sikh temple would play for the school, either as part of a class assembly, or on their own, as one boy did, having asked his class teacher if he could bring in his tabla [drums] to play.

While the shared and public areas of the school reflected the multicultural make-up of its pupils, this policy was not uniformly carried through into classrooms. Number lines and alphabets were shown only in an English script. European artists, such as Monet, Matisse and Van Gogh, and European art techniques were most frequently used for inspiration during art sessions. It was noted that few children coloured in pictures of themselves using their actual skin tones, unless directed to do so by teachers – most often pictures were not coloured at all. This was true also of pictures drawn by children in both nurseries. This may reflect the limited number of images of people from ethnic minorities presented to the children, particularly in professionally produced resources – for example the reading and maths scheme books, which, while screened for their suitability in terms of multicultural content, were still dominated by images of white people. Derman-Sparks (1989) recommends that more than half (though not all) images and materials in schools should reflect black people, to counter the predominance of mainly white images in society.

Coping with Intensification

Teachers are not entirely free to apply their beliefs and values. As noted in the Introduction, they operate within a political context which in important respects runs counter to their own values, and which has led to an intensification of their work. All our teachers complained about the increased workload that had been brought about by the changes in legislation, and in many ways these were considered a distraction from the real purpose of their jobs. Rosalind talked of the predominance of what she saw as 'low level tasks' which impinged on and transformed her own professionalism, detracting from her role as a headteacher:

> Some days I feel upset because if I've tidied up my desk I find I'm congratulating myself, saying, I've got through all that admin and I've tidied my desk and I've got a nice, tidy office to come into in the morning, and I think, 'Is that what I'm about? Is that what gives me pleasure? Is that satisfying? Is that what I call job satisfaction?' Because it's crap. It's not what I wanted to do in life.

Equally Chris felt that much of her job as a head was concerned with peripheral tasks (see Boyle & Woods, 1996; Woods *et al.*,1997):

> I worked it out one week: I'd actually done over 80 hours, can you imagine? And then it made sense, no wonder you get fed up with it, because otherwise you think 'What's the matter with me, why can't I keep working?' You've actually done a lot of paper work, but because it's not interesting or challenging ... and then we have other things to do with such as costs, staffing costs, maintenance, buildings, colour of the staffroom chairs *[laugh]*.

The expansion of managerial responsibilities appeared to encroach on both Chris's and Rosalind's teacher identities, as Chris illustrated: 'I like teaching. I've learnt more than anything that basically I am a teacher. I'm not a manager or accountant, a maintenance woman. I'm basically a teacher ... and I really wouldn't want to give it up.'

Rosalind and Chris had little control over these particular aspects of managerial duties, which had become a large part of their roles as headteachers. Yet in other areas they were able to maintain control. Rosalind felt it necessary to be in complete control regarding the overall management of the school: 'I don't think that true democracy works in a school, if I'm going to be honest, I think there has to be a leader who makes the final decision.' She believed that in taking full responsibility she was able to steer the school in the direction she felt most appropriate and that by working in this way she could alleviate pressures on her staff who would then be able to get on with their jobs as teachers:

> The head's job to me is to take all those pressures off the staff, to take the pressure from above. Your job is to take that as a head and deal with it and say, 'No I'm not going to change and this is the way my school is' and not allow that pressure to filter down to the staff [who are left] to get on with the job and not involved in other political issues that they don't need to be involved with and not feel all the time worried.

Chris's leadership style contrasts somewhat with that of Rosalind's. We have described in detail elsewhere (see Boyle & Woods, 1996, Woods *et al.*, 1997) Chris's management approach regarding policy formulation as one of 'controlled collegiality'. There is a sense of teamwork that is viewed as collaborative, responsibility is shared and Chris is willing to delegate tasks to her staff. At other times, as with Rosalind, there is a realisation that the final decision has to be hers:

> I want to be the one that will always accept the total responsibility for the things that are not going well, [not just] for what's going well ... I feel we talk it through. I think everybody has their say, everybody, and when I walk away, that this is what we're going to do. But how am I going to get from there to their thinking the decision was theirs? Most of the time I've managed to do that but it still leaves me feeling I'm seen as taking full responsibility.

Jenni's role as the co-ordinator of the nursery unit at Westside had also resulted in a proliferation of paperwork and extra tasks, yet many of these were due to lower school initiatives, such as keeping records for children entering Year 1, rather than the impact of changes from government. Jenni also commented that much of the paperwork involved in the preparation for an OFSTED inspection had been beneficial, providing an opportunity for reflection of the nursery curriculum: 'We did have to sharpen up and we did have to get it very clear between the three of us [nursery staff] exactly what was happening and what was going on.' In this sense control from others, including both the school and agencies such as OFSTED, was not seen as negatively as in the case of Rosalind and Chris. Jenni also had responsibility for a staff, but chose a particularly collaborative approach in working with them. This was due very much to the fact that she herself had originally trained as a nursery nurse and believed that her nursery nurses should be given opportunities to contribute to nursery policy, though again there was acceptance that she made the final decisions. As one of her nursery nurses commented: 'I think we've got a great deal of responsibility in the way things are planned, we do tend to share everything, it's just at the end of the day it does come down to Jenni.'

Theresa, as subject co-ordinator, had some managerial responsibility in the lower school in specified areas of the curriculum, and was involved in certain aspects of overall school development. Like Jenni and the staff in the nursery, however, her main sense of control came in the day-to-day running of her classroom:

> I don't get bored [with teaching]. I get tired, I get fed up sometimes with the workload, I get frustrated with ticking boxes but actually when I'm with the children, I'm always interested in them and I always enjoy them, even when you have difficult classes. You get exhausted by them but the challenge is still there. Sometimes you despair, but it's still satisfying when you actually crack it ... there's a lot of freedom in how you do things and what you chose to do on a certain day.

Though our teachers are affected by intensification, especially with regard to the growth in managerial responsibilities, they feel that their personal control is maintained. This is also the case with regard to teaching methods. There used to be agreement that government would not interfere with teaching methods (Hutchinson, 1994). However, since the introduction of the 1988 Education Reform Act, teaching methods have increasingly come under scrutiny. There have been increasing criticisms of so-called 'progressive teaching methods' and of the Plowden Report (1967) with which they are associated. These have been blamed for poor educational standards, and there have been frequent calls for a return to the basics, particularly in reference to literacy and numeracy teaching. The inference here is that whole-class teaching and more traditional pedagogies would be more effective than child-centred practices (see Alexander *et al.*, 1992). This process has now been furthered by the recommendations regarding teaching methods in the National Literacy Strategy (DFEE, 1998). Yet our teachers were critical of such interventions.

Rosalind, for example, accepted that there were certain things which children must be taught, but firmly held on to her beliefs that learning would be best achieved in an atmosphere where the children's own interests are the starting point:

> I think there would be times with the National Curriculum when you're covering things that aren't of interest to the children and I think that's fair enough,

but perhaps you could still try and link them and make them more interesting. They've still got to do things, they've still got to learn to read and count, I know that, but if you can link them to interests ...

She was not willing to compromise her beliefs in order to accommodate the expectations of OFSTED inspectors:

We're not going to match up to their lesson observation schedules, and we're not going to start teaching lessons in the nursery because it wouldn't be right or appropriate to teach lessons to children at that level of their development. But OFSTED demands lessons, so we know that the dice are loaded against us before we start. So it's a bit like waiting to be shot and not being able to have a gun yourself, or waiting to be punched in the playground. You just have to stand there, you can't run away because you know that your hands are tied before you start because of the principles of nursery education. We actually can't fall in with the OFSTED format in which we do not believe, so we have to deal with that.

Jenni also asserted that '[if] the OFSTED report comes up and says this woman should be doing more worksheets with her four-year-olds I'd totally ignore it because I don't think I would want to do it.'

The teachers in the lower school similarly criticised outsiders' attempts to control their teaching methods. During the course of the study, Westside Lower School underwent an OFSTED inspection that led to feelings of concern and anticipation amongst the staff of the school. It meant that not only would their philosophies and forms of management be subject to close scrutiny and examination by people outside their school context, but also their own identities as teachers since, as for Nias's teachers, 'to adopt the identity of "teacher" was simply to "be yourself" in the classroom' (1989: 182). Although Chris's feelings about herself as a head were positive as a result of the inspection, nevertheless during the pre-inspection period, as a professional embracing a special knowledge of her own school, she expressed her resentment at this intended scrutiny of her role: 'I just feel that there are people making judgements on us and [they] may not be in a position to ... It's easy to come in and criticise, it's not what the school is about.'

Chris was adamant that no changes would be made to teaching methods in the school simply to accommodate perceived expectations of inspectors (see Woods *et al.*, 1997). Theresa, too, felt that she would not alter her preferred mode of teaching for the inspection, but after the event she acknowledged that she had been forced to abandon some of her usual teaching methods:

I'm not ashamed of what I do in class. Sometimes it looks chaotic but if anybody just walked in, like today, I would have been quite happy – I wouldn't have minded. I could justify what I was doing. I wouldn't have worried at all about it, but I agonised over every lesson ... I wouldn't run a lesson like that usually, would I? ... And I wasn't relaxed, you know I'd got: Stage 1, Step 2, Step 3, do this, do that, go there, do this, you know and it was like – regimented.

These feelings of deprofessionalisation for the week of the inspection were temporary, however, and Theresa soon returned to her normal classroom practice. Hutchinson (1994) points out that there are many positive aspects of the changes which have occurred in the wake of the ERA, for example the development of whole-school policies and collaborative cultures that have encouraged primary teachers to develop clearer consensus approaches. However Hutchinson (1994: 141) also argues that:

> ... in moving into the field of curriculum organisation and classroom practice the government is risking direct intervention in the one area that was always supposed to come outside the scope of the Secretary of State – teaching method. It is also an area that is notoriously hard to monitor. Could any OFSTED team ... force a primary teacher to teach in a particular way from Monday to Friday?

Our teachers have indicated their resistance to this form of control. Yet control of management, curriculum and pedagogy appeared to be relatively 'culture-free' issues. If we accept that education is a primary way in which culture is passed on from one generation to the next (Chinoy, 1967; Durkheim, 1956; Singh, 1993), then control of the education process determines what that culture is. The question is – how is control used by the teachers? Is it for the benefit of the pupils, or more to do with maintaining their own professional identities? To answer this question we need to examine the relevance of their teaching, which we go on to do in Chapters 2, 3 and 4.

Chapter 2
Teaching the National Curriculum

The National Curriculum and Bilingual Learners

In the Education Reform Act of 1988, children of all cultural and linguistic backgrounds were promised 'equal opportunity' and 'equal access' to the curriculum. All subject working parties were urged to include consideration of racial and gender issues in their discussions. As Siraj-Blatchford (1996a: 45) says: 'Most multicultural and antiracist educators tried to be optimistic and set about attempting to make the best of the windows of opportunity made available by these limited innovations.' What developed, however, was a varied commitment to multicultural and antiracist content within the different subjects.

In 1989 a multicultural task group was appointed to provide teachers with guidance on how to develop multicultural aspects of the curriculum and to 'take account of ethnic and cultural diversity and the importance of the curriculum in promoting equal opportunities for all pupils regardless of origin or gender' (Tomlinson, 1993: 21). The group, which consisted of nine experts in the field of multicultural education, suggested the planning of a curriculum for bilingual and ethnic minority pupils. The report was never published, which Sally Tomlinson, one of the task group members, felt was due to a growing right-wing populist belief that 'such development threatens the nation's heritage and culture and erodes educational standards' (1993: 26). Since then the National Curriculum subject documents have been revised and slimmed down in the light of the Dearing Report (1994). Although the new version was welcomed in many ways it was still considered over-prescriptive by many teachers, and has also been criticised because the focus in the last two years has been on subject knowledge and content (Siraj-Blatchford, 1996a). More recently schools have been encouraged by government to introduce daily literacy and numeracy hours into their curricula, creating not only additional planning and assessment, but also a need to examine teaching methods in the light of the new requirements. What has been forgotten, Siraj-Blatchford (1996a: 47) claims, is that 'the real subjects in the education system are the children'.

While nursery education has not been subject to the same constraints as statutory schooling, it has been included in the OFSTED system of inspections and codified to some degree by the publication of Desirable Outcomes for Children's Learning (DLOs). These cover six areas of learning: Personal and Social Development;

Language and Literacy; Mathematics; Knowledge and Understanding of the World; Physical Development; and Creative Development. It is suggested that children should have attained certain skills in these six areas by the time they leave pre-statutory provision at the age of five. In addition to the DLOs, 'base line' assessment has recently been introduced, whereby children are assessed in their skills as they first enter school. Both recommendations have the potential for generating a more prescriptive curriculum in nursery education, bearing a much closer relationship to the National Curriculum. These proposals form the framework for the OFSTED system of inspection of pre-school settings. It is in this context that early years educators have to work and maintain a sense of worth as well as of commitment to the education of their pupils.

Within the curriculum documents of Bridge nursery, it was noted that the long-term planning contained in the School Development Plan was modelled on the DLOs. However, the school's policy indicated ways in which the learning experiences arising from the DLOs and the National Curriculum would 'be integrated into the whole curriculum', for example:

> When children cook they learn to count and measure, they combine solids and liquids and learn what happens to substances when they are heated and cooled. Woodwork, sewing, gluing and brick-play are particularly important for developing children's problem-solving skills.

Rosalind sought to modify and extend the DLOs. However, she did feel under pressure to defend her curriculum provision:

> It's very difficult to get the nursery message across that the curriculum's delivered through play, that we're doing very high-level concepts. So all the time you're trying to explain these ideas to parents or even in practice to people in your own profession, to other teachers or even convince our own profession of our worth.

At Westside, by contrast, Jenni felt the need to prepare the older children for their move to the reception class of the lower school, and to increase the proportion of structured activities in relation to free play. Jenni told us: 'I think I wouldn't be doing the reception teacher a service if I hadn't drawn the line and said, "OK, the game's over now."' Jenni's nursery curriculum policy reflected National Curriculum subject divisions and was arranged under the same headings of Personal and Social Education, Language Development, Mathematical Experience, Science, Information Technology, Technology, Music, Creative Arts, Physical Education, Religious Education and History/Geography. The unit's curriculum policy emphasised that many of the National Curriculum areas 'were always found to be in existence in a well-planned and balanced curriculum' and as a result an awareness of the National Curriculum should permeate the curriculum of the nursery.

Despite these divisions into subjects the policy explained that 'the wholeness of our curriculum must be emphasised'. However, the obligation felt for some form of adaptation to outside curriculum control was greater at Westside than at Bridge.

The lower school was obviously more directly influenced by outside curriculum controls in the form of the National Curriculum, which they had to 'deliver', and teachers were subject to the pressures of 'handing on'. At the end of the school year there was much discussion among the teachers about the nature and ability of individual children who were moving into new classes. Teachers felt it imperative that various aspects of the curriculum should have been covered before the children moved. Elaine particularly felt the pressures of 'handing on', as her class would be sitting SATs in the following year. Theresa similarly felt there were pressures in 'handing on', and that certain aspects of the school day had to be side-stepped, for example the amount of time children had for play:

> If they actually need play, well there's nothing wrong with it ... if they're actually at the stage when they can play – but there does come a point when you haven't got time, you've actually got to force them through hoops. Sometimes I know that I'm pushing children on too quickly but, they're going into Key Stage 2, there won't be any play! ... The poor old Key Stage 2 teachers get a bit stressed about how much there is to cover.

During the school's OFSTED inspection play became a real issue, especially for Theresa. Despite her feelings of not wanting to change too much, some alterations were noticed during the week of the inspection, particularly with regard to her customary practice of allowing children the opportunity of free-choice activity once they had finished their work. When asked about this later she commented:

> I didn't let them go and play, except on planned activities. If they'd finished on maths, they played on maths things, that's all ... I think it was something I just did for the OFSTED *[laugh]*. Because I actually think the time that they're playing is really valuable. But I just didn't want to have to justify it ... I didn't particularly want them to say, 'Look, this is maths time, why are they playing with Lego?' *[laughs]*. I don't bother about that normally. I think it actually does them far more good, then they're actually interacting.

However, the National Curriculum was not seen by the teachers as a straitjacket. Theresa did not feel restricted by it, though she had at first:

> In a way you had to go through that process to actually come to grips with it ... I think it's just practice really to get to know roughly what you're going to teach. I tend to pick out the bits that are more appropriate and leave the bits that don't particularly matter. It's been good in a lot of ways because there are a lot of areas that we never touched upon that are interesting to children, that are valuable –

that we probably wouldn't do, or wouldn't have done. We've more or less got over the stage of actually rigidly sticking to the National Curriculum to the exclusion of everything else ... Otherwise you're just rushed off your feet, and they're not really learning, and you do take time and go back over things.

Thus rather than resisting its changes, Theresa incorporated and reinterpreted the National Curriculum to suit her own pedagogy and the needs of the children.

Chris similarly did not feel totally restricted by the National Curriculum, and commented:

It might have been at the beginning, but that's not to say we've slacked off. Every aspect of the curriculum is covered, but there are lots of ways you can take things on. Most of the time it does work, but you must take the time to react. It's so important to react to the needs of the children, because you must remember these are people you're dealing with. They are not going to sit there quietly waiting for an input. It is there, and we do follow it, but we also take on the interests of the children.

In essence it did not appear to be the nature of the National Curriculum itself that caused difficulty, but the amount of work that was expected to be covered. This meant that the lower school teachers at least were forced to marginalise activities such as play, and use all available time to cover National Curriculum content. It was not unusual to observe teachers calling children in at lunchtime in the lower school, to see them complete some work or hear them read.

While the recent changes have affected all pupils, they hold additional significance for bilingual learners. In relation to the National Curriculum, the original guidelines emphasised approaching the curriculum through cross-curricular themes and dimensions that 'promote personal and social development, include equal opportunities, and education for life in a multicultural society. They require the development of positive attitudes in all staff and pupils towards cultural diversity.' (NCC, 1989, para. 11.) Subsequent guidelines continued to promote this approach:

Dimensions such as a commitment to providing equal opportunities for all pupils, and a recognition that preparation for life in a multicultural society is relevant to all pupils, should permeate every aspect of the curriculum ... Teachers have a major role in preparing young people for adult life; this means life in a multicultural, multilingual Europe which, in its turn, is interdependent with the rest of the world. (NCC, 1990: 2–3)

However a more recent guide to the National Curriculum (1996) made no statements relating to cross-curricular themes, and gave guidance on individual subjects only. Despite this, our teachers still believed that it was flexible enough for them to be able to adapt it to the needs of children of other cultures – and yet there were relatively few examples of their doing so. Various festivals were celebrated, and one year when celebrating Diwali all the teachers dressed in saris and shalwar kameez; religious stories were explored in assembly, in particular a series of stories about the childhood of the major religious figures of Christianity, Islam and Sikhism; but these events were on a whole-school basis and focused on religion. In class, examples of multicultural teaching usually occurred solely in those aspects of the curriculum that particularly lent themselves to it.

In the remainder of this chapter we examine specific areas of the curriculum and their significance for bilingual children.

Language Development

In the Common Requirements of the Programmes of Study for Key Stages 1 and 2 under the heading 'Use of Language' the following paragraph appears:

> Pupils should be taught to express themselves clearly in both speech and writing and to develop their reading skills. They should be taught to use grammatically correct sentences and to spell and punctuate accurately in order to communicate effectively in written English or, where the medium is Welsh, in written Welsh. (DFE, 1995)

The emphasis is heavily on the use of English as the language of learning:

> English is not only a core subject in the National Curriculum but, together with Welsh in Wales, is also the medium for teaching and learning in all subjects. Opportunities across the curriculum to develop pupils' abilities to speak, read and write English are reinforced by the Use of Language requirement in other subject Orders. This requirement is important for all pupils, including those who are learning English as an additional language, since such teaching will help them to succeed in these subjects and to communicate effectively in English. (SCAA, 1996: 19)

Children of all backgrounds, then, on starting school, are expected to embrace standard English as the official language, and there is an assumption that learning in what might be a second language for many of them will 'help them to succeed' in communication and learning. Learning in a mother tongue other than English appears to be ruled out, which is especially unfortunate for those children who are skilled in their community languages but lack confidence in English (Martin-Jones & Saxena, 1996; see also Edwards & Redfern, 1992).

In schools where the majority of children are learning English as an additional language, language development may especially be considered a central aspect of any learning. Language generally is held to be at the heart of intellectual and personal development (Vygotsky, 1978; Bruner, 1983), and a strong influence on the structure of thought (Mercer, 1995). As for bilingualism, it is claimed that it can get to 'the process of objectification' earlier than others (Cummins, 1976; David, 1990); and that it can be a strength for all language development (Siraj-Blatchford, 1996a). This is because children develop language in order to communicate meaning, and to do so draw on their own culture and community (Kress, 1997). In consequence, bilingualism is a strength, rather than a disadvantage, and this was the generally held view at our schools.

However, within the nurseries, despite the expressed support of community languages, the predominance of the use of English by teachers contributed to the culture-specific nature of the curriculum. The majority of teachers in the nurseries were monolingual and shared neither a knowledge of the community languages spoken by the children nor an understanding of those communities. Communication in community languages, therefore, became a medium for private and unofficial interactions between children playing with or in the company of their peers. This also meant that these same uses lacked the status afforded to English.

Both nurseries benefited from having bilingual Section 11 members of staff, Nadia at Westside, and Sonia at Bridge. Nadia's and Sonia's presence provided the children with opportunities to speak their community languages with an adult. Nadia, for instance, was observed responding to children's approaches to her in their community language and she emphasised that the younger and less confident children would always speak Panjabi to her as a way of building their communicative and social confidence. In general, her role appeared similar to that of the other teachers in helping individual children and taking groups for practical activities such as cooking, and for stories at the end of the afternoon, some of which she would read in Panjabi. Sonia was also used as an additional teacher, generally interacting with children on a one-to-one basis. She also took a story in Panjabi once a week with a group of children in each classroom. The presence of bilingual educators clearly provided the potential for developing the status of community languages in the nurseries. However, there were no planning, recording or assessment systems for the encouragement and monitoring of children's use of community languages. As a result these remained private and unofficial, and English predominated in the curriculum, as the majority of teachers were excluded from the children's first languages. Thus the potential provided by the presence of bilingual teachers had not, as yet, been fully explored.

At the lower school the teachers and children were more constrained by the National Curriculum. As stated earlier, standard English was the medium through which the teachers were expected to teach and the children expected to learn. We might have anticipated, therefore, a particular focus on English language learning. However, the learning of English was seen by Theresa as something which pervaded all aspects of school life, was therefore constantly attended to within the general context of learning and did not require specific teaching: 'The language is a problem because it goes through everything ... it's almost so much engrained in us now that we almost don't think of it as a problem, we actually teach the language with everything that we do.' She did not consider language to be 'the main problem', but said, 'I think that when they're very, very small that some of these children suffer at a crucial time from lack of stimulation, lack of language and nobody to play with and I think that is sometimes never caught up.'

There is an inherent assumption here that there are certain experiences that children should encounter before they begin school. In part this is based on Western society's notion of the family and the needs of the child (Woodhead, 1990). In a cross-cultural study of family, Hoffman (1987) found that parents in the USA were most concerned that their children become 'good people', 'independent' and 'self-reliant'. In contrast, parents in countries such as Turkey, Indonesia and the Philippines, who often relied on the economic contribution of their children, placed greater importance on 'obedience' and the 'respect of elders'. Emblem's study (1988) of primary education in India, Pakistan and Bangladesh found the educational system reflected the family expectations of their children, that they be obedient and show respect. At the same time, Emblem illustrates that the children were taught a great number of traditional skills and values at home. Clearly some of the children in our study had alternative early years experiences (rather than a 'lack of' experience) from those expected by teachers and the English school system. If these experiences could only be incorporated into the curriculum they might provide an opportunity for teachers, parents and pupils to explore alternative methods of teaching and learning which could be more appropriate for children of varied backgrounds.

In contrast to the constrained approach of the teachers, the children themselves exhibited a fair degree of knowledge of language. In the nurseries they were observed using their community languages together on a number of occasions, generally on a one-to-one basis, but also amongst small groups of friends. These uses arose naturally out of the relationships and ways of working which the children were developing, providing means by which they were able to find common ground together. The process revealed a flexible set of skills that the children used quite naturally as part of their cultural repertoire. This knowledge about language was a common feature manifested by even the younger bilingual children. While having their milk on the carpet Tariq and Fatima sat close to each other and talked quietly in Panjabi, a conversation which lasted several minutes while the other children went outside to play. Similarly, Jabidul was observed one afternoon sitting on the tandem outside with his friend Ali and as they drove around they stopped occasionally and spoke together in Panjabi, laughing and tickling each other. These examples of the affirmation of friendship by means of what children have in common was exemplified also by Iqbal and his friends, who often chose to speak Panjabi together as they played, responding naturally together in the language chosen by the group.

In the lower school, language appeared to be a central aspect of the children's cultural identity. In their first year at school, our researcher Mari discussed with them the languages they spoke. The children talked of speaking in Pakistani or Indian rather than Urdu or Panjabi, and always spoke positively of themselves in these terms. They were 'Pakistani' or 'Indian', though all of them had been born in Britain. Discussions about language with the children in their second year indicated their growing awareness of their language-rich environment. For example, Azmat, an Iraqi child, revealed her knowledge of the variety of languages she spoke with her best friends, Parminder, a Panjabi speaker and Fatima, an Urdu speaker. Azmat herself spoke a limited amount of Arabic, English having become her strongest language:

Azmat: Yeah, I understand people speaking Arabic, but I can't speak Arabic. I can only understand Arabic, what they're saying.

Mari: So you want to try and learn more?

Azmat: How to say it.

Mari: How to say it ... in your class lots of children speak, they don't just speak English do they?

Azmat: No, no. But, there's only about four children that's Arabic in this school, no five children, about three of them are in another Arabic country, because there's eight Arabic countries.

Mari: So would you understand, if they were to speak Arabic would you understand them?

Azmat: Yeah, they speak a bit the same but a little bit different.

Mari: And what about Parminder and Fatima, are they your best friends?

Azmat: They're my best friends, yeah.

Mari: Because Parminder speaks ...

Azmat: ... Indian ...

Mari: ... and Fatima speaks ...

Azmat: ... Pakistani.

Mari: And you, well you understand Arabic, but you say that you don't really speak it. So when you're playing together d'you just speak in English or ...?

Azmat: I sometimes speak in Arabic because they only, I tell them some stuff and but most I just speak a lot of English because they don't know that much.

Mari: Uhuh, and so does Fatima sometimes tell you words in Pakistani?

Azmat: Yeah, because Parminder knows Pakistani so they sometimes say words.

While our teachers were impelled in many ways to work in English due to their own monolingualism and the focus in the National Curriculum on English as the language of instruction, we see that the children took opportunities, if only between themselves, to share their knowledge of language, broaden their understanding and reinforce part of their cultural identity through language (see also Chapter 7).

At the same time, the children were constantly adding to their understanding of English, needing to listen to and follow teacher instructions for work or general behaviour and needing to communicate with children and adults who did not share the same mother tongue as themselves. The following example indicates how in some cases it is not the understanding of an exercise that can cause confusion for children learning English as a second language, but basic vocabulary.

In a phonic lesson during the children's second term at school the teacher had explained that she wanted them to find the 'end sound' of certain words. She had gone through the exercise with them orally and then gave each child a sheet with a variety of pictures on it. Under each picture was the name of the object with the last letter missing, for example slu_ [slug], quee_ [queen]. Mari sat with the children as they did the exercise and the following extract shows how Ali tries hard to get the right end sound but unfortunately for the wrong word. The picture was of an ice-cream cornet. Written underneath the picture was 'corne_':

Ali: *[showing picture of a cornet]* I have to do this one.

Selina: Ice-cream.

Ali: Ice-crea-mma
[emphasising the last part of the word in order to identify the sound and letter].

Mobeen: No. Not
ice-cream. It's another word. Arks Miss Boyle.

Mari: What?

Mobeen:	Look. It's not ice-cream.
Mari:	Well it is. Some people call it an ice-cream, and sometimes it has a special name, and it's called a cornet.
Ali:	Cornet. Corne-*t*, t. Ticking Tom, t. Ticking Tom. I'm gonna do the next one, snail, snai-*l*, snai-l *[picture of a slug]*.

Ali has clearly understood what is expected of him and he imitates his teacher's method of sounding out words and emphasising sounds. He also uses the characters from the phonic scheme 'Letter Land', used in the school, to identify the sounds and letters. Yet as Gregory (1996) notes, for bilingual children in particular, sounding out words which are not understood may in fact serve only to confuse them. We see here Ali sounding out only words he understands and which are meaningful to him, 'ice-cream' and 'snail'.

Shortly after this more formal language lesson, Mari observed Ali looking at books in the reading corner. The following conversation took place:

Ali:	Read this story *[a non-fiction book entitled* All About Colours*]*.
Mari:	Ooh ...
Ali:	*[pointing to one of the words on the cover]* Colour.
Mari:	Colours. *[Reading the title of the book]* 'All about ...'
Ali:	I, I know that word, 'c'. 'C', 'c', 'c'. 'O' for orange, em Oscar Orange, an, em Umbrella, and 'r' for Ali, and 's' for ...
Sabida:	Sabida
Ali:	No, 's' for Semina.
Sabida:	And my name.
Mari:	And Sabida.
Sabida:	Look, this is my name ... *[pointing to the names under their self-portraits, part of a display on the wall]*
Ali:	... and looka that's my name then *[pointing to his name also]*.

We see here that Ali appears to be collecting sounds and letters and also indicates those that are meaningful to him. He completely misses out the letter/sound 'l'. Essentially in both these examples Ali shows the importance of relevance within the curriculum. The first example in part reflected the adherence to the National Curriculum, and also the problematic nature of using professionally produced schemes which may not always suit the needs of individual children. The second example reflects Ali's own interests and new-found skills which he is eager to illustrate.

English language, as Theresa commented earlier, was something that pervaded all aspects of the curriculum, and there were many examples of the teachers using opportunities to advance children's English language development (see Chapters 3 and 4). The opportunity for mother-tongue language development came outside the school in the children's home environment (see Chapter 8) and in the religious classes many of them attended after school (see Chapter 7).

Mathematics

Mathematics is a subject often viewed as being relatively 'socially neutral', in that it deals with universals and 'its content is held to be independent of the material world' (Jenner, 1988: 73). Yet there is much within the mathematics curriculum that is problematic in relation to the teaching of bilingual children (Gregory, 1994b). Theresa gave another example of how she saw the children disadvantaged by their backgrounds in relation to mathematical understanding:

> It's just a gut feeling because there are so many children who come in and they can't count – they've got no concept of counting and colours or anything like that ... there's not many but a few do come into this class every year, maybe three who haven't got numbers and it is blood, sweat and tears to get those numbers in their heads ... and it's not necessarily that they aren't intelligent ... but it's this whole sort of thing that a number means a set of things ... and they've probably done it for two years before and in the nursery and yet it doesn't go in. Eventually they do get it, often this year if they are poor, and then sometimes they're away like Asria. She took ages and ages and ages to get the numbers concept.

Yet the concept may not be the problem. The difficulty may lie in the language:

> The Panjabi youngster learns different sorts of language rules [from the English-speaking child]. The *colour* of the door may not be emphasised by the mother, but the gender of the door is vital. The *tense* may not be absolutely correct, but the use of the polite 'you' when speaking to adults is vital. The number of spoons may not be emphasised, but where they go in the kitchen is vital. He will know the Panjabi words for maternal grandmother, paternal uncle (older than his father), paternal uncle (younger than his father), maternal uncle, etc. But he won't know about a definite and indefinite article – they don't exist in Panjabi. He will have trouble with pronouns (in English) – there is just one word for he/she/it in Panjabi. 'Yesterday' and 'tomorrow' may also be a problem. In Panjabi it is the same word for both, the context explains which is meant. (Garcha, undated: quoted by Mayor, 1987: 16)

Thus Asria's difficulty as a Panjabi speaker in grasping mathematical concepts in an English curriculum may be due to the importance of and use of numbers, colours and shape in her home language. Her home experiences have simply not prepared her for an early years mathematics curriculum which is focused on these concepts. Language and conceptual development are strongly linked (Vygotsky, 1978). It is not surprising therefore that many bilinguals find it difficult to talk about maths in a language other than the one in which they were taught (Grosjean, 1982; Mayor, 1994). Furthermore, much of the language used in early mathematics is confusing. General terms such as 'more than', 'bigger than', 'less than' and 'smaller than' can be used in many situations. On one occasion Chris as Year 1 teacher had just completed the register and asked the children to guess how many boys and how many girls there were in class. Having been given the answer, she then asked if there were more boys or more girls in the classroom, and the majority of the children said there were more girls, at which point Damian commented that 'the boys are littler', meaning there were fewer boys. If terms like this are confusing for native English speakers such as Damian, they must be even more so for children learning English as an additional language, and especially if we view mathematics as a form of communication:

> As the language of mathematics is so tightly defined, the ability to use mathematics to communicate in a particular language may take longer to develop than we would expect, and this may lead us to underestimate pupils' grasp of ideas, particularly since language is so closely related to culture. (Jenner, 1988: 73)

The view that mathematics is 'culture-free' appears to be a prevailing one, too. However, as Maxwell (1988) illustrates, if we examine the problem-solving questions that occur in English maths textbooks, and indeed those of other countries, there is much to be found in the way of a hidden curriculum. Maxwell cites examples of questions involving the struggle of peasant farmers in China, freedom fighters in Tanzania and pay disputes in England, all of which take on specific cultural significance. For children of ethnic minorities this can be a subtle way of enculturation.

There is also the problem of under-representation of ethnic minorities in maths schemes and curricula. Westside Lower adopted the Ginn maths scheme, popular in many schools to accompany a very practically based mathematics curriculum. The booklets are brightly coloured and there are a great many pictures and cartoon-type illustrations, and the pictures of children do include some from ethnic minority backgrounds. However, whilst the school was able to choose its scheme carefully, it had no choice over the Maths Standard Assessment Task booklet. The Key Stage 1 booklet for 1996, which was the test the children of this research took, contains 11 pictures of children. None of them is from an ethnic minority. The lack of positive images and role models within texts such as this does little to build up self-esteem for such children. This may have a detrimental effect on their achievement within the subject (Jenner, 1988; Siraj-Blatchford, 1996b), a particularly salient point when we consider that success in mathematics is one of the subjects through which achievement is measured.

Science

Language can present similar challenges within science. In a lesson focusing on planets during the children's first year at school, the teacher had a number of difficulties exploring the concepts of the Earth, moon and sun. The children were seated in a circle and individuals were asked to come out and hold different-sized balls to represent parts of the solar system: a large yellow football was the sun, a tennis ball the moon; and a blow-up globe the Earth. Vocabulary appeared to confuse many of the children, particularly when they were later asked to draw what they thought a spaceman might see from a rocket. Some children were perplexed by the difference (or rather the lack of difference) between the Earth and the World, and so drew both on their pictures. A number of the Panjabi-speaking children talked about the 'night-sun' in reference to the moon. The moon also caused problems because of the different shapes it appears in. Damian talked about a 'curly one', meaning a crescent-shaped moon, and wanted to know if there was one moon or many different ones. The teacher felt the children's conceptual understanding had not been advanced by the visual aids, and that she would need to revisit this work in other ways.

The adoption of simpler, more practical illustrations, based on the children's own experiences, enabled them to begin to understand complex scientific concepts, as shown in another lesson. Again this took place during the children's first year at school and was part of a topic on forces. The class had already done some work on pulling and pushing, and the teacher had begun to introduce the concept of gravity covering science in the National Curriculum Attainment Target 4 (this is pre-Dearing). The word 'gravity' had been introduced to the class in connection with pulling, and the teacher now wanted to reinforce this concept. She stood at the front of the class, with the children sitting on the mat, and the lesson developed:

Teacher:	(*holding up a pencil in front of the class*) What's going to happen to the pencil, Sabida, when I let go?
Sabida:	It's going to go down.
Teacher:	Down. Do you think it's going to go down, Manjid?
Manjid:	Yes.

Teacher: *[to Manjid, with appropriate gestures]* Do you? It's not going to go up? It's not going to stay there?

[Teacher then asked a number of children 'Where do you think it's going to go?' and all replied 'Down'. Teacher let go of the pencil and it fell on the floor.]

The teacher started the session by asking the children a rather simple question, to which there was only one correct answer, though she hinted at the possibility that something else might happen. This simple action helped to create an atmosphere of anticipation, drawing the children in. When she dropped the pencil there was complete silence in the class, and then smiles from the children when they realised they had got the right answer. Whilst this was clearly something the children knew about, trying to figure out the reason why the pencil fell to the ground required more abstract thinking.

Teacher: It did go down, didn't it? Why did it go down? Why did it go down? Why didn't it go up? Why didn't it just stay there? Why did ... ssh *[one boy interrupting to give an answer, but the teacher waits for the children to have some time to think]* Why did it go down? Why? Come on Semina, think. Come on Azmat, think. Why did it go down? *[Teacher waiting for all the children to raise their hands before choosing someone to answer]* ... Damian?

Damian: Em, 'cos you dropped hold of it.

Teacher: I didn't, I just let go, I didn't make it go down, I didn't push it down, I just let go of it. Why did it drop down? Fatima?

Fatima: *[no response]*

Teacher: Don't put your hand up until you've thought about it, 'cos it's silly when I ask you and you go 'hmm'. Think about it. Taylor?

Taylor: 'Cos you threw it.

Teacher: Yes, but I didn't throw it, I just let go of it and it went down. You weren't here, though. You weren't here when we were talking about this. Most of you were though, and I told you about something, but you've forgotten, and you can't remember the word. Shiraz?

Shiraz: Gravity.

Teacher: Good boy. What does gravity do?

Shiraz: It pulls it down.

Teacher: Good boy. You used the right word, you used the word 'pull'. Gravity, gravity, we can't see it. We can't see gravity, like we can't see the air, we can't see gravity. But gravity pulls things down to the ground *[making appropriate movements to go with pull]* and that's why things fall down, when you let go of them.

The initial answers given show the process of the children's thinking. The teacher's questioning challenges their reasoning and asks them to go beyond the obvious. A series of steps is developed; Damian points to the most obvious, that the teacher dropped the pencil. Taylor moves on from Damian's reasoning and suggests that the teacher threw the pencil down, realising perhaps that there needed to be an external force, but it is Shiraz who makes the connection with work done in a previous lesson. When Shiraz remembers the word 'gravity' he also remembers the explanation of what gravity does. In part this is helped by his teacher's visual and practical display, but also by the manner in which she talks. The language she uses has hints of the narrative of young children's stories. There is constant repetition of the central theme, 'pull', and sentences are kept short and to the point. She also uses her voice to build up a certain atmosphere, emphasising particular words to create the sort of rhythm often found in such stories.

The explanations continued:

Teacher: Watch again. The gravity's going to pull it down. You can't see it, but gravity's going to pull, pull it to the ground *[drops the pencil]* and gravity did it. We couldn't see it doing it, could we?

Damian: It was quick.

Teacher: But gravity pulled the pencil to the ground. Gravity's pulling me to the ground. I can't feel it. I can't see it doing it, but if it wasn't pulling me I'd be floating round the classroom *[teacher and class laugh]* and I'm not.

Fatima: It's pulling us too.

Teacher: It's pulling you on the carpet, you're right Fatima, good girl. Gravity is pulling you on the carpet.

Fatima: Everyone.

Teacher: Yes, and all the things in the classroom as well. It's pulling all of them, good girl. Remember that word, that was a good word you used Shiraz, 'pull', it's pulling. Gravity pulls things to the ground, it pulls them to the ground.

Compared with the earlier part of the dialogue, in which the children responded to the teacher's direct questions, the latter section shows how the children are allowed to add their own voice and given encouragement for doing so. Fatima shows her understanding of the concept by relating it to herself.

The teacher then moved the idea of the pull of gravity to talk about air resistance by using the example of a toy parachute, which many of the children recognised and said that they either had one, or knew someone who had one. The teacher showed them how to make a parachute using squares of tissue paper. This became quite animated, as the teacher got up on to one of the tables to show how the parachute worked. The children later made their own parachutes, which they tested. Once all of them had made their parachutes the teacher allowed them to play with them outside during playtime. Some lasted for a few days, and the children enjoyed playing with them. The whole experience remained with them for a long time. In the last week of the school year, over four months later, when they were allowed to choose an activity, a number of them made parachutes and were able to reproduce the same skills on this occasion without any teacher help.

The example indicates the importance of verbal interaction with young bilingual learners (Levine, 1996), the necessity for frequent repetition of instructions or new concepts, and a need to develop far more visual methods of explanation, together with practical demonstrations, of what is expected of children. Thus the emphasis on particular words which are accompanied by actions such as 'pull' helps the children to understand the meaning of the words. The rhythm and repetition that the teacher uses in her delivery draws the children into the situation, and because the session is followed by practical work the children are able to learn through concrete activity.

All of this links closely with Levine's (1996: 118) view of the crucial need for bilingual children to develop their learning within a social and physical context: 'Pupils' language and learning repertoires grow both by means of their participation in meaningful interaction with other people, with resources and texts, and by direct instruction.'

History

The history curriculum is heavily weighted toward British history. Some argue that this bias is necessary, that children should know the history of the country they live in (Dyer, 1982, Musgrove, 1983). Nicholas Tate, the former head of SCAA, argues that the promotion of a strong sense of British identity for all children in British schools will help to counter racism:

> Misapplied cultural egalitarianism that wants to give equal attention to everything simply makes the problem worse ... We tackle racism, jingoism and the

lack of identity and collective self-esteem which underlie them ... by developing a sense of pride in the dynamic and multifaceted majority culture of our society, while respecting diversity. (Tate, quoted by Pyke, 1997: 3)

Others believe that as Britain is a multiracial society the adoption of a *world* history curriculum would serve to combat stereotypes (Goalen, 1988). They feel that National Curriculum subjects such as science and maths may, like history, also prove to be inherently ethnocentric in content. This is not least because most mathematical and scientific discovery is considered to be 'Western' in origin, and there is a general lack of consideration that children from other cultural backgrounds may approach similar problems in different ways, and achieve different, but equally acceptable, kinds of results (Glauert & Thorp, 1993).

The Areas of Study for Key Stage 1 in history (DFEE, 1995: 74) specify that:

(1) Pupils should be taught about the everyday life, work, leisure and culture of men, women and children in the past ... In progressing from familiar situations to those more distant in time and place, pupils should be given opportunities to investigate:

    (a) changes in their own lives and those of their family or adults around them

    (b) aspects of the way of life of people in Britain in the past beyond living memory.

(2) Pupils should be taught about the lives of different kinds of famous men and women, including personalities drawn from British history.

(3) Pupils should be taught about past events of different types, including events from the history of Britain.

Although there is room for negotiation in that the areas of study say that children should study famous people and past events which *include* those represented in British history, the reality is that it becomes difficult to consider anything other than British (or at the most, European) history. One reason for this is that many of the teacher aids and early years textbooks produced since the National Curriculum have concentrated on British history. Finding resources which relate to world history outside Europe and which are suitable for early years learning is more difficult, and also more expensive, since the demand is not as prominent. In our two years of observation at Westside the children studied in detail the Romans and their invasion of Britain, the reign of Queen Elizabeth I, Louis Blériot, Florence Nightingale and Louis Braille, some of which were single history topics, others tied into other topics. The following observations of two lessons show how the very nature of the first lesson and the use of materials created problems in understanding for all the children in the class, not only those from ethnic minorities. The second lesson (interestingly on one of the few topics that fell outside the national framework) was more relevant to the children's experiences and provided different responses. The contrast shows how the curriculum can be made relevant to children's concerns.

Boudica

The first lesson occurred during Year 1 and was based on the story of Boudica, as part of a topic on the Romans. The teacher had already told the story of Boudica, using a Ginn history reader designed specifically for Key Stage 1 history topics. The scheme included worksheets and suggested follow-up activities. The teacher began the session by trying to establish how much of the story the children had remembered. They listened quietly throughout the recap, concentrating on what she was saying and looking at the pictures in the book. She did not use the text of the book, but told the story through the pictures. However there seemed to be some confusion regarding who was who in the story:

Teacher: *[pointing to a picture in the book of Roman soldiers]* Who are they? Who are they?

Ali: Soldiers.

Teacher: Yes, what sort of soldiers? What sort of soldiers? What sort of soldiers are they? *[pointing to the picture in the book]* Ali, what sort of soldiers are they?

Ali: *[no response]*

Teacher: What sort of soldiers are they? Who are they? They're the ...? Who are they, Shiraz?

Shiraz: *[no response]*

Teacher: Roman soldiers. They're the *Roman* soldiers, they're the Romans ...

The fact that the children do not give an answer is significant. Essential to an understanding of the story is the fact that there were two groups of people who were fighting. The children, at this stage having heard the story at least twice, are still unable to distinguish between the two groups, indicating that they have not yet grasped one of its main aspects. Throughout the question and answer session the teacher spent a great deal of time trying to elicit answers from the children. Having got to the end of the story she held open the last picture in the book, showing two of Boudica's men, and the following interaction took place:

Teacher: Who was the strongest?

Damian: *[pointing to two of Boudica's men with bulging muscles]* Em, them two.

Teacher: Why were they the strongest?

Damian:	'Cos they got muscles.

Teacher: Ah yes, they've got muscles ...

Pupil: Muscles?

Teacher: ... but they weren't the winners in the fight, were they? Who won the battle? Which ...

Pupil: Soldiers.

Other: Romans.

Teacher: The Roman soldiers won that battle, yes. The Roman soldiers.

Damian: It's not a race.

Pupil: Everyone got killed.

Teacher: Well not everybody got killed, some of them were made slaves ... Do you think some of the Romans got killed?

Ali: No.

Peter: Yes.

Teacher: Don't you think any of them got killed, Ali?:

[Ali shakes his head]

The children are attempting to make sense of the story on their own terms. Damian, for instance, when asked who was the strongest, uses the contextual clues from the picture he sees and relates that to his own understanding of strength, that is, the person with the biggest muscles. When the teacher talks about winning the battle, again Damian's understanding of winning is restricted to his own experience of what winning means – the person who comes first in a race. Exactly what Damian understands of the story is difficult to ascertain, particularly as when he attempts to sequence the story later with Mari he seems to have difficulty in figuring out which picture comes next:

Mari: Who were the Romans fighting with?

Damian: With Matica's guards.

Mari: Boudica's army.

Damian: Army.

Mari: Boudica's army. She would have probably had some guards.

Ali: What's a guard?

Mari: *[to Damian]* What's a guard?

Damian: A policeman's, policeman's guard. I know, guards look after people when they're naughty.

Mari: Well some guards do, and some guards look after people to protect them.

Damian: Yeah.

Again, Damian attempts to make sense of the story through his own knowledge. Within child-centred education there are often attempts to develop knowledge based on what the children already know. For Damian this becomes a central feature of his attempts to understand the story, setting the new situations against knowledge he already possesses in order to make the story relevant. Unfortunately he does not have enough experience on which to superimpose this new knowledge. The pictures in the book and those he has been working with probably bear little relation to his existing concept of soldiers and armies. This may account for his difficulty in connecting with the story. He replaces the term 'soldiers' with 'guards', which he appears to understand better and then, in response to Ali's question, likens them to policemen. He uses the word 'naughty', again one more familiar to him than concepts of war, fighting and killing. He seems to be trying to make sense of the story in terms he already understands.

Blériot

The second lesson, which took place one week later with the same class and teacher, was based on the story of Blériot, the first person to succeed in flying across the English Channel. This lesson was related to a project on movement. Again the teacher started the session by telling the story using a book – although it was a very different type of book from that of the previous session: it was a story-book. The picture style was less detailed than in the Boudica reader, and the language closely related to the general storytelling style of many of the books in the classroom, as opposed to the text-book style of the Boudica book. The teacher introduced it to the class as a true story and there were immediately aspects that the children could relate to. The central character had a family that included children of their own age and a baby, and the opening picture showed the family riding in their car. The following extract shows how the children associated their own knowledge with the story:

Teacher: And you can see them in the car. All the children are there.

Touzia: And the baby.

Teacher:	And the baby sitting on Mummy's knee. Is it a car like we have now?
Pupils:	No.
Teacher:	No. What sort of a car is it?
Shiraz:	Old.
Teacher:	It's an old car.
Pupils:	Old.
Teacher:	You're right, Shiraz.
Shiraz:	We've got a number.
Teacher:	Oh well we have a number-plate. We do have a number-plate, you're right.
Manjid:	*[pointing out something else she could see in the picture, but unclear]*
Teacher:	An old car.
Damian:	You can get ones with where you can get them.
Teacher:	Get what?
Damian:	You know, you know there's something on the front.
Teacher:	The number-plate.
Damian:	Yeah. It tells you em where you get it. A car.
Teacher:	Oh sometimes in this country sometimes there's some little writing that tells you where you bought the car.
Damian:	Yeah.
Teacher:	Not always, not always. You'll have to look at all the cars on your way home, Damian, sometimes they do, sometimes they don't.
Shiraz:	Miss what is that?
Teacher:	Ah now that...
Imran:	That will wind it up.
Teacher:	You're right, it's called a starter handle. It is a bit

like winding it up, you used to have to turn it to make the engine go. You had to turn it to make the engine go. Not like now when we put a key in and turn the key and that starts the car, doesn't it?

Pupil: Yeah.

There are recognisable characters here, and the children compare and contrast the car in the story with modern vehicles. Later in the story there were pictures of an airship that the children recognised, as they had seen airships passing over the school. Comments were also made with regard to the flying machines that appeared in the book and the children compared them again with modern planes and helicopters. While telling the story the teacher also put up her own pictures on the easel board, to accompany the narrative. At the end of the story she went over the pictures again. She did not use the script directly, but often talked around the pictures – comparing and contrasting them with life today. As against the previous lesson the children contributed far more during the telling of this story, often making comparisons themselves between modern life and that depicted in the book.

The children were also able to sequence and retell the story with much greater ease than they had done in the previous session. This may in part have been due to the fact that the teacher herself had drawn the pictures for the sequencing activity and done the writing that accompanied it; they were much simpler than those of the prepared scheme for the Boudica story.

Following the whole-class session the children talked about the story in groups, which provided opportunities for discussion between them while they worked on sequencing their stories. The following extract focuses on the children's discussion about France.

Mari: Can you remember what country Louis Blériot lived in?

Peter: I know. France.

Mari: In France.

Selina: My uncle went to France.

Mari: You could've went to France?

Selina: No, my uncle.

Mari: Your uncle went to France.

Damian: Brian went to France one day. *[Brian was Damian's mum's partner]*

Mari: Did he?

Peter: I think my grandma went to France one day, I think.

Damian: And I went with Brian in Flance, France.

Mari: In France, did you?

Damian: I went with Brian in France. And I buyed a, em I buyed a [thing] in France, and you've seen it, Peter.

Peter: What is it?

Damian: A castle, isn't it.

Mari: You bought a castle in France?

Damian: Yeah.

Azmat: *[laughs]* Toy castles?

Damian: Yeah.

The children continued talking about France, asking how to speak French, wanting to learn how to count in French, particularly in regard to the fact that Blériot had made 11 flying machines. In this way the story of a French aeroplane-maker provided an appropriate context for extending their learning and going beyond the story in the book.

There was still some confusion for one of the children with regard to the story, but this was related to remembering new terms rather than the overall concept. In the original telling the teacher had described the airship as an 'airship ... a ship in the air', which may explain Ali's later confusion:

Mari: This is Louis Blériot. He was out in his car, and he looks up and what did he see?

Ali: Er, a boat.

Mari: He saw a ...? Do you get boats in the sky?

Ali: No.

Mari: I know what you mean, it's a bit like a boat. He saw an airship.

Ali: Airship.

Comparing the two sessions, appropriateness and relevance seemed to be the main distinctions. Both had had the same children and teacher, and a similar format, yet with one lesson there was a great deal of general confusion; with the other there was understanding. Appropriateness and relevance in these two lessons occur (or not) at the conceptual level and in the use of materials. At the conceptual level, the complexity of understanding concepts such as invasion, battles, killing, armies, soldiers and slavery seems a very heavy burden for the teacher to unpack for the children and for the children themselves to understand. The invasion of Britain almost two thousand years ago, as presented, seems to bear little relation to the experiences of children at this stage of their development. By contrast, relating to something that happened just over a century ago, where there is much to be recognised, families, cars, fashion, planes, airships, may have enabled them to understand the story better.

The use of materials also had an impact on the lessons. Hughes (1993) points out a number of ways in which many of the current materials produced for primary school children in history are inappropriate. Most have been produced by subject specialists, often secondary school authors rather than language or primary experts. Pupil materials are usually designed to cover a range of age-groups; for example the Boudica materials were developed to cover both Year 1 and Year 2 children. Books frequently include a high factual content, and though readability levels may be technically correct, the mass of subject-specific language may serve only to arrest understanding. Furthermore, though texts may be more attractive than in the past, the publisher's house style may take precedence over any 'child-friendly' one. These points concern all children, but for those learning English as an additional language they become even more pertinent, specifically in relation to the materials used in the Boudica session. In the second session, by comparison, where the teacher had to create and gather her own resources, she had the opportunity to adapt her materials to her class, using her own knowledge of the children by which to gauge the level of work. In this way she was able to make the session far more meaningful. In particular the use of the story-book may have been more appropriate for children at this stage, as Kress and Knapp (1992: 5) point out:

> In any one society there are types of texts of particular form: because there are recurring types of social encounters, situations, events, which have very similar structures. As these are repeated over and over and over, certain types of texts appear over and over and over. They become recognisable and recognised in a society by its members, and once recognised they become conventionalised.

The children may have had more difficulty in recognising the genre of the Boudica text than the Blériot one simply because the former was not as familiar to them as the latter. Being confronted by unfamiliar ideas and unfamiliar language both at the same time appeared to confuse them.

Geography

Geography would appear to offer particularly good opportunities for multicultural teaching. One of Theresa's projects, for example, included a study of the world. Children drew pictures of themselves which were placed around a map of the world and connected by a thread to their country of origin. They were also asked to bring in items such as stamps and money from their home countries and were encouraged to talk about them. In another project on food, which included geography, art and cookery, the children looked at foods from around the world. Fruits and vegetables from local shops were brought in for them to draw.

Despite this, on the whole the curriculum followed the direction of the National Curriculum. In essence it seemed that there were aspects of the National Curriculum that did not lend themselves to alternative cultural interpretations. The teachers did make use of the local community in studying geography, for example mapping out the local area and going on walks to look at the local shops, religious buildings and other sites of interest. In this way they sought to relate the curriculum to the everyday experiences of the children, but the wider multicultural view impacted far less on the topics explored in class.

In the following example the class teacher was developing some work on physical geography, covering Attainment Targets 2b, *make representation of real or imaginary places* and 2e, *identify familiar features in photographs* (National Curriculum pre-Dearing). The children had done some preliminary work about features of islands, and were now going to make their own islands using papier mâché. The discussion is about geographical structures that they have been asked to identify from a series of commercially produced photographs.

Teacher:	We're going to make something, I'm going to show you something, so you know what to do. Who can tell me what's this? *[Teacher has a variety of pictures of different types of islands and features of islands. This particular picture shows an island with sandy beaches and sheer cliffs.]*
Pupil:	Sand.
Teacher:	Sand.
Touzia:	Sand.
Teacher:	Sand is on a ...
Pupil:	A isla ...
Teacher:	Something beginning with 'b'.
Touzia:	'B'.
Mobeen:	Bedge.
Teacher:	Nearly right.
Peter:	Beach.
Teacher:	The beach, beach ...

Touzia:	Beach.

Teacher: We call this the beach. It's next to the ...

All: Water.

Teacher: What sort of water?

Various: Sea.

Shiraz: River.

Teacher: The sea. No not next to a river, it's next to
the sea.

The teacher continued with this observation exercise, looking at various types of islands, pointing out features such as cliffs, volcanoes, snow-capped mountains, pine
forests and so on, but while the photographs were often quite spectacular, they bore
little relation to the local environment in which the children lived. Their town is far
from any beach; it has a river, but the surrounding area is prone to flooding because
of the low-lying landscape. There are certainly no cliffs, volcanoes or snow-capped
mountains. The result is a 'guessing game', where the teacher hints at the answers
she wants and the children try for the correct one. The task is made more difficult because the children have little knowledge of these features – note Mobeen's
approximation of the word 'beach' and Shiraz's offer of 'river', something he is familiar with, rather than 'sea'.

The introduction of specific geological terms through the use of photographs
seemed less successful compared to the children's understanding of these terms
when they were making their own model islands in the second part of the lesson.
This involved physical activity using papier mâché and was wonderfully messy.
The context and focus of the lesson changed at this stage. The first part of the session
involved whole-class teaching that followed the popular form of teacher question,
pupil response. Though in this mode the children are seated together, in many ways
there is little opportunity for discussion. Whole-class teaching has been strongly
advocated by the Chief Inspector of Schools (Woodhead, 1996), but for many children learning English, including those just starting school, such a session, though
useful for some purposes, may not be beneficial for others. It becomes difficult for a
child to ask for clarification, and there is an emphasis on 'right answerism' (Holt,
1969) whereby the tendency is to value the 'yes' and other positive answers over the
'no' or negative ones. When the children were involved in making their own
models, however, they worked with partners and were able to interact with the
teacher on an individual level, as she went from group to group commenting on
their models and discussing the features they were creating. There was no longer a
right or wrong model; the focus was on the children's imaginative and creative

development, through which the teacher was able to extend their knowledge of mountains, volcanoes, beaches and cliffs.

There is scope within the geography curriculum for children to cover a variety of topics relevant to their backgrounds and cultures, for example studies of the local environment and world studies. However, there is still a danger that professionally produced geographical materials are inappropriate, for similar reasons to those cited earlier for the history topics. It was a feature within the staffroom that when brochures for new materials were sent to the school there were frequent discussions about how relevant these materials might be, particularly with regard to language and representations of other cultures. The school was constantly adding to its resources, and from a variety of sources, often buying artefacts which were representative of some of the many cultures present. Despite this, the pressures on teachers, in terms of both budget and time, made it impossible for them to be constantly creating their own materials for use in the classroom.

The National Curriculum and Assessment

Assessment, whilst always an important aspect of teaching, has developed dramatically through the National Curriculum. Prior to the ERA most schools and teachers carried out formative assessments, but the National Curriculum called for national testing in the subject areas of English, mathematics and science for children aged 7, 11 and 14. The original assessment procedures proved an unwieldy expectation of both teachers and children (Anning, 1995), and it was recommended in the Dearing Report (1994) that 'urgent action by the School Curriculum and Assessment Authority [be taken] to find ways to cut down the administrative work connected with national tests' (para. 3.31). Subsequently new Standard Assessment Tasks (SATs) were devised, in English and maths only.

Despite this reduction our teachers were still concerned about the SATs, particularly in relation to their bilingual pupils. Theresa felt that the tests were 'definitely culturally biased':

> The spelling test, the kind of words they used in that were dreadful, and the language in the stories, in the comprehension thing, it really was ... The maths, they love all the doing, action, practical maths, and what do they give us for a SAT maths test? A nice little booklet, with loads of reading in and sums.

Chris indicated how, despite the fact that some children understood little of the content, they were able to complete SAT exercises simply because of the coping strategies they had learned along the way. She had observed the following incident:

> One of the children was reading a piece for a SAT comprehension exercise and it was something about the Himalayas, and the question she read out was,

'Where do all the arses live'. She read 'All the arses live in tibbit', so she wrote down 'All the arses live in tibbit', but she had actually written beautifully, 'they all live in Tibet, all the asses live in Tibet', ... it didn't matter, 'I don't know what asses are, I don't know what Tibet is, but that is what they want to know, that's where all the asses live – Tibet'.

The object of this particular test, which it signally failed to achieve, was to assess the child's understanding of a passage. There is much concern about how well bilingual and ethnic minority children perform in school assessment, particularly in national tests (Gillborn, 1995; Troyna; 1991). However, as Savva (1994) points out, where their bilingual children have only the beginnings of English, teachers have little choice, other than to withdraw from the National Curriculum and its testing procedures. Where children are in a transitional phase, teachers, parents and the children themselves must accept that their test results are likely, particularly in English, to be lower than those of their monolingual peers. The government's initial response to this situation, as noted in the Cox Report (set up to review the English Curriculum, 1988), was that where lower attainment levels were recorded this would not reflect a child's general ability, but rather their need for 'special help in English language skills' to 'overcome their problems with the English language'. Savva (1994: 38) notes:

> We are presented here with a deficit view of bilingual children and an inade-
> quately crude model of their language learning development. No mention is
> made of the crude, invidious comparisons likely to be made within and be-
> tween schools as a result.

A recent example of this kind of comparison was made regarding the reading levels of seven-year-olds in three Inner London boroughs in an OFSTED research report where low literacy levels were found (OFSTED, 1996). The report blamed poor teaching methods as being at the root of the problem. However it was much criticised by the teachers and schools which took part, not least for its failure to consider the fact that up to 50% of the 80% of seven-year-olds who were considered to be behind in their reading achievement were learning English as an additional language (*TES*, 10 May 1996). In such instances assessment simply identifies what children have failed at, rather than what they have achieved (see Drummond, 1993).

There is little recognition of the children's ownership of new knowledge in many of the summative assessments, yet parents were very aware of their children's progress at school, as indicated by the following transcripts:

Mrs C.:   [Guvinder] remembers everything what he does do. And they were
                 doing the weather chart. And he goes to me, 'Mum, it's sunny,' and I
                 goes, 'Yeah, and can you see anything else?' and he goes 'Yeah, I can
                 see the clouds, and I think it's going to rain,' and I said, 'It might.' And I
                 thought, 'Well, I don't teach him all that, but he knows when the sun is

out, and it's sunny and it's rainy and it's snowing.' And I didn't thought he could come up with clouds as well, or it's gonna thunder or things like that. Yeah, he's really catched up. Because, well it's the teachers are learning him, but you know, really nicely, and em, some of the kids maybe tell him what it is, and he's really learning, and I'm really pleased.

Mrs A.: [Shiraz] comes home talking about he done, work about the Romans, and he was telling me about, they'd been doing some work on glass, or about glass I think, and he came home and 'Oh Mum, do you know what "opaque" means?' And I was, I didn't, I didn't! I knew it was something to do with glass or plastic or whatever, and then he was going on about 'transparent' and 'translucent' and I was just sitting there! *[laughs]* ... He's always full of stories about 'We done this today, we done that today', and bring his paintings and everything home.

By contrast the reports the parents receive with results of their children's SATs scores merely provide them with a level of achievement, though Theresa talked to individual parents about their children's progress in all areas of the curriculum and explained the SAT procedure. However as Chris noted, for her the most disappointing aspect of the SATs was the inability to show individual development and achievement:

I think there are some very good things about the National Curriculum, and there are other things that are not so good, there are some things that needed to be done and things that should have been removed ... But there is no celebration of children's learning through SATs, what they have accomplished or achieved.

Conclusion

Since 1988 there have been profound changes in the education system in the UK. The role of teachers has changed dramatically, as have the responsibilities of schools (Pollard *et al.*, 1994; Woods *et al.*, 1997), and we have indicated here the effects of these changes on our teachers and their responses. Clearly there are a number of constraining features inherent within the National Curriculum, for example the removal of multicultural statements from the revised curriculum document, the emphasis on English as the language of instruction and learning, the inappropriate forms of assessment which again rely on the use of English, and the ethnocentric nature of the curriculum overall. There are additional factors outside the curriculum that affect our schools' abilities to develop a more culturally appropriate curriculum. The cuts and changes in Section 11 support and the fact that there are few bilingual teachers available in the area means the schools may not be receiving adequate professional provision. Furthermore, training courses offered by the Local Education Authority deal more in content-based programmes (for example, how to teach Key Stage 1 science) than in issue-based ones which could address matters like equal opportunities within the curriculum.

Examples of lessons have been used in this chapter to illustrate how these constraints impact in the classroom, and how the following of National Curriculum subjects, recommendations and forms of assessment to the letter can be detrimental to the learning development of children from ethnic minorities. At the same time we have indicated that teachers do have the opportunity to find more appropriate teaching methods which are beneficial to these children's learning. Further examples of innovative approaches will be given in later chapters.

Perhaps one of the most significant constraints for teachers lies within their own attitudes to learning. As Valerie Emblem (1988: 91) points out:

> In any class the children will bring a wide variety of experience to school. Whether this has been in Bangladesh or Bradford or East London, the teacher must learn to accept the children as they are as the starting point of her teaching. Rather than seeing children as 'deprived' she can identify each child's strengths and build on these.

Suggestions

(1) A lot of information about bilingual children's level of development can be obtained from talking to parents or carers. This and information about the children's progress can also be obtained not only from their written work, where that is appropriate, but from observing and talking with them. Bearing this in mind the following considerations might be useful:

- Are you setting aside time in the classroom to observe children at play or carrying out activities, not only those connected with the National Curriculum but on other occasions also?

- When observing bilingual children what are you looking for? For example, can you observe examples of children bringing their cultural and linguistic knowledge to bear on their activities? How are the children using language? To what extent do they use their community languages with others, including adults and other children? In what contexts do they use these languages? (For example, in the house?)

- If you have a bilingual support educator you might think about how you could encourage her, or him, to take an active role in observation of the children and talking with them. You might encourage her to use her community language consistently with the children and join with you in planning and observing work on this basis with groups of children.

(2) Your bilingual support educator can join with you occasionally in activities with children. She could perhaps take a leading role, using her community language with them while you act as the assistant. In this way, the children not only have an opportunity to use their community languages but also recognise that their languages have status and can represent a normal part of classroom work. It also gives them an opportunity of seeing that the bilingual educator has status within the classroom environment.

(3) Recognition and use of their first languages by teachers would show bilingual pupils that they were valued (Edwards, 1983). How could you as a monolingual educator encourage the use of community languages in your classroom? You could make it an aspect of your policy in your classroom to learn a few words of community languages, such as greetings, and make a point of using them with the children. You could also ask them about their languages – they could teach you words and phrases that you can use in your work with them. In this way the children are themselves becoming educators, using their skills to establish the status of their own cultures and languages.

(4) As a monolingual educator you can also encourage the children to use and develop their community languages with you in activities planned for that purpose. For example, you might use a dual-language story-book (the picture-book *Topiwalo* is an example) with a group of children, not only to develop the potential of the story itself but also to draw attention to the written language. For this you will need to learn a little about the way the particular community language works, for instance, in which direction is it read? Where do verbs come in the sentence? Are there words for definite and indefinite articles? All these can be discussed with the children and you can also ask them if they can recognise differences in the ways in which English and the community language are written. The children could then be invited to make a tape of the story in their community language, perhaps taking it in turns to retell pieces of the story in sequence. One child may like to translate their version of the story for you. The children can add their own songs to the story and then the tape is available for others to listen to in the book corner. This activity could form the basis for moving on to other activities including, for example, puppets which could be used by the children in a performance of the story in their community language for other children. In this way you as a teacher retain your role, but in a partnership with the children on which they bring their cultural and language skills to bear.

(5) Look at the provision you have made in your classroom. Does it reflect the cultures represented amongst your children? Does the house have appropriate

artefacts and equipment? Do your dressing-up clothes reflect the cultures represented in your classroom? Do the posters, pictures, and puzzles show ethnic minority children?

(6) Are different cultures and languages represented in print in your classroom? Is there a substantial proportion of children's books in your class and school libraries that reflect the cultures of your children? Do you have dual-language story-books or books specifically in the children's respective community languages? Labelling of equipment and displays could also reflect the languages of the children, and labels on displays could be in community languages as well as in English (your bilingual support educator or a member of the community could help to do this). All labels on displays should invite a response from the children by, wherever possible, being in the form of a question, so that they have to observe the displays closely and talk about them. Even if they are not yet able to read their community languages the visual presence of those languages throughout the classroom will not only give the languages status but will also give you opportunities to look at the languages with your children and discuss features of them.

(7) If you are the language or multicultural education co-ordinator in your school you will probably consider it important to disseminate the notion of provision for cultural and language diversity to your colleagues. A first step might be for you, in collaboration with the headteacher, to establish these initiatives in your own classroom. Perhaps you may have a colleague who would be interested in collaborating with you. You might then want to introduce the work you have carried out in your classroom to the staff at a series of meetings, offering your advice and support to other teachers who may feel confident about beginning these initiatives in their own classrooms. For an example of an effective whole-school inclusive language policy in a bilingual school, see May (1994a and b).

Chapter 3
Creative Teaching

Introduction

In this chapter we consider two particular aspects of creative teaching in the educational practice of the teachers in our study – relevance and innovation – and their significance for bilingual learners. We have discussed the notion of 'relevance' in a general context in a previous study (Woods & Jeffrey, 1996), where we considered how teachers strive to construct knowledge that is meaningful within the child's frame of reference. We described teachers' strategies in sharing and creating knowledge, stimulating 'possibility knowledge' through imagination, utilising children's 'prior knowledge', and developing 'common knowledge' (Edwards & Mercer, 1987). If knowledge conveyed to the children is relevant to their concerns (Woods, 1995: 2) and reflects their societal and cultural knowledge (Woods & Jeffrey, 1997: 1), then it is more easily internalised by the child, developing into 'personal knowledge' (Woods & Jeffrey, 1996: 116).

We might posit some alternative notions of 'relevance'. Teachers might feel obliged to try to deliver the prescribed National Curriculum and 'teach to tests', regardless of whether these are serving the causes of 'common' or 'personal' knowledge or not (Parker-Rees, 1997). We saw in Chapter 2 some examples of how children 'learned by test'. The relevance here is to some others' conception of pupils' and society's needs, and as we have seen, the needs of bilingual learners are not prominent in the National Curriculum. Chris Woodhead (1995), at the time of writing HM Chief Inspector of Schools in England, has criticised the belief that 'education must be relevant to the immediate needs and interests of pupils'. He argues that 'our school curriculum must provide young people with the knowledge and skills they need to function effectively in adult working life'. We would agree with this latter point, but see relevance to 'immediate needs and interests' – and in particular pupil cultures – as an essential aid towards that adult state. As Martin and Stuart-Smith (1998: 251) have shown, 'children are affected by the relevance and cultural nearness of what they are learning about' (see also Ferdman, 1990; Kress, 1997). We develop this argument here in considering the application of relevance to different situations and within different aspects of the overall curriculum in relation to our bilingual learners.

Our teachers sought to establish relevance in various ways: encouraging children's play; starting with the child; developing home-school links; revisiting topics and skills; 'teaching in the margins'; and through spontaneous reaction to children's interests.

The Relevance of Play for Bilingual Learners

Play provides outstanding opportunities for creative teaching and learning. It offers a means of developing knowledge through practical experience in a way that is highly relevant to young children. Moyles (1994: 4) describes how the emphasis is on involvement in processes and the knowledge children bring to bear on their activities. Bruce (1991: 22) argues that in 'free-flow play' children possess a higher degree of ownership of learning than in more structured work. They are not forced to generate a product for its own sake, and are consequently free to act creatively (Sutton-Smith, 1975, in Gura, 1992: 117). This is why in play children will attempt things they might not risk in other activity (Meek, 1985: 49).

For bilingual learners, play has special significance. In such activity they are able to bring their own cultural knowledge and understanding to bear, to collaborate with others, and to make optimum use of their first language. The importance of this is noted by Moyles (1989: 47):

> Collaborative play situations across cultures and gender, such play as in the home corner or variations of this pretend-play situation, where different cultural media are added, supplement the variety of language used and value the diversity of cultures from which children emanate.

Both nurseries expressed a commitment to play. At Westside, teachers are asked to provide 'every opportunity ... for the children to explore all areas of play provision'. The first responsibility of adults was seen as providing a 'stimulating environment'. The policy at Bridge was to give children:

> ... time to experiment, create and reflect, time to be listened to by adults and time to actively engage with them. Space to use, organise and link materials in ways that they themselves choose, in a setting where learning through play is valued by adults and children alike.

In the nurseries we witnessed many examples of the educational value of play. One hot afternoon Attia was playing outside with the water tray. She had found it difficult during her time in the nursery to make friends and to feel confident about sharing activities with other children. She had, however, recently made friends with Rabeela who enjoyed similar activities and did not try to dominate their relationship. But Rabeela was Attia's only friend and when she was absent due to illness Attia returned to playing on her own. On this particular occasion Attia became absorbed in filling and emptying different plastic containers with water and experimenting with how many containers of water it would take to fill a kettle. After trying this with different containers she then filled each of them with spoon-fuls of water, counting the number of spoonfuls it took to fill each container. She was careful to fill each container to the limit of its capacity without overfilling it, revealing an early understanding of the rules and nature of capacity and using a variety of containers to exemplify the fact that these rules remain constant. Her absorption in this activity seemed complete and lasted for several minutes until a younger girl and boy approached the water tray and asked her if they could play with her. She helped each of them to put on a waterproof apron and showed them what she had been doing, encouraging them to join in. Thus it might be claimed that the opportunity to explore was not only educative in itself, but also contributed to Attia's confidence, enabling her in turn to share her knowledge with others. We might then expect the collaboration to lead to further discoveries.

The educational potential arising from children co-operating and talking together in their play was observed in both nurseries. For example children were regularly observed playing together. On one such occasion Tariq and Tony were experimenting with the vertical properties of a long rod which they had constructed from small interlocking plastic tubes. They began by comparing the rod vertically with their own heights. After adding more pieces they noticed, as Tariq, showing an appropriate use of mathematical language, remarked: 'this is taller than me'. Testing the rigidity of the rod they began to walk with it round the nursery, until eventually it broke. They returned to the remaining pieces and rebuilt it, adding still more pieces, watched it bend and then took it round the unit again. This process of constructing and comparing heights in a vertical plane enabled the boys to experiment together through co-operative play with building concepts of comparison and the properties of rigidity and flexibility.

Bruce (1997: 97) emphasises the value of adult and child 'developing play together':

> Supporting begins where the child is and with what the child can do. Extending might be to give help with physical materials, create space, give time, dialogue and converse about the play idea, or help with access strategies for the child to enter into play with other children. Extending also involves sensitivity and adding appropriately stimulating material provision, and the encouragement of the child's autonomous learning.

Bennett, Wood and Rogers (1997: 12) also consider the need for the teacher to be 'pro-active ... in creating challenging learning environments and providing appro-priate assistance at the right time even in play activities'. Bruce (1997) stresses the need for what she describes as an 'interactionist' approach to teaching and learning through play, comparing it firstly with a *laissez-faire* or 'stand back and light the blue touchpaper approach' (David, 1990: 86), and secondly with the didactic form of teaching where a body of knowledge is imparted to the pupil:

> The *laissez-faire* approach tends to leave children where they are. The didactic approach gives children only the 'right' ideas. The interactionist approach begins where children are, helping them to use what they know, and to move with them into new knowledge and understanding.

The importance of communication with others was recognised in both nurseries. At Bridge adults were regarded as facilitators:

> They observe and extend the children's play, interacting with them either individually or in groups and providing extra resources to develop play where appropriate. Staff are aware of the value of helping children to increase their independence.

At Westside the role of the adult was also seen as important. In the unit's policy this role was described as involving four stages of intervention: to observe the children 'play, participate, structure, extend'.

Children were observed interacting and co-operating with adults in different situations. Many interactions between adults and children constituted part of the day-to-day routines common to all nursery settings, including group stories and clearing up at the end of sessions. There were additional instances of more extended interactions between individual children and adults, representing individual support and development in the children's learning. For example, at Bridge Nursery School the children were free to play for as long or as short a time as they wished. The role of the teachers was to observe the children's play and intervene only on the basis of providing them with opportunities for extending it. One afternoon Lyn spent time exclusively with Naveen at the woodwork bench. Although she restricted her interaction to words of encouragement and to specific questions, her presence acted as an encouragement and reassurance for him, and when he did need help she was close at hand enabling him to move on and carry out the next steps in his model-making. On another occasion Kate approached Naveen to help and talk with him while he was sticking paper shapes on to a card he was making for his mother. She sat with him, asking him about his card and holding shapes for him as he stuck them. Naveen knew what he wanted to make, but with Kate's help and suggestions, for example about the amount of glue he was spreading on the shapes, he was gaining important knowledge in a situation which was relevant to his interests and which would help him in similar activities. This collaboration between Kate and Naveen continued when she shared a story with him in the book corner after he had finished his card. The collaboration consisted of the teacher reading and talking about the story with the child, while the child pointed out aspects of the illustrations and turned the pages when the teacher was ready. This provided an opportunity for them to talk together in the context of an alternative activity that was meaningful to the child. It also represented over a period of almost half an hour an important means for a variety of learning opportunities in the company of an adult in an unhurried and focused environment.

Regular interactions between educators and children took place in the context of the planned group activities that were a feature of both nurseries, for example story-time, or activities built around exploration of the indoor or outdoor environment. Cooking represented a regular example of just such an activity. Linda had been working with a group of three children preparing and cooking some mixed vegetables. She had introduced each vegetable to the children and talked with them about where and how it grew. She then showed them how to cut the vegetables, encouraging them to copy her, helping the children with their preparation and giving them an opportunity to try out the techniques after she had explained them. When the vegetables were cooked Linda divided the food between three mugs, gave each child a spoon and sat down with them. At this stage she asked them about the division of the food, how many portions there were and whether they thought the portions were equal. As they ate, she asked them if they could remember which vegetables they had used and which ones they liked best. One of the children mentioned the onions and how these had made them cry, and Linda explained why this was so. Although this example represents a more formalised activity, it also provided an opportunity for a small group of children to conduct a practical exploration and a collaborative experiment with an adult in a situation that provided a focus and an interest for all of them. Thus through a combination of instructions, suggestions and questions, the potential was created for the development of skills that could subsequently be employed in similar contexts.

Collaborating in their play provided good opportunities for children to use and develop their knowledge of language, whether their own community language or English. Where teachers joined in such collaboration, further opportunities were presented, but were inevitably limited to English in cases where teachers did not speak community languages. However, there were occasions on which bilingual children could have benefited from the opportunities afforded by the use of their community languages in their interactions with adults. One such example occurred one morning when Attia was playing on her own with the sticklebricks. Although engrossed, she nevertheless stopped and began to tell Nick about an event that had happened in the family. She started by saying: 'Nana's gone to Bangladesh.' Nick asked her about her family and she told him that 'Mummy, Nana and Daddy do the cooking.' After a further discussion about her family they began to talk about getting up in the morning and she said: 'In the holiday I can stay in bed but Nana tells Mummy to get me up. Nana gets up early and then Mummy and then I get up before my sisters.' The following week Attia proudly told Nick that she had come to school that morning with her Nana who had returned from Bangladesh a few days before. Nana's absence and return were obviously of great importance to Attia. The opportunity to talk about it in school allowed her not only to rehearse her feelings and anxieties about the fact that her grandmother was away, but also enabled a potentially important emotional and educational connection to be made and developed. If Attia's feeling of loss at the absence of her grandmother could have been shared in the nursery in her own community language, it might have had an even deeper meaning for her. Finding ways of encouraging children's use of their community languages in their play and interactions with relevant adults provides a potent force not only for the bilingual child's cognitive development, but also for her social and cultural development.

Starting from the Child

In keeping with their child-centred beliefs the teachers frequently used individual children's interests as starting-points. The flexible organisation of Bridge Nursery School enabled educators to respond to and develop themes of enquiry which initially began with the children, as Rosalind illustrated:

> The other day for instance we had a child who brought in a plastic spoon which changed colour when it was put into cold water, so ice was got out and people brought in T-shirts that changed with heat and we looked at how things change with temperature, so you can go with it, and if you can see the possibilities you can extend things to a high level with children.

The outdoor areas in both nurseries provided important sources of teaching and learning as children discovered aspects of an environment that changed with the seasons. For example, one morning two children had chosen to do some digging with trowels in one of the flower-beds. They asked Kate to come and look at a worm that they had unearthed. From this initial discovery Kate and the children talked about the different flowers that were growing, including their colours and sizes and whether they had a scent. The children noticed that there were some plants that did not have flowers, Kate pointing out that they were probably weeds and needed to be removed from the flower-bed. The children said that they wanted to keep these plants in their classroom to watch them grow. As a result they and Kate dug them up and planted them in flower-pots which the children had fetched from the school garage.

The teachers at Westside appeared more constrained in their approaches, partly because of the National Curriculum (see Chapter 2), but they all sought opportunities to follow up on children's interests. For example after a performance of Irish dancers at the school some of the children in the nursery asked to listen to the music again, which Jenni encouraged. On another occasion during outside play a number of children had found ladybirds and Jenni quickly located magnifier jars to enable them to look at these more closely. In Theresa's class, whilst doing topic work on poetry many of the children during choosing-time began to learn poetry by heart that they collected themselves from the bookshelves. Theresa gave the children the opportunity to recite poems in front of their classmates and it was observed during reading-time that a number of children, both boys and girls, spent a great deal of time reading and finding poetry.

Chris was frequently observed using the children's experiences as starting points to lessons, but she also sought to support the children's emotional needs. This reflected her belief that education was concerned with 'person-making' (Brehony, 1992; Woods & Jeffrey, 1996), as well as with academic needs. The following lesson shows Chris putting her philosophy into practice. It illustrates the way in which she would take pedagogical advantage of a particular event which might have excited the children's feelings and through which she might arouse a high state of awareness as well as exercising care.

At the start of a morning session with the reception class, Saadia (aged 5) complained to Chris that she had cut her finger. Chris asked if the researcher could take Saadia to see the teacher who had responsibility for first aid in the school whilst she herself continued with registration. When Saadia and the researcher returned, the finger suitably dressed with a clean sticking-plaster, Chris chose a story which she felt might help Saadia feel better, *Don't Cry Little Bear*, about a small bear who hurts himself. She compared Saadia's story to that of Little Bear, and used her name card to place over the words 'Little Bear' in the text when she wanted to refer to Saadia's story. The following extract is from the start of the story:

Teacher:	Ssh, Nora, you come and sit near me, you're being silly. You sit near me. This is to make Saadia feel better. *Don't* cry Saadia. *[Points to letter 'c' in 'cry']* What sound does this make?
Pupils:	'C', 'c', 'c'.
Teacher:	*[turns page]* Let's see what's on this page. *[Points to writing on book, putting Saadia's name over words 'Little Bear')* What's the story called?
Pupils:	*[led by Attiqa]* 'Don't cry Saadia'.
Teacher:	'Don't cry Saadia'. Did Saadia fall off her bike? *[picture in book shows Little Bear falling off his bike]*
Pupils:	Yeah.
Teacher:	Did you fall off your bike, Saadia?

Saadia:	*[shakes head]*
Teacher:	No, I don't think she did. What did Saadia hurt?
Nadia:	Her leg.
Teacher:	No, not her leg.
Pupil:	Arm.
Teacher:	Her *finger*. Saadia hurt her finger. What did Little Bear hurt?
Attiqa:	Arm.
Teacher:	His arm, good. Who's this coming? *[picture shows Little Bear's mother coming to help]*
Pupils:	Mum.
Teacher:	Mum. What did Mum say to Little Bear? She said 'Don't cry Little Bear'.
Pupils:	'Don't cry Little Bear'.
Teacher:	What do we say to Saadia?
All:	'Don't cry Saadia'.
Teacher:	Mum said 'I will pick you up'. Who picked Saadia up?
Pupil:	Her mum.
Teacher:	No. Who picked Saadia up?
2nd Pupil:	Mrs Boyle.
Teacher:	Mrs Boyle. Mrs Boyle said 'I will pick you up'. She said 'So *don't* cry. Don't cry Saadia.
Alia:	Little Saadia.

We see within this small extract a considerable amount of learning developing. There is some attention to phonics in the opening stage. Throughout the telling Chris points to the words 'Don't cry Little Bear/Saadia' as she and the children read them out, encouraging the children to become 'partners' in the reading process. There is the early development of scientific understanding, labelling parts of the body 'leg', 'arm' and 'finger'. The story also provides a strong scaffolding process for English language development. The repetition of phrase throughout the story enables all the children to join in, even those who may have little English. Further, because this story is well known to the children, new language can be brought by telling in parallel Saadia's experience, while maintaining the basic structure. Later in the story, other children began to talk about their own experiences of falling over or being hurt. However, the lesson did not end with the completion of the story. Chris asked the children if they would like to make a class book of Saadia's story, and they agreed enthusiastically. They drew the pictures and 'wrote' out the story, and the book was placed in the reading corner of the classroom. Mari observed the children on several occasions reading the book in class. Later in the term the book was used by the class as the focus for their class assembly and they shared Saadia's story with the rest of the school.

This example shows the pedagogical advantage that can be gained by recruiting children's feelings stirred by things that have actually happened to them or to a friend or colleague. It illustrates what can be achieved when teachers are creative about finding relevant opportunities within everyday occurrences. This had not been the planned morning activity.

Home and School Links

We shall consider relationships between parents and teachers more generally in Chapter 8. Here we examine the pedagogical advantages of links between home and school. How teachers sought to make such connections is illustrated in the following lesson. Elaine, a Year 1 teacher at Westside, had set up an experiment with the children (aged 5) to see what happens to various foods such as carrots, milk and biscuits left out on a window-sill.

Teacher: Perhaps tomorrow we'll put a few more things on, and then we're going to leave it, we're going to leave them and see what happens to them. Where do we usually keep, Imran, where do we usually keep carrots? Where does your mummy keep carrots?

Imran: Home ...

Teacher: Ssh, are you listening, Fatima ? [*Fatima is talking with Mobeen about the things they've left out on the window-sill.*)

Imran: In the shopping, in a bag ...

Teacher: She keeps them in a bag, does she? Where does she keep them, in the kitchen or in the cupboard or where?

Imran: In the cupboard.

Teacher: In the cupboard. Yes, we don't usually leave them lying out like that, do we? [*referring to the foods left on the window-sill*]

Mobeen:	Not in the fridge.
Teacher:	Well you can put carrots in the fridge ...
Mobeen:	You can, but then they get cold ...
Teacher:	... or you can put them in a special basket for vegetables.
Touzia:	And in the bowl ...
Shareen:	My mummy do.
Teacher:	Where do we usually keep biscuits? *[Some children speaking out]* Put your hands up, put your hands up.
Mobeen:	In the packet.
Teacher:	Ssh, put your hands up. Where do you put the biscuits, Touzia?
Touzia:	In jin.
Teacher:	In a ... ?
Touzia:	Jin. *[Goes incredibly shy at this point, realising she's said something incorrect.]*
Teacher:	*[puzzled by her answer, bends toward Touzia, talking quietly and directly to her]* In a ...?
Touzia:	Jin.
Teacher:	Jind? *[pause]* Is that a Panjabi word, Touzia?
Touzia:	*[shakes her head]*
Teacher:	*[still puzzled by Touzia's answer, suggesting possible meanings for her]* No? Do you mean a packet, or a tin?
Touzia:	*[very quietly, still looking unsure of her answer]* Tin.
Teacher:	Tin, a ti*n*, a ti*n [emphasising the sound of the word]*.
Touzia:	*[repeating it after her]* A tin.
Teacher:	*[tries to provide a context for the answer, relating it back to some work done earlier in the week]* Do you remember when we did that work and there were some crackers, and there was a tin for the crackers, do you remember the tin? A ti*n*.
Touzia:	*[nods, remembering the work]*

Teacher: *[returning to talk to the rest of the children]* You can put them in a tin, sometimes people just keep them in the packet and then they pull the top over, don't they, so that the biscuits are covered over, they don't usually just leave them out.

Mobeen: We're leaving our biscuits out.

[Other children talking at the same time about biscuits.]

Teacher: Pardon?

Mobeen: We're leaving our biscuits out.

Teacher: We're going to leave them out to see what happens.

Here Elaine is seeking to use the children's own experiences to provide a relevant context in which to place the new learning. It is a successful approach in many ways, as shown by the children being so eager – sometimes too eager – to volunteer their answers, and Elaine falls back on certain classroom controls, asking the children to raise their hands, requesting quiet and choosing individual pupils to answer. Yet when Elaine asks Touzia a question there is some confusion. We see Elaine attempting to make sense of Touzia's answer, suggesting possible explanations: is it a Panjabi term? Does she mean 'tin'? Though it appears as though Elaine is providing answers for Touzia, such prompting may be necessary, since the linguistic abilities in both English and Panjabi of these very young children will not yet be very well developed.

Mandell (1988) has shown that for young children to be asked to repeat themselves because adults have difficulty understanding them can prove very frustrating and embarrassing for both child and teacher. At the same time, bilingual children may appear to have attained a certain level of fluency in their second language, but may not have achieved an equal level of understanding (see Rix & Boyle, 1995). Touzia may not have understood the discussion. She may not have known or remembered the correct English term for what she wanted to say; she may even have had problems with the term 'Panjabi', since many of the children, including Touzia, referred to their mother tongues at this stage as Pakistani or Indian, rather than Panjabi or Urdu. While Elaine successfully provides an opportunity for both herself and Touzia to create an understanding, by providing an answer and referring to previous work, the example indicates some of the problems that teachers encountered in addressing cultural and linguistic relevance in the classroom.

Morning registration also brought opportunities for children to talk about events at home or to bring things into school that they had made. This activity had both strengths and weaknesses. On one occasion during their first year at school the children had been making books in class, and several of them brought in books they had made at home to show their teachers and peers. On another occasion Taylor brought in some butterflies he had made, copying an activity he had been involved in the previous day. Many of the children frequently brought in pieces of paper on which were lines of writing (letters and words) or rows of numbers which they had practised at home. The fact that they were able to re-create at home skills and activities which they had learned in school indicated how meaningful and relevant such activities were to them. Bringing in 'homework' was an opportunity for the children to have their abilities publicly acknowledged in front of their teacher and peers, and to experience some control over proceedings by being allowed to talk.

However, Baker and Perrott were critical of this sort of session in the schools of their research. They concluded (1988: 36) that while teachers might consider 'news sessions' important in that they allowed pupils the opportunity to learn 'to develop topics', 'how to listen' and 'rules of public discourse', in reality children were merely being initiated into school culture. They argued that the teacher maintained control over the whole procedure and that what the child was learning was most likely to be:

> ... discovering what the teacher likes to see and/or hear: the ability to interpret questions asked by the teacher in an 'adult' or 'curriculum' way; and an ability to act appropriately in the classroom setting and thereby be or become an acceptable pupil. Thus some pupils will 'fail' the teacher's expectations in news sessions. What is required for successful participation is advanced judgement and fine tuning on both 'form' and 'content' criteria. This involves considerable interaction.

We consider in Chapter 5 other aspects of starting school which influence the transformation of children into pupils, but Baker and Perrott highlight here the significance of the language skills that children need to possess in order to partake in this form of activity. This is particularly relevant for bilingual children. All of the 'news sessions' were carried out in English, and children's individual participation in them indicated not only their general confidence about standing up in front of their classmates, but also their confidence about talking in English.

Links between home and school could also be developed in a private way. On one occasion when Chris was taking the Reception class children she was given a letter from a child in an older class who was doing some work on letter-writing. Chris wrote a reply to the older pupil, explaining what she was doing with the Reception class. The following day, Alia, one of Chris's pupils, came to school with a typed letter for Chris that her mother had helped her with.

DWAR NRS MCFALAN

I GULSHAN FAROOQ like to came to school
a nd i love to paly in the home coner.
i love to come school bsu bayse i have got lot o
of farids and i love my teachers
too.
i ill like to siting on the pa carpat
plice come to my house on eid you can have cap o
of tae
thank you
yourg gulshan FAROOQ?

Chris read out the letter to the class, and later that day wrote back to Alia thanking her. During the afternoon session Alia then wrote a letter to the researcher, Mari, who also wrote back to her, and for a few days a number of the children wrote letters to each other during free choice at the writing-table. Whilst Chris could have used this as a starting point to encourage all the children to write letters, containing the letter-writing just between those children who chose to join in meant that this was a meaningful, real and relevant activity to those children involved. It was not simply another school language exercise.

Revisiting

In the interests of developing relevance children were also allowed to revisit activities in both nursery and school. At their first attempt they had learnt the physical skills necessary to performing an activity. Revisiting encouraged them to develop conceptual skills. For example, Naveen (aged 4 years 1 month) of Bridge Nursery School frequented the cooking area on a regular basis. Over a period of time he had built up a knowledge of how to make a rice crispy cake. On one occasion he was observed making a crispy with the help of Kate and was able to carry out some of the steps by himself, for example adding the Rice Krispies to the melted chocolate without being prompted. Kate asked him what he needed to do after he had mixed the ingredients and he replied 'cake case'. She then asked him what he did with the case and he replied: 'put name on it'. He was getting so used to the activity now that he was able to point at the sentence under the pictures in the recipe book and say: 'That says ...'. Being given the opportunity to do something he obviously liked over a period of time, rather than just as a one-off cookery lesson, not only enabled Naveen to cook, but also showed that he was beginning to understand print, and to be able to follow instructions and sequence. No doubt this activity gave him other opportunities for learning – counting, measuring, what happens to chocolate when it is heated, what happens when you add Rice Krispies to it and so on.

The teachers in the lower school also frequently used the children's previous experiences to build on and extend the children's knowledge. During their first year at school they were often asked to mix paints, using primary colours to make secondary ones. The example below, taken from their first term at school, illustrates how they were beginning to develop their understanding of colour. Elaine is talking to them about painting some clay patterns they have made.

Teacher: Now you're going to paint them next, and you can mix the colour to paint. I've put the colours out, and you're going to have one of these little pots to mix in, there you are. I've put some brushes there. Can you put that over there for me, Fouzia, thank you. Now you can use two colours. You can choose two of the colours to mix. So you can look and think which two colours you might like to mix. Just two colours, please. Now you should know, a few of the colours that you can mix, you should all know that if you mix the blue and the yellow, you should know what colour you're going to get. Put your hand up if you know what colour you're going to get if you mix those two colours together.

Pupil: *[unclear, trying to give away the answer]*

Teacher: Ssh. Can you remember, Imran?

Imran: *[hand not up]* No.

Teacher: No?

Touzia: I can

Shiraz: I can

Teacher: Can you remember, Fouzia? What colour?

Fouzia: Green.

Teacher: Green, good girl.

Touzia: Green.

Teacher: If you mix blue and yellow together you get green ...

Children: Green.

Teacher: We were doing that, if you remember. We also mixed these two together.

Touzia: *[referring to the paints]* I know.

Teacher: We also mixed ... this red and this yellow.

Mobeen:	I remember doing them things.
Teacher:	Can you remember what colour we made? Can you remember, Ali, what colour?
Ali:	We made red.
Teacher:	We didn't make red, didn't make red when we mixed them together.
Imran:	[*calls out*] Orange.
Teacher:	Put your hands up, please.
Touzia:	[*calls out*] I know.
Teacher:	Some children have their hands up. Can you remember, Semina? What colour did we make?
Semina:	Green.
Teacher:	No not green, that was blue and yellow that made green.
Touzia:	I know.
Teacher:	Red and yellow made something else.
Asria:	A green.
Teacher:	Em, Fatima.
Fatima:	Orange.
Teacher:	Orange.

This was an exercise the children did frequently throughout the year, but always within the relevant context of painting something. During their second year at school Theresa continued with this practice. During one lesson she was explaining to the same class about light and shade in painting techniques. She had drawn a flower on a piece of art paper and was painting in the leaves. As she did so she continued to talk to the class, explaining what she was doing:

Teacher:	I'm going to make this side a bit lighter and then see if I can find a darker green.
Mobeen:	Not very dark.
Teacher:	Not very dark, no. A bit darker, I think I'm gonna put a darker colour on this side. See that's a bit darker?

Children:	Yes.
Mohbi:	It looks bit blue.
Teacher:	It does look a bit blue. Em, I made that green darker by putting more blue in it, I put more blue in that one, I mixed yellow and blue together to make green. And I put more blue in it. And this one's got more yellow in it so it's a lighter green.
Mobeen:	That's light green now.
Teacher:	Now does that look like a leaf?
Children:	Yeah.
Teacher:	Good.

Theresa revisits a concept the children had been developing during the previous year, but develops it and adds a little more information. It was noticeable that she did this frequently across the curriculum, reminding children of work they had covered in their previous class before moving on to the next stage. It reflected the important communication also that went on between the teachers in the school.

Teaching in the Margins

It seemed as if our teachers never stopped teaching. Although there were definite times of the day when one could identify a lesson as starting or ending there were points at either end of the lessons which were frequently used for teaching purposes. For example during a term when Elaine was covering the topic of forces with the children, she was helping some of them put on their coats for playtime. As she did so she was talking to them about 'pulling' up their zips and 'pushing' open the doors, emphasising both the words and actions. Both Elaine and Chris also used registration for counting and mental arithmetic: how many children were at school, how many more boys were there than girls? On Thursdays the children were allowed to bring money into school to buy cakes at breaktime. The children were asked to give their money to the class teacher on arriving and then collect it at break. This opportunity was used by Theresa to look at money, pennies, 2p, 5p and 10p pieces. Lining-up times were used by all three teachers as opportunities to develop learning, for example by allowing children wearing certain coloured or patterned jumpers to line up first, or those who had particular letters in their names, or who could answer a specific question. Elaine used these opportunities to develop maths work using plastic coloured shapes. She would ask children about various attributes of the shapes, for example their colour, or their name, or how many corners they had, how many straight sides, how many curves and so on. When the children answered correctly they were allowed to go and wash their hands ready for dinner.

There was a strong element of fun in these situations, and differentiation by the teachers indicated an acute awareness of the abilities of each child. In fact Elaine used them specifically as a sort of informal assessment. If a child was struggling with the colours or names of the shapes then she was able to identify and support that child in more formal situations.

There were other occasions when teachers gave an impromptu reaction to events within the classroom or to children's questions. On one occasion in Theresa's class the children had been working on an exercise in which they had to draw an overhead plan of a set of different sized pots and pans on a toy cooker. At one stage one of the boys in the class asked Theresa if the cooker was real. She said that it wasn't but then asked the group what it would need if it were real. They came up with the following suggestions:

Mohbi: make it get hot with fire

Fatima: 'lectric and matches

Taylor: electric

Ravinder: matches

Fouzia: matches

Damian: gas

Theresa discussed the workings of a cooker with the group for a short time before bringing the children back to the original exercise. There were many occasions when our teachers provided opportunities for children to ask relevant questions within a meaningful context and to respond appropriately. On some occasions these involved individuals or small groups, on others the whole class. For example when Taylor informed his class teacher that his aunty had just had a baby the whole class made suggestions for a suitable name, and the children began to talk about their own experiences of baby brothers, sisters and cousins.

Incidents such as these create a great deal of interest. They often require an immediate response from the teacher, otherwise the moment and the relevance can be lost. Once the tangential inquiry has been dealt with, the children and teacher continue with the main focus of the lesson. These teaching and learning opportunities differ from those investigated in the following section because they are brief interludes and do not disrupt or alter the focus of the original lesson.

Spontaneous Reaction

An important aspect of creative teaching (Woods & Jeffrey, 1996: 9) is innovation – finding effective ways of engaging with pupils; of shaping, contextualising and developing the knowledge to be shared; and of turning apparent constraints into opportunities (Woods & Jeffrey, 1996: 7). Much of this comes from spontaneous reaction to clues offered by children that represent opportunities to advance their learning.

As we have already seen at Bridge, part of the innovative approach lay firmly in the way in which the nursery was resourced and in the belief that children learned best through the use of play. The structure in the nursery was particularly flexible, so that the teachers could make the best use of developing themes that would encourage the children's interest. Rosalind gave an example of this innovative approach:

> It might be that you wanted to introduce Spring so you brought in a whole load of flowers and just put them on the floor and the children said, 'Why are you sitting there with those flowers?' And you could say, 'Well I was cutting up these stems because I thought I'd arrange these flowers.' Then they would want to help me, and then they might be involved in using scissors, but then they might be involved at a higher level on: 'We've got these flowers because it's spring-time, and that's when flowers grow. If you cut off these stalks it helps them to drink, it'll be better than if we don't.' So they're learning all kinds of concepts.

Also important at Bridge was the use teachers made of observations of children's play. Rosalind pointed to the emphasis on progression:

> You could come in and do a piece of woodwork at your level even though you're skilled. You could actually go to the woodwork bench and select appropriate materials and do something yourself. Same as the painting, so that you can always progress. That's why the provision was chosen and perhaps if the children had their interest, like at the woodwork they have an interest in transport and one puts out things that might suggest wheels on that day, so a lot of the structure comes from provision.

At Westside nursery there were perhaps fewer opportunities for more flexible approaches to learning in the way there were at Bridge. Constraints were greater at Westside, partly because of preparation demands made on the nursery by the lower school, but also because of the way in which the curriculum was designed. In practice there was a greater emphasis on structured than on free-play activities in relation to planning and assessment, although at the same time there was a belief that unstructured play was beneficial to the development of the child. There was no specific definition of the purposes of unstructured play, except indirectly in a section of the policy document on 'The Role of Adults in Play'. This role was perceived as 'initially to provide a stimulating environment with materials and opportunities for the children to develop socially, emotionally, physically and cognitively'. It was left to Linda, one of Jenni's nursery nurses, to provide a more specific description of the function of free play in the unit:

I quite like the free structure of the nursery as well where they just come up and do things when they want to do it. Co-ordination, their social skills, depending on what they're doing they learn a lot of other things, day to day life and learn their skills from it.

Unlike at Bridge there were no observations at Westside of children's free play, their development being noted only during the structured activities they carried out with their teacher. However, there were opportunities for the development of children's interests, and though structured activities were by their very definition teacher-directed and planned, elements of 'fun' were inherent in them. The educators sought to use materials that they believed would appeal to the children and would be interesting to use. For example different types of paper, items such as wool, pulses, small paper shapes and junk material were provided in art and craft. Various games such as Snap, matching number puzzles and object-counting games were used to encourage mathematical development, and stories to develop language and reading skills. However, again unlike at Bridge, tabletop equipment, such as small constructional apparatus, was generally changed on a daily basis, a practice which was designed to give the children a width and variety of experiences, but which meant that at times they were not given the opportunity to exhaust the potential of a particular activity if they wished to return to it on the following day.

At Bridge children were encouraged to observe each other's play and take their time in choosing activities. At Westside, on the other hand, they were encouraged to be busy and fully occupied rather than wandering around in an apparently unfocused way. Attia, for example, found it difficult on occasion to identify activities that particularly interested her. One morning in quick succession after looking at a book on her own she visited a number of additional activities, including the Lego table and the jigsaws. At each one she interfered with other children, putting a book on a child's lap, taking a piece of a boy's puzzle and pulling away a chair from under a child. Eventually she settled, but only after Anne had intervened and directed her to a painting activity which she was supervising.

This illustrates a classic teacher dilemma. In the encouragement of socially acceptable behaviour there could be on occasions the potential for misunderstanding the interests of children and thus the opportunities for taking advantage of teachable moments. Attia might have benefited from a longer period of free observation and experiment. While Tariq and Tony, in the example described above, were comparing their heights with the rod which they had constructed from plastic tubes, they were twice instructed by a teacher to return to their table as they moved around the nursery testing the rod's rigidity.

In the lower school, the constraints already discussed – such as certain aspects of the National Curriculum, the need to ensure children are at a certain stage before moving to a new class, the impact of an OFSTED inspection – can limit teachers' scope for innovation and reduce them to a mode of 'getting done' (Apple, 1986):

> 'Getting done' is characteristic of bureaucratic systems, where an objectives-led approach, with the emphasis on outcomes and monitoring, focuses attention on getting the prescribed task finished and records completed regardless of what other opportunities for learning occur during its course. (Woods & Jeffrey, 1996: 34)

Yet there were times when teachers chose to abandon planned activities and to 'go with the flow', which 'puts the emphasis on process, and involves intuition, spontaneity, "tacit knowledge", enthusiasm and fun' (Woods & Jeffrey, 1996: 34). Chris was perhaps the one most inclined to this mode of teaching and was observed on numerous occasions pursuing the 'teachable moment'. One particular example of this occurred as she was taking the register with the Year 1/Reception class. This had followed the pattern of most registrations, calling out children's names, marking them in and the children then trying to work out exactly how many were in school that day. As a follow-up to some maths work they had done earlier in the week Chris asked the children if they could work out if there were more boys than girls. They came up with a variety of answers to the question and Chris suggested that they work out the real answer by using patterning, which they had been doing the day before. The following fieldnotes illustrate what happened.

> Chris asked the children how many more girls than boys there were in the class [*there were ten girls and five boys*]. Peter said ten, Damian said three – she asked Damian how he knew and he said he had counted them. She then reminded the class of how they had solved a similar problem the day before through patterning and said they could find out by making a pattern of girl/boy/girl/boy etc. Chris began the pattern for the class, picking a boy and girl to stand at the front of the mat, then asked the children what came next. Rather than choosing herself which child should come next in the line, she encouraged the children to volunteer themselves. When Imran's turn came there was not enough room at the end of the line so he stood at the front without disturbing the pattern. After the last boy joined the line the children were aware that there were four girls remaining on the carpet [*the pattern had gone g/b/g/b/g/b/g/b/g/b/g*]. The focus then shifted to considering how they could get everybody in the line in a proper pattern, which mainly came from the children's own interest, because there were still four girls left on the carpet. This turned into a very dynamic piece of practical problem-solving. Peter felt that he had a much better way of doing the pattern, gg/bb, and Chris asked if the children could organise themselves into Peter's pattern. Selina was asked if she could do this but she declined, so Chris asked Mobeen who was more than eager and needed little help ... Many of the

children were aware that this pattern also would not work once there was only one boy left on the carpet, and had no problem explaining to Chris that there were not enough boys. Chris asked if anyone else had any ideas. Mobeen came up with a very complicated pattern – ggg/b/ggg/b. Chris asked her to organise this pattern. Again the pattern did not work out fully, with one boy and one girl left on the carpet, but Chris praised the efforts of the children, commenting on how well they had done. She then suggested that they could make some patterns of their own, using strips of card, and drew some examples of patterns on the easel board. The children went off to make their own patterns whilst Chris worked with individual children with their reading ... Most of the children copied the pattern Chris had put on the board, except for Mobeen who chose to make a pattern of boy/girl and then of different coloured flowers. Chris also set up patterning activities on other tables for the children to do when they had finished their initial task – peg-boards and beads, which were mainly chosen by the girls. The boys tended to drift toward the mat when they had finished, to play with Lego or one of the games available.

Afterwards Chris explained that this had not been the planned session, but because the children had taken such an interest in the patterning exercise she felt it was more beneficial to pursue that activity. (Fieldnotes, 2 November 1994)

Chris encouraged 'going with the flow' with all her staff. A typical example was when Mary, one of the Key Stage 2 teachers, whilst working on a topic on food, had wondered with her class how many Cornflakes packets it would take to feed everyone in school. They pursued this problem, which finally resulted in Mary's class making breakfast for the whole school. The children measured out portions of Cornflakes and milk, planned seating arrangements and organised the service requirements, who would be serving and who would be clearing away. They also made their own uniforms for serving.

Our teachers indicated their innovative approaches through the variety of teaching methods they employed. Chris particularly enjoyed using drama and story to enhance the learning experience (see Chapter 4). Theresa spent a great deal of time on practical lessons. Circuit boards were used to develop an understanding about electricity. Magnets were used not just to explore magnetism but to work with a variety of materials which led on to practical problem-solving. Artwork was particularly varied. Not only were painting skills developed, but the children also worked with chalk, clay, collage and weaving. Importantly the children were given the opportunity to start again on art projects. When working with new materials, such as clay, Theresa allowed them to experiment with the material first before asking them to work on a particular theme. This meant that they had the opportunity to discover at least some of the properties of these materials before being asked to 'make' something. Additionally, Theresa encouraged the children to start again if they felt that what they had done was not really their best effort. Children were also given the opportunity to develop work over a period of time. In their final half term in Theresa's class they created their own story-books. They were encouraged to do some research on stories and books, taking note of the way in which book covers were designed, how pictures and words needed to match up, and they then had to make a choice as to whether they wanted theirs to be a 'flip' book or a picture-book. Some children chose to create their own stories or adapt ones that they knew, others used known rhymes and stories and put their own pictures to them, and some made information books. Because they were given time to work on their books the standard was very high, and there was a very tangible sense of achievement amongst them.

Teachers were not innovative *all* the time. To be so would be exhausting, both for the teacher and for the children, as was illustrated during the OFSTED inspection when the teachers attempted to demonstrate their ability to be innovative in their teaching. Through trying to incorporate all their best ideas into one week, both teachers and children were visibly tired by the end of the inspection. Theresa commented afterwards:

> [The OFSTED inspectors], they're expecting such a lot, aren't they, they're expecting everything to be excellent all of the time and average isn't good enough is it? And you just can't keep it up. There's no way in this job that you can be wonderful all the time.

There were times when lessons followed a noted routine, and this routine in itself helped to balance the school day. It was important for the children that they had this balance between innovation and routine. The highly practical nature of the curriculum enabled the children to develop problem-solving techniques, be experimental and innovative themselves. For the bilingual child it provided physical explanations for new concepts, allowing the child to overcome in part the linguistic mismatch that might otherwise occur with a less practical approach. At the same time, more structured activities provided a sense of security. The children knew what was expected of them in these situations, and again for the bilingual child, having a knowledge of the routine of certain exercises at least meant that they were not constantly having to struggle with understanding a new set of instructions every day.

Suggestions

(1) A discussion of the importance of play has been a feature of this chapter. If you use play in your classroom the following ideas may help to develop it as a tool for children's learning:

- Creating opportunities to observe and record children's play can provide you with important information about their level of development. This information can inform and supplement your general planning and assessment.

- You may find it useful to review the consistency of your provision in your classroom. It is likely that your large apparatus will be available from day to day, but what about the smaller apparatus? Is it displayed in such a way that the children know where it is stored and are able to use it when they wish?

- Your own role in children's play can be an important part of teaching and learning, not only in your choice of the physical provision. As part of your observations of children's play you could make it a feature of your teaching to look for opportunities, where appropriate, to join in with the children and develop some of the ideas suggested on p.67 of this chapter by Tina Bruce (1997: 97). See also Kelly-Byrne, 1989.

- How relevant is your provision for play for your bilingual learners? We have made some suggestions for this in Chapter 2.

(2) In your work with Key Stage 1 of the National Curriculum you will, as a normal part of your planning, be aware of the need to build on children's previous knowledge as a foundation for each body of work carried out in the classroom. Do you also provide opportunities for responding to children's immediate interests arising from the current piece of work? These opportunities may arise from work already planned in another context and to which the children will be bringing their own ideas and personal experiences, sparked off by the present activity. You need to feel confident about responding positively to these 'going with the flow' situations, particularly if you are trying to provide opportunities to make your National Curriculum work relevant to your bilingual learners. The following suggestions may be of help:

- You may not at first feel confident about responding every time to children's immediate concerns and interests. In this case try slowly to increase those occasions, keeping in mind the potential opportunities provided by the examples in this chapter.

- As you would with normally planned activities, monitor closely the learning which has taken place as a result of situations arising from 'going with the flow'. Return to the attainment targets and check which have been achieved. You may find in these circumstances that the attainment targets are not necessarily the ones you originally planned to cover! In that case you may need to replan some of your subsequent activities to ensure that those particular targets are visited.

- Discuss with your colleagues your use of 'going with the flow' strategies. Perhaps they might want to develop some of these ideas as a matter of regular policy in their own classrooms. Talk also with subject co-ordinators and the headteacher in order to gain support and advice.

Chapter 4
The Educational Significance of Stories

Introduction

Stories represent an important way in which children from the earliest age come to make sense of the world (Meek, 1977). Children are often told stories by peers and adults in the form of talk, songs, nursery rhymes or storytelling. They also construct their own stories from personal experience, and in so doing give such experience a plausibility in the context of their own lives. This process is described by Wells (1987: 194) as the construction by children of stories in the mind, or 'storying', in which they attempt to create 'a mental model of their world':

> ... in every act of perception, the world 'out there' is interpreted in relation to the inner mental model in terms of which that world is represented. Making sense of an experience is thus to a very great extent being able to construct a plausible story about it. (p.196)

Storying is a personal process which becomes a story when it is shared with others through words (Wells, 1987: 194), and which we use to explain events, actions, feelings and motivations (Meek, 1991: 103). Hardy (1977: 13) suggests that such stories are expressed in the form of narratives, by which we express 'that inner and outer storytelling that plays a major role in our sleeping and waking lives':

> For we dream in narrative, daydream in narrative, remember, anticipate, hope, despair, believe, doubt, plan, revise, criticise, construct, gossip, learn, hate, and love by narrative. In order really to live, we make up stories about ourselves and others, about the personal as well as the social past and future.

Whilst story is an important medium through which we all represent our lives and experiences, there are also immense educational benefits in it for all children, with added advantages for children learning a second language. Barrs (1990) points to the importance of sharing stories in the classroom that can support language-learning and growth in addition to developing children's storytelling skills. For children learning an additional language, 'stories provide an important route into the sounds and rhythms, vocabulary and structure of the new language' (Barrs, 1990: 12). Yet they can provide more. Where stories from other ethnic groups are told in class, then all the children can share in the rich variety of cultures in the world and 'such stories have an added importance for (ethnic minority) children when they realise their cultures are recognised and valued in school' (Aylwin, 1992: 71).

Stories and storying of various kinds were very prominent in our schools. In this chapter, we discuss their significance.

Creating Meaning

It has long been recognised in educational research that continuity of learning experiences between home and school is important for the child's successful learning development (Heath, 1983; Tizard & Hughes, 1984). Where there is a mismatch between home and school cultural practices, research has shown children experiencing learning and reading difficulties (Heath, 1983; Gregory, 1993; Kook & Vedder, 1995). Firm links are required, therefore, between home and school in terms of knowledge content and structure. But firm cultural and personal links are also required. Our children tried to make these through informal acts of storying, constructing meanings from their experiences of home and school which were taken into each environment to be re-enacted as links between the two. The experiences of home and school were thereby legitimised as part of the process of induction into the respective cultures through children making them their own (Wells, 1987: 195). Stories emerging from the children's own inner storying also provide an integrating function. They are helping to promote holistic pupil-knowledge across a number of divides. We select examples from the nurseries to illustrate these points.

Parents considered storying facilitated their children's engagement with the culture of the schools. Mrs Ali described how Iqbal had become absorbed in his life at school and the influence it was coming to represent:

> When he's doing anything in school similar he does like this he says, 'I done this in school', 'I will make this cake like this'. When we make cake he wants to help me. At home when he plays with his toys, he's talking himself like his friends when he's doing things and his other friends in nursery he imagines he's playing with them.

For Rushan the experience of the nursery took the form of observing and re-enacting the role which he had seen the teacher play from day to day. His mother said:

> Sometimes he get his book and he make up stories and just like one of the teachers do at school he'll pretend that there's some kids sitting there and he'll get the book and start reading the story out, but he can't read the words but he makes it up.

Children sometimes used storying in a form of role-play to re-enact at school experiences they had had at home. This form of 'story play' (Meek, 1991: 108) enables them to 'be themselves in a real world or in an imaginary world. Or they can be imaginary people in that world, or imaginary people in the real world'. For example, Aisha was observed on her own sweeping up in the house with a dustpan and brush. She put on a pair of oven-gloves, went to the cooker and opened the door. She then visited the house which had been set up in the corridor before returning to the main house and taking off her apron. On another occasion she had decided to prepare drinks for Kieran. She took two cups from the house where Kieran was also playing and carried them to the milk table where she filled them from a jug of water. She carried the cups back into the house and put them down saying to Kieran: 'There's some water for you. That is mine [*pointing to one of the cups*] and that is yours'. After drinking some of the water she went out of the house taking two dishes with her, saying to Kieran: 'I'll come back in a minute'. She chose some pieces of small coloured paper and scrap from the gluing table and returned to the house saying: 'That's mine and that's Victoria's [one of the dolls in the house].' Meanwhile Aditya arrived at the house and asked: 'Can I come in?' to which Aisha replied: 'No you can't come in, it's my house, it's not your house.' This example shows how role-play which was centred around the house enabled Aisha to make links with actuality, moulding and re-creating through her own narrative the language and habits of home to give them meaning for her personally within the nursery environment.

Re-enactments of experiences at home through the mental process of storying could also provide the basis for the child embracing a more wide-ranging view of the world. Tariq was making a car with the large Lego, experimenting with moving it backwards and forwards on the table-top. He told Nick that his dad had crashed their car and that he wanted him this time to buy an 'ice-cream car'; 'I said to my dad yesterday, can he buy an ice-cream car?' This imaginative transfer from the Lego to an ice-cream van he had seen outside enabled him to create this connection between the activity and home. Again on another day he was playing with the Lego, this time making a train, but the subject of cars was still fresh in his mind:

When my dad was driving up a hill it was all broken and the car fell down and it was on fire and I did fall out of the window and I was bleeding and then blood was coming from my foot. Then my daddy did buy a new car like an ice-cream car.

There was then a short pause during which he was obviously thinking more about his car at home, after which he said: 'My car's called Chitty, Chitty, Bang, Bang.' (He had heard Nick talking with another boy about a flying car that he had made.) He then walked away, but returned a short time afterwards to add: 'The white car's called Lighty, Lighty, Bang, Bang.'

The ebb and flow of Tariq's thoughts was returning constantly to his life outside school, whether real or imagined. He thus created a direct link between the reality of his father's car and the imaginative potential provided by it, including the connection made with a story he had heard. Of significance also was his awareness, through his use of the alternative name for his white car, of the potential for playing with language through a use of its patterns. He was using this knowledge to re-invent his language while at the same time relating it to his own experience.

In a similar way, children used storying to imbue events experienced at school with personal meaning and relevance. It also gave them an opportunity to join the adult world and externalise their storying as a form of re-enacted adult wisdom, as in the example of Aisha's play in the house. One such opportunity occurred when a fire broke out among a pile of discarded tyres in a yard behind the nursery garden. The children, who were already outside, went to the railings to watch. After a few minutes Sonny began building with the wooden building blocks what he described as a 'fire car'. After adding a plank of wood to the structure to complete it, Aisha asked if she could sit in it. She sat inside while he went to collect another plank of wood to put on the structure. By this time Deepak had arrived and he, Aisha and Sonny sat together in the 'fire car'. The materials that were available enabled Sonny to use the moment to translate an actual event and to enter into the adult world of firefighters in his imagination. Sharing that with others gave what he had made a reality and validity of its own.

In another example Naveen became absorbed in playing with some large wooden blocks that he fitted closely together to create a grid. He then fetched some plastic vehicles and put miniature people in them. Next he drove the vehicles on to the grid, providing a commentary as he did so: 'The baby's going in the lorry', he said, as he fitted a figure in the tractor, and 'All this stuff is going on', as he put the vehicles on the blocks in a line. After that, he picked up some of the vehicles and announced: 'Going to put these in the sand.' Again, storying provided a way of making sense of what he knew of the world outside.

Stories read and told to children can also offer them a means of personal discovery and exploration of ideas (Meek, 1991: 113). An example of this process occurred in a discussion between Mari and Azmat about stepmothers, after Azmat had read Mari *Hansel and Gretel*.

Mari: Why do you think the stepmother wanted them to leave?

Azmat: 'Cos she's a stepmother.

Mari: Oh! Is that what stepmothers do?

Azmat: They do bad.

Mari: Sorry?

Azmat: They do bad.

Mari: They're bad. Are all stepmothers bad, do you think?

Azmat: Yes.

Mari: Is it just the stepmothers in stories that are bad, or is it real stepmothers as well?

Azmat: Real stepmothers too.

Mari: Too? Why do you think that?

Azmat: 'Cos it's in films and stories.

Mari: 'Cos it's in all the stories? What about stepdads? Do you think stepdads are bad?

Azmat: Dunno.

Mari: Have you heard any stories with stepdads in?

Azmat: No.

Meek (1987) talks about the 'life-to-text, text-to-life' relationship in story, in which children are able to explore and reflect issues regarding emotional growth and maturation, without having to test them out in real life. Azmat has made judgements about stepmothers, which are negative in their outlook, based on her knowledge of these relationships from the stories and films she has read and seen. Her own experience of real step-parents may have been very limited. Indeed within the school, the family unit overwhelmingly consists of two parents, siblings and in many cases, a large extended family. Divorce and one-parent families were uncommon; only three children in the class were from single-parent families. Two of these children were white (one of the parents was divorced), and the father of the third child had recently died. This particular example indicates how influential the story medium is in shaping children's views and how literature can challenge or reinforce stereotypes within fictional tales.

Creative Teaching and Learning

As we have seen earlier, creative teaching and learning require innovation, ownership of knowledge, control of the teaching and learning processes, and relevance to the needs of the learner. Given opportunity to flourish they will lead to growth and development. Stories provide an excellent way of promoting all these requirements (with a special significance, for the bilingual child, in relevance) since they bear not just on learning needs, but also on cultural ones. We shall explore these creative functions through consideration of the 'Rainbow' story project that took place in the lower school. We give first a short synopsis of the overall structure of the four story sessions, before going on to consider their educational significance for bilingual children. The teacher and children spent an hour to an hour and a half each week preparing and developing a story about a giant and a rainbow. The sessions included oral storytelling, drama and art work, and culminated in the children presenting the story to the whole school.

Session 1

Mainly directed by Chris (the headteacher). Using a photograph of a rainbow, Chris led a discussion with the children before beginning the story. She told them how the rainbow in the story had been painted by a group of people whose responsibility it was to make sure it remained bright and clear and repaint it when necessary. One day when all the townsfolk were about to go on holiday they went to check the rainbow, but found that large shapes had been cut out of it. On the ground was a giant footprint, the only clue. The townsfolk decided to find out who was responsible. Chris then developed some drama work with the class, based on the story so far.

Session 2

Chris recapped on the story and the children joined in, reminding her of parts she had left out. With their input she developed the story further. The townsfolk went to confront the giant, initially angry at what he had done. However, when they met him they found he had used the shapes to decorate his house for his birthday. The giant, repentant for spoiling the rainbow, asked the townsfolk to stay and celebrate his birthday with him. They had a lovely time and forgave the giant for cutting their rainbow, but stipulated that he should not do it again. The children then went on to make their own pictures of the rainbow.

Session 3

Chris and the children recapped on the story and she completed it by telling them how the townsfolk had taken the shapes back from the giant to mend their rainbow. This session also included some drama work.

Session 4

Rehearsal for the children before telling the story to the whole school.

The following sections examine the learning development which took place during the story sessions in three main categories: language development, conceptual development, and social, emotional and cultural understanding.

Language development

Throughout the sessions Chris provided opportunities for all the children to take part in the story, regardless of their fluency in English, through the use of repetition of phrases:

Teacher: Ready to help me? Now don't shout, I'm not shouting. I'm just using a nice voice so you can hear me.

All: This story happened a long, long, long, long, long time ago.

Teacher: And it's a story ... *[some of the children trying to join in]* no, you listen now. And it's a story about some people who lived in a village, and they lived in their houses with their ...

All: ... mums, and dads, and brothers, and sisters, and aunties, and uncles, and grandmas, and granddads and babies.

Teacher: And they lived in their houses and they had a very special job to do. They ... *[some of the children trying to join in]* shush, they had to paint a beautiful rainbow. And in their houses they had big, big, big tins of paint. They had red, and yellow ...

All: ... and pink and green, purple and orange and blue.

It was noticeable that even the most reticent of children in the classroom joined in with these chorus phrases, their unchanging nature and rhythm helping to scaffold the language development. Paley (1995: 95–96) comments on how powerful stories can be for children learning to speak a second language, as they have available to them 'fully developed sentences borrowed from someone else.'

> The dialogue can change a child from inarticulate embarrassment to confidence, as if by a magic wand. The only task required is to memorise the words. With enough practice, anyone can do this, because the practice is part of the reward.

By joining in with the 'Rainbow' story the children at Westside began to develop some control and ownership, both of it and its language. Ownership was furthered by Chris encouraging individual children to become storytellers themselves. As they sat on the 'storytelling chair' (the teacher's chair) she supported each child by repeating what they had said, expanding, prompting and encouraging. She pointed out changes they had made to the original storyline, demonstrating the flexibility of storytelling, that each telling can be different. The following extract highlights this scaffolding process (Bruner, 1985):

Teacher: Ready, Jatinder? Are you going to tell us the story?

Jatinder: The man painted the rainbow.

Teacher: Good boy. The man painted the rainbow. He painted a beautiful rainbow. Now in Jatinder's story, Jatinder's changed it. Jatinder said the man painted the rainbow ... we said in our story there were mums and dads and babies, and grans and granddads. Jatinder said in his story today the man painted the rainbow. What colour did he paint it?

All: Red, and yellow, and pink and green, purple and orange and blue.

Teacher: And what happened then?:

                 [Jatinder nominated Peter to continue the story.]

Peter: The man and the lady painted it.

Teacher: Peter said 'and the lady painted it' too, and she painted it ...

All: Red, and yellow, and pink and green, purple and orange and blue.

Peter: And they painted it every day, and one day the man and the woman said 'Let's go on our holiday.'

Teacher: They did. They said. And one day they said 'Let's go on our holiday.' And everybody went in their house ...

Peter: *[interrupts to add]* But first they checked the rainbow.

Teacher: But first, before they went on holiday, they went to check the rainbow.

There is a strong sense of ownership and control over the story by Jatinder and Peter in this practice session before the telling to the whole school, the teacher validating their contributions by her repetitions. Many of the children were given the opportunity to be the storyteller. All of this gave the children the opportunity of using English within a supportive context and enabled them to hear their peers using English in a storytelling context, not just their teacher or other adults.

One particular child, Simera, received a noticeable boost to her language confidence through the sessions. Though she had been born in England she had spent a considerable amount of time in Pakistan before starting school and rarely spoke in class. When she did, her head would lower, her hand would cover her mouth and her answers were generally inaudible. Both Chris and Mari had noticed in the early sessions how Simera had joined in the 'chorus' lines of the story and appeared more attentive, following the action and speakers closely. During the above session Peter passed the story to Chris. When Chris came to pass the story on Simera immediately adopted the pose of the other children, sitting up straight, arms and legs crossed, chest out, indicating that she wished to be chosen, and Chris chose her as the next storyteller. She sat in the storytelling chair looking directly at her classmates and at Chris, smiling. She contributed only nods and 'yeses' to Chris's questions, and then passed the story on, but returned to the mat smiling proudly. Though she had not actually spoken, this was a major breakthrough for Simera. Shortly afterwards, she began tentatively to raise her hand in class to answer questions, though she still spoke very quietly if chosen. On a one-to-one basis she became more talkative with her peers and teachers. This activity took place midway through Simera's first term at school. By the second term, she was occasionally checked on the mat by the teacher for talking. Her involvement in the story was perhaps a 'critical incident' (Woods, 1990), indicating a substantial advance in her willingness to become involved in whole class activities.

Conceptual development

Mathematical concepts were constantly being reinforced through the story. As can be seen in the previous extracts, colour names were repeated frequently (the colours were taken from the song 'Sing a Rainbow', regularly sung in assemblies). During the second session Chris asked the children to draw their own rainbows, using crayons. She then encouraged them to extend their patterning by making more than one rainbow. As they worked, a number of the children kept repeating the sequence of colours from the story to guide them. In more 'formal' mathematics work, many of the children were at the stage of patterning two or three colours; here they were sequencing seven. This highlights Egan's (1988) point that story helps to develop abstract thinking, and thus conceptual development. Furthermore, Langer (1953) and Meek (1991) suggest that narrative is strongly linked to the way we experience memory, and provides a means of putting things into some sort of order. Clearly the children were using the narrative of the story to aid their sequencing in this exercise.

Other mathematical concepts reinforced in the story included those of shape and size. Chris discussed with the children the appropriate size of paintbrush that might be used to paint the rainbow. The size of the giant's footprints were used to compare and contrast feet sizes in the classroom, and the children were asked to consider the size of scissors the giant would have needed to cut out the shapes from the rainbow. They then considered the shapes (Chris used coloured plastic shapes as props):

Teacher: Oh no, said the people, they have cut a red square, they have cut a ...?

All: Yellow ...

Teacher: Yellow ...?

All: Triangle.

Teacher: Triangle. They have cut a ...?

Some: Blue ...

Some:	Circle.
Teacher:	What is it?
Sabahit:	Circle.
Teacher:	What colour is it?
Some:	Blue.
Teacher:	A blue circle, and our rainbow is spoilt!

This transcript has the familiar pattern of question and answer, similar to one that might be used in a more 'formal' learning situation. However, because it is embedded within the context of the story there is a greater impetus to achieve the correct answer, as doing so contributes to the meaning of the story. The children are not being 'quizzed' or given worksheets to complete, to enable a teacher to fill in certain checklists which meet the requirements of the National Curriculum. Yet the situation provides the teacher with the same information.

The story provided several problem-solving opportunities, too. Hasanan, for example, wanted to know how the townsfolk stuck the shapes back on to the rainbow once they had retrieved them from the giant. Sticky tape, it was decided, would not be strong enough. After discussion, the children thought it would be better to sew the shapes back on, and acted out this part of the story through role-play. The fictional aspect of stories allows children to explore, interrogate and investigate issues and problems in abstract ways, in a 'what if ' context, within the safety of the narrative (Fox, 1993). Exploration, interrogation and investigation are other attributes which teachers try to foster in children where the aim is to develop autonomous learners. Story can provide a suitable context for their development. For the bilingual learner, the safe context of the story enables them to involve themselves in 'what if' situations without the pressure of needing a 'right' answer, which they may not always be able to express clearly because of the need also to have the 'right' words.

Social, emotional and cultural understanding

The storytelling experience was very much a social event. It involved all of the children both in its development and telling. The children and the teacher worked together to develop *their* story (not individual efforts), and as a class they presented *their* story to the rest of the school.Some of the children had only been at school for four weeks when this project began. Through this activity the class were given the opportunity to work closely together, to 'gel' as a class and be supported by their peers.

There were times also when Chris explored the children's emotional and moral connections with the story. She frequently asked them about the reactions of its characters. How would the townsfolk *feel* regarding the damage to the rainbow? Would the townsfolk be frightened of the giant? Chris also discussed with the children whether they thought the giant had been silly or bad when he had cut out the shapes. The children decided he was 'just silly' and had not meant to be naughty. Although the characters were fictional, the context of the story enabled an emotional link, allowing the children the opportunity to bring their own experiences of anger, sadness, fear and naughty behaviour to bear. The story became relevant to their own emotional experiences.

The confidence of individual children was developed, as well. Simera, for example, was supported by both her teacher and her peers when she became the storyteller. Chris supported her initially by asking if she would like to be the storyteller, then through her use of questioning and prompting. Simera's peers supported her by acknowledging that she was the storyteller, listening quietly and patiently to her. Similar support was given throughout the sessions to all the children and when the class came to tell their story to the whole school, they had the confidence to speak to an audience of about a hundred of their school friends. These were the youngest children in school. They were not reading from a script, but using their own words to tell the story, and for some the telling was in a language second to that which they spoke at home. Yet they rose to the challenge and returned from the assembly with smiles on their faces.

Finally, Chris sought to make the story culturally relevant, stating for example that the townsfolk were going to Pakistan for their holidays and would need to pack their saris and shalwar kameez. This related directly to the experience of travelling for many of the children who had themselves been, or else had relatives who had been, on extended visits to their home countries. A particular image of family was also used which many of the children would recognise, as Chris talked about the people in the village who 'lived in their houses with their mums, and dads, and brothers, and sisters, and aunties, and uncles, and grandmas, and granddads and babies'. To a number of the children this kind of living arrangement was familiar. Acknowledging the cultural diversity of the children, not setting the story within the 'mainstream' culture, heightened its relevance.

These examples represent the potential for creative teaching and learning which arose from Chris's work with the children. She was innovative, using story, drama and art work together, and the children responded to this innovation with enthusiasm. Had they not, the project might not have lasted for the four weeks it did. The ownership of knowledge had clearly begun with Chris, who initiated the story, but as the children began to take a greater role in its development they too experienced feelings of ownership and took control of their own learning process. Finally, because Chris had sought to make the story relevant to the children they responded positively, and probably made far more connections with it than have been shown here. Perhaps the most significant aspect of the project was that the story itself became the main focus, providing the children (particularly those learning English as an additional language) in a creative and meaningful way with the opportunity for a whole range of learning outcomes.

Literacy skills

Stories are considered an important way in to literacy, especially in the Western world, where children are more likely to be read stories than 'told' them (Wells, 1987). In our schools, too, stories were seen as a powerful aid to developing literacy skills and phonic awareness. Again we select one prominent example for detailed examination – Chris's working of the *Annie Apple* story with a group of children from the Year 1 class. These children were in their first term at school, and the aim of the lesson was to develop their phonic awareness through the use of the Letter Land phonic scheme. This scheme gives each of the letters of the alphabet a character, for example Annie Apple, Clever Cat. Each of these is represented by a finger-puppet, and a story in which it is the central character. In this session Chris chose the story of Annie Apple. The children had already been introduced to the character of Annie Apple in previous phonic lessons and so this one was used as a reinforcement exercise in identifying characters and letter sounds from the scheme. Though the principle aim of the lesson was to develop phonic work to accompany the children's learning in reading and writing, the story itself provided a number of opportunities to introduce a whole range of new concepts.

Before beginning the story Chris used the finger-puppets to reinforce the children's awareness of the difference between the phonic character and the concept of a letter. Also, by using the puppet and wandering into the world of make-believe, playing with the character of Annie Apple, Chris constructed a 'storytelling' atmosphere – an important element in teaching and learning (Woods & Jeffrey, 1996). She drew the children to her, relying on their ability to suspend reality and work within their own imaginations and thus giving them an opportunity to take some control of the learning process. She began the session by introducing the finger-puppet of Annie Apple. The children discussed who had an 'a' in their names, all shouting out, some shouting out that other children had an 'a' in their names. The session went on:

Teacher: Oh, she looks very happy, and she's got a nice smiling face, and Annie Apple says ...?

Child: 'A'.

[Teacher and children at various points saying 'a'.]

Teacher: Annie Apple says 'a'. And if I turn her round *[the finger-puppet character* *face is toward the children]*, if I turn her round, you can see her ...

Nazneen: I can see a number.

Teacher: No it's not a number, it's called a letter, and that letter says, 'a', 'a'.

Children: Annie Apple, Annie Apple.

Teacher: *[to Ahmed]* You're not looking, now you turn your bottom right round, because if you're not looking you can't see it ... Can you see her, Hannah? Annie Apple. I like Annie Apple.

Jatinder: I like Annie Apple.

[Others join in with 'I like Annie Apple'.]

Teacher: If I turn her round *this* way, are you watching? I won't make her dizzy, I'll do it slowly, you can see Annie Apple's l-etter. Annie Apple's let-ter, it says 'a', it says 'a', it says, Taylor what does it say?

Taylor: 'A'.

Teacher: 'A'. Annie Apple. What do you like to look at, Taylor? Do you like to look at Annie Apple's *letter,* or do you like to look at Annie Apple's face?

Taylor: I like to look at both!

Teacher: Oh well I'll show you both then, let me turn her round *[turns finger-puppet round slowly]*. Annie Apple's face *[turns puppet again slowly]* and Annie Apple's letter. Lots of people have got Annie Apple in their names.

By using the opportunity of Nazneen's comment, 'I can see a number', Chris was able to introduce to the group the concept of letters within a relevant context. In previous sessions many of the children had shown awareness of what written language looks like, pointing to the writing in a book rather than to the pictures. Some were already beginning to recognise whole words from the reading scheme. At this stage Chris introduces the basic building block of written English, that of a letter. It is interesting that within this context Nazneen remarks that she can see a number. This is not surprising. Nazneen uses her knowledge of single marks on a page within a new context. When number is being taught in class, written numbers are introduced singly. The children are shown how to write them on an individual basis. Words, however, are introduced in their full format: 'help', 'can', 'you'. Nazneen, though able to recognise that her name contains an 'a', as yet has not made the distinction between letters and numbers, and perhaps their differing functions.

Nazneen's confusion in this context highlights a problem that many bilingual children may encounter, as Gregory (1996) indicates. She endorses the validity of using a variety of approaches to learning to read, including phonological awareness, for children whose English is their additional language. However, she also suggests (p.65) that in learning English as an additional language children begin by recognising individual words as labels which they can use in order to draw personal meanings. Examples (p.60) are words such as 'writing-book', 'pencil', 'ruler', 'work', which represent the key identifying words of important aspects of the culture of school. An understanding of individual words thus possesses a particular importance for bilingual children in their early meaning-making, and the development of phonological knowledge, it can be argued, needs to work in parallel with this (p.69): 'Without this understanding, it is very difficult to know where sounds end and words begin ... "sounding out" a word is likely to be a meaningless activity unless that word is understood.' Gregory suggests instead (p.111) that pointing out phonological structures can arise incidentally and where relevant from the children's work with their teacher, by calling 'attention to letters which recur'. In our own example, Chris used the children's names as a relevant and personal means for them to identify the letter 'a'.

As children develop their English and enter the early stages of starting to read they need to extend their use of language to embrace more extended and meaningful utterances. Walkerdine (1981) examined how in her research children were able to use what she described as 'chunks' of language in their role-play as a result of watching television. These 'chunks' are represented by pieces of language that are used in speech or writing and are conventional forms used to verbalise ideas and feelings. Gregory (1996) argues that such 'chunks' can be developed in a number of ways. The first (p.106) is by means of children's play, in which the language used is 'predictable, repetitive and well contextualised'. The second can be as a result of the language used by the teacher, who will need (p.101) to be 'constantly alive to her role as language model, carefully considering vital "chunks" of language needed, initiating and practising them in a variety of spoken and written contexts'. The third way (p.115) is by means of the stories that children hear and from which they can 'store story-language' to re-use in their own stories. In part, Chris was able to do this by emphasising the story aspect of the Letter Land scheme.

After further discussion with the children and some scene-setting, Chris began to tell a story using the character of Annie Apple. Although the story existed in written form in a book which accompanied the Letter Land scheme, Chris told her own version, using the pictures from the book, in order to create an overall story with the children. Her ability to take control and ownership of the story, rather than relying on the text, enabled her to relate it to the children and to make it more relevant to their own experiences. It centred on an astronaut called Alan who had landed on

Letter Land in error. The astronaut had in the written version been on his way to the moon. In this version, Chris, after consulting the children, decided that the astronaut had been on his way to Pakistan.

Teacher: One day, somebody very special came to Letter Land. He didn't mean to come to Letter Land, he wanted to go to ... *[question to the children]* where shall we say? Where did you go, Nazneen? You went to Pakistan, didn't you, let's say Pakistan, shall we?

Nazneen: *[nods smilingly]*

Teacher: He wanted to go to Pakistan, he didn't want to come to Letter Land.

Ahmed: I went Pakistan.

Teacher: You did, and look, he wanted to go to Pakistan *[pointing to the man in the picture]* and when he opened the door, he was in Letter Land with Annie Apple and Clever Cat, and when he opened the door he said, 'Look,' he said, 'I didn't want to come to Letter Land, I wanted to go Pakistan', and he said, 'Where am I? This isn't Pakistan. Where am I?'

Other alterations were made to the story, but most stayed true to the pictures. However, at one point, when the characters of Annie Apple and Ticking Tom went for a flight in the spaceship Chris changed the story quite significantly. Ticking Tom, having mended the spaceship, went with Alan and Annie Apple for a ride. However, Annie Apple became ill on the journey. At this stage Chris asked the children if she could take Annie Apple out of the story.

Teacher: Poor Annie Apple. Then Ticking Tom said, 'Come on Annie Apple, I can help you'. I think it's a bit sad. Shall we take Annie Apple out of the spaceship?

Various: No.

Teacher: No? *[Directed at a particular group of children]* Shall I take her out?

Children: No, no.

Teacher: Shall I leave her in?

Jatinder: But you can't.

Teacher: I could, I could. Yes I could.

Jatinder: You can't!

Teacher:	Shall I take her out, Taylor?
Taylor:	*[nods]*
Teacher:	Shall I take her out, Asria?
Asria:	*[nods]*
Teacher:	Look, she feels very poorly. Can I take her out? Can I take Annie Apple out?:

[Some of the children nod in approval, Jatinder however is not happy with this, and sits with arms folded and a furrowed brow to indicate his disapproval.]

Teacher:	Right, come on then, come on. *[Puts away the Annie Apple finger-puppet and takes out the Clever Cat one.]*

Although Chris quite obviously wanted to take the Annie Apple character out of the story and managed to do so by contrived decision-making, Jatinder did not approve of her action. Much of this was to do with the fact that the Annie Apple character was still shown in the pictures of the story and Clever Cat was not. Jatinder became even more frustrated later when the story was finished and there were no more pictures, and yet Chris continued with the tale, in spite of his commenting more than once, 'it's finished'. Chris picked up on his growing concerns with regard to the changes being made and relented:

Teacher:	Let me ask you, Annie Apple, because we took her out of the story didn't we? Annie Apple, are you cross you came out of the story.
Jatinder:	Yes.
Teacher:	Yes. Oh, let's put her back in. Quick, quick, she's cross! We took her out of the story. Quick, quick she's cross *[trying to find the page in the book that she had taken the character out of]*. Let's put her back. Where shall we put her back?
Sabahit:	In the end.
Jatinder:	In the rocket.
Teacher:	Shall I put her back there where she's poorly?
Jatinder:	Yeah, yeah.
Teacher:	But she's poorly there. Oh all right then. *[Chris then recommenced the story from that point; Jatinder seemed happy with this.]*

Why did Jatinder act in this way? In part it may have been due to the fact that Chris had centred the story around the book, particularly around its pictures. One of the main differences between oral storytelling and written storytelling is the permanent nature of written tales. As Jatinder became increasingly aware of the nature of print (he was already beginning to take reading books home with him at this stage) he was also becoming aware that the story does not change. What this situation further indicated was that Jatinder was aware of how much pictures can tell one about a story, but also knew that pictures, like print, do not alter; hence his unwillingness to allow Chris to alter the story.

At the same time, Chris's reason for deviating from the original text in the book was that she wanted to introduce more characters from the phonic scheme within the context of the story. As she pointed out to the researcher afterwards, the way stories were written in the phonic scheme meant that often they were not easily understood by her class, and therefore to tell them in her own words enabled her to tailor them to the children's language needs. This is particularly important when we consider that the majority of the group was learning English as an additional language and the initial purpose of the lesson was to develop their phonic awareness. Yet Chris's actions also indicate to the children that stories are not inflexible, that they can be changed to suit the needs of the individual or the group. Furthermore she is encouraging the children to 'take a risk' in changing the story. In many ways risk-taking is part of learning. If a child is not prepared to try something new or move on to the next stage, then learning development may remain at a hiatus or focused on one area. It would seem that Jatinder is not comfortable taking risks, sticking to the rules and order which he has experienced in the written genre of stories. Jatinder was becoming very engrossed in the written genre. Perhaps for many bilingual children in particular there is a certain comfort in knowing that the story one hears in a second language will be the same every time one listens to it. For Jatinder the permanence of the written text appeared essential in order to develop meaning; there was a structure on which he could rely and this reliance was reflected in his own tellings of story. This conversation took place the following term between Jatinder and the researcher:

Jatinder: I made a story, but I made it to my mum.

Mari: Oh, can you tell me that story?

Jatinder: All right.

Mari: Can you remember it?

Jatinder: *[nods]*

Mari: OK.

Jatinder:	Where. Where is it? Is it here? No it's not in here? Here it is? *[spoken staccato, head raised and eyes looking up to the ceiling]*
Mari:	Is that the end of it?
Jatinder:	*[nods]*
Mari:	And is that a story you made up or is it ...?
Jatinder:	Shall I write it down here?
Mari:	Can you write it? Right.

[Jatinder starts to'write' his story down on Mari's jotter-pad.]

The story Jatinder tells here is virtually identical to one of the stories from the reading scheme. Out of context, with no pictures, it makes little sense, but for him it is a story because he has seen and read it in his reading book.

Opportunities for Stories

In Chapter 3 we stressed the need for 'opportunities' in creative teaching and learning. What opportunities, therefore, were provided for the use of stories and storying on a consistent and regular basis, and what was their cultural relevance for our bilingual learners?

The children in the two nurseries experienced stories at home, whether read or told, both before and during their time at nursery. All the parents recognised the importance of stories in the lives of their children and in every home there was interaction with stories and books, whether introduced by the parents or by older sisters or brothers. For example, their mothers read to Iqbal, Jabidul, Tariq, Aditya and Rushan on a regular basis. On the other hand Naveen, Aisha and Attia shared purely oral stories with their mothers.

Some children, however, generally relied on older sisters and brothers for the experience of books and stories. This was usually because those children had brought books home from school and were reading them for enjoyment. Zeeshad had to rely entirely on his older brothers for books, as he did not have any of his own and his parents did not share books with him. Aisha's mother Balkis, although she told and read stories to Aisha, relied also on her older daughters to share books with their younger sister:

> When my daughters come back from school and they're reading their books with them she'll sit down and she'll watch and she'll try and see if she can say it, she's sort of memorising it. She's having a look and she's having a look at the pictures as well, so she thinks she can understand what's happening.

The languages and cultural forms of the stories and books used by the parents varied. With the exception of those used by Jabidul's mother, which were in Urdu, the books were in English and reflected an English cultural background, including those used by Mrs Mousaf with Rushan, which she would translate into Bengali after reading them to him first in English. Stories and nursery rhymes told orally would also generally be in English, and where they were traditional, would usually be from the same cultural source. The exception to this was Mrs Islam, who made a point of telling Attia stories in Bengali.

In the nurseries books consisted mostly of a wide variety of picture-books, mainly in English, although some did portray children from ethnic minority cultures. The same situation applied in the lower school. Many of the children were exposed to stories which were predominantly written by Western authors, and which were mainly available in English. The following example of an interview with Manjid, a six-year-old Indian girl, indicates how close the links are between reading English and stories:

Mari: Right, Manjid, you know at home, does your mum tell you stories?

Manjid: She can't read stories.

Damian: *[laughs]*

Mari: No, but does she ... *[to Damian]* Damian, no, that might be because she can't read English. *[To Manjid]* She can't read English? So does she sometimes tell you stories in Pakistani? Or in Indian?

Manjid: Indian.

Mari: In Indian, she tells you stories in Indian? And what sort of stories does she tell you in Indian?

Damian: Like, like, erm, like, erm, this boy, yeah, sit on a dog and the dog bent. The dog's back bent.

Manjid: That's not, that's not read to me.

Damian: That's a story. Or a little fairy went in this tree, and a bear got her and eat her all up. That's a story.

Manjid: *[laughs]*

Mari: Does, does she tell you stories about India, in Indian? No?

Manjid: *[shakes head]* Don't have stories in India.

Mari: You don't have stories in India? Do they not? I bet they do.

Manjid: We went to India, but there were no stories.

Initial reactions to Manjid's comments that there are no stories in India might be of sadness and loss that she was missing out culturally in some way because of a lack of exposure to such stories. Rosen (1988) contends that through story one comes to learn the value systems of society, and that it is a way in which we become part of the society in which we live and with which we identify. For bilingual learners it may also be a way in which they become aware of the two cultures of which they are a part. Yet considering more carefully what Manjid said it is possible to understand what she means. Manjid associated story closely with books and reading activity. Damian's laugh at the fact that Manjid's mother was unable to read English indicates another problem that many bilingual children might encounter, that their parents are literate in a language other than that in which their children are taught.

Even when Damian defined what a story could be, Manjid rejects this on the grounds that his story was not from a book. Interestingly, Damian was one of the few children who said that he was regularly told made-up stories by his stepfather, and this experience had made him aware of the variety of ways stories can be shared. The children generally in class were less exposed to this form of spontaneous storytelling and as already noted, the majority of stories were read from books. In Manjid's classroom there was a large number of books available for the children to enjoy, but within this selection there were few stories representing the countries of origin of the children and many of the dual-language texts were often adaptations of modern Western stories. Rani Kumar (1989) points to a number of problems concerning dual-language texts.

(1) Often translations of texts may be poor because the onus tends to be on translating the words rather than the ideas of the story.

(2) Some languages are written from right to left, but publishers may print these languages the wrong way round to accommodate the English version. Additionally, the English script most often appears first with the translation underneath and therefore sending a message about the status of the two languages.

(3) Where stories from the Indian subcontinent are available they are frequently over-simplified so as to lose much of the essence of the stories.

Viv Edwards' (1995) study of dual-language texts also shows how problematic the concept of a 'good' book can be. She contrasts pupil and teacher choice of dual-language books. The teachers preferred glossy and colourful Western-style texts; their bilingual pupils sought faded Indian books with traditional illustrations. This was because they believed them to be more serious and adult-looking (see also Edwards & Walker, 1995). Such book styles may have also been more familiar to the children, reflecting the mother-tongue language books their parents might have had at home, rather than new books with modern illustrations of the type that were prominent in our research schools.

In the lower school library there was a much greater selection of both fiction and non-fiction books from various countries, yet most of the children during library-time still tended to choose English storybooks. Only one girl, Asria, consistently chose books about Pakistan to take home with her. The availability of books of traditional tales from India, Pakistan and Bangladesh (these were the main ethnic groups of the children in the school) is sparse for the very reason that many have never been written down. Availability is also limited because, as a children's book representative commented, it is often very expensive to produce dual-text language books. In the light of this, and since Manjid associated story so strongly with reading, her comment that 'there are no stories in India' was not surprising: she may never have read any Indian stories, or had any read to her.

The same problem arose with reading-books. In some cases, as with Manjid, the parents were not literate in English, and so reading-books were frequently shared with siblings. Mobeen faced this situation:

Mari: Do you read a lot of things at home?

Mobeen: *[nods]*

Mari: Yeah?

Mobeen: I read my library book, my reading-book and my home book. And this is, and my book is called the *Puzzle World [talks about one of the puzzles in the book, with mazes in it].* I read that book ... And there's another, that my sister brought to my mum to read, 'cos she only knows a little bit English an I used to read that, and now my sister sended it back to school.

Mari: Uhum. So, you say that your mum only knows a little bit of English, so does she tell you stories in Pakistani?

Mobeen: *[nods]*

Mari: Yeah? Does she read in Pakistani as well? Does she read Pakistani?

Mobeen: *[nods]*

Mari: Yeah, so does she read books that are written in Pakistani to you?

Mobeen: Yeah, an she read my reading-book, and my library book. She getting used to, she trying to get used to English.

Mobeen's comments about her mother not being able to read English very well were echoed by one of her older sisters who attended the middle school. Mobeen's sister talked about how her mother tried reading with her older children, but she was not particularly happy with this situation:

> My mum, she reading it to us innit, 'cos she think we're reading higher, but she just read it, but she takes quite a long time reading it, she probably takes about half an hour or something reading it, but she can read it but she read it like you know, she say one word, and then she say it again, you know, she not quite sure, she not comfortable with what she reading, so till she got it right she won't go on, and er we just read on innit, and she went, 'Slow down I can't go that fast' [laughs] and we go 'It's so boring', we reading it together right, we have to wait for her for a long time.

Again we see the difficulties encountered by parents and children where they do not share literacy skills in the same language. A similar situation was found by Gregory (1994a); many of the parents from her research group of Bangladeshi children claimed that they were unable to assist their children in reading due to poor literacy skills in English, though they eagerly awaited their children teaching them to read.

Research evidence points to the importance of parents sharing in the reading development of their children (Kook & Vedder, 1995), and the advice often given to parents is to talk about and extend the story through the pictures. If parents are not able to read the story with their children, though, then they might also feel restricted in discussing it further. Many of the children said that they often read their reading-books to older siblings, but the older children may not have had the maturity or experience to discuss the text and develop understanding and meaning within the context of the story.

The growing awareness of written story appeared also to limit the children's confidence to simply 'tell' a story. On a number of occasions Mari asked children if they could simply tell her a story, in particular if they knew any stories from Pakistan, India or Bangladesh. The most frequent reaction, like Manjid's, was that they did not know any, but that they could read her one. The example of Fouzia indicates in part this initial reluctance to tell a story. Mari asked Fouzia, in her second year at the lower school, if she could tell her a story from Pakistan. Fouzia immediately got up and went to the bookshelves and came back with *The Gingerbread Man*. They had the following conversation:

Mari: The Gingerbread Man. Can you tell without, without the book? Can you just tell it to me?

Fouzia: Pakistan?

Mari: Well you can tell it in Pakistan first and then perhaps you could tell it to me in English, because, the problem is I don't understand Pakistani.

D'you think you could tell it in Pakistani?

Fouzia: Yeah.

Mari: OK then, you tell it to me in Pakistani first, and then ...

Fouzia: What should I tell? The Gingerbread Man?

Mari: The Gingerbread Man if you want to.

Fouzia began the story in Panjabi, but seemed to get stuck translating. Mari suggested she use the pictures in the book to help her. As soon as she began to use the pictures, Fouzia told the story mainly in English:

> Mummy said to the children and the man, 'We want something to eat for tea.'
> The mummy baked a, em, gingerbread man *[unclear]*. The the old woman, hey,
> phir [again] old woman she tooked it out. Then it baked. Then after she, er, she,
> er, she tooked it out from the oven. Then, then, gingerbread man runned out,
> then out the farm *[unclear]*, then he, the old woman, the old woman says to the
> gingerbread, 'Stop.' Then the man said to the old woman, he seed a little puppy,
> and em, 'Stop little em gingerbread man.' The gingerbread man he jumped on,
> on the, on the leaves. Then then he runned under the log, he said, 'Hey little gin-
> gerbread man.' Then he ran and he ran, then he ran. Then, then he stopped and
> he a little stop, right, then, then, then, the horse now he says, then the horse now
> he says 'Stop little gingerbread man', then he carries on running. Then he
> stopped again then the cow says *[deepened voice for this part]* 'You look nice for
> my tea', the cow says 'Ma tanu kha lana ha [I will eat you up].' Then he ran, and
> then ran. All a sudden and then little dog goes, 'Hey little gingerbread man, nice
> to eat.' Then he ranned and ran and oh no, gingerbread man uh billy labhda si
> [he was looking for a cat] and he stopped again, he stopped uh billy labhda si
> and he ranned in the river, and he ranned in the river, and he went, and the fox
> came and he said, 'You need, I'm just going to talk to you.' Then he said, 'Come
> back on my tail.' Phir una billy labhda si phir una kha lia si [then he found the
> fox and cat and ate it].

The repetitions, the uncertainty about what to say next, the experimentation with tense, and the incidents of code-switching during this telling, all indicate Fouzia's language development in both English and Panjabi. She begins by switching from Panjabi into English, possibly because English is the language she first heard the story told in, and perhaps also because she realises that the researcher does not understand Panjabi, thus showing an awareness of audience (Rosen, 1982). She remembers the structure of the story well and uses the pictures for contextual clues. Much of the language she uses could be described as story-book language (Fox, 1993) 'Then he ran, and he ran, and he ranned.' Fouzia also borrows language directly from the story, for example 'you look nice for my tea' and 'stop little gingerbread man'. In many ways, as noted earlier, the written word of the story can provide a strong language scaffold for children learning English as an additional language. It is not surprising therefore that Fouzia initially wants to read the story rather than tell it. Where she does not have the English language skills to express herself she switches to Panjabi, using expressions that perhaps best fit what she is trying to say, a common feature among bilingual children (Romaine, 1989; Baker, 1996; Blackledge, 1994).

The structure and process of storytelling is not independent of culture. Children will often use the narrative patterns that they are familiar with and, as Kress (1982) points out, 'texts have a high degree of internal structure'. Though Kress was referring more to the process of children's writing, what he says applies equally to telling stories. This was shown in the research of MacFall (1993), Fox (1993) and Barrs (1990), in which very young children were aware of many of the conventions of telling a story with regard to openings, endings, and the need for some action to take place. Interestingly, the typical opening of 'once upon a time' was not present in Fouzia's retelling, though once into the narrative she adopted the language conventions needed to relate this particular story. However, as Moore (1993) illustrated, bilingual children may use different story structures in which to place their narratives from those the dominant culture is used to. Moore's example of a Year 10 Bangladeshi pupil writing a love-story highlighted how the teacher's views of how a story should be written became the 'right' view, ignoring the structure the student had created, which was perhaps more in line with the oral tradition of storytelling to which he was accustomed. By contrast when Mari asked Fouzia what kind of stories she heard at home she replied that she was read stories similar to those at school. If this was so, then for Fouzia the dominant narrative structures were those she was aware of through written texts, rather than any oral culture. This is a reminder that stories can integrate and legitimise within the dominant culture.

Conclusion

In many areas of the curriculum for early years education, stories are seen as a useful medium for learning and conceptual development. For children who are learning English as an additional language the use of story to develop language has been shown here. Children gained motivation, developed new language skills, and some acquired new-found confidence to speak up in class. There were opportunities in the stories for them to develop concepts and to begin to debate moral issues, whilst re-evaluating their own emotional experiences through a third person. Woods and Jeffrey (1996: 100) comment that 'the structures pupils use to interpret these issues and experiences [in stories] are the same structures they need to explore the cognitive world of the sciences and of the arts'. Stories can therefore support the development in new and appropriate contexts of many of the skills considered to be important in other parts of the curriculum.

A further consideration lies in the issue of culture. There is a prevalent view that children who come from ethnic minority backgrounds come from a rich oral story-telling tradition (Rosen, 1988; Moorhouse, 1989; Minns, 1990; Austen, 1992; Blackledge, 1994). This is, perhaps, an over-simplification of the situation. Most of the children in this study said that they had books at home, and all the titles of books they mentioned were popular English texts, including 'Barbie' and 'Power Rangers' books. All of the children said that they were read rather than told stories, and that these stories came from a Western culture. Some of the children in this group are second generation English and therefore assumptions regarding cultural activity at home cannot be generalised. The children are growing up in two cultures, and as Kearney (1990: 12) points out:

> Culture is a complicated business, as diverse and contradictory as the human beings who create it and as complex as the networks they create to carry it. It is no static phenomenon: and neither is language. Both depend on the kinds of contacts human beings make with each other and the kind of networks that are formed which sustain these relationships.

The contacts and networks that are being created for these children are formed between their homes, school and the wider community of which they are a part. There is a possibility that where children are introduced to book stories at home then they may be at a certain advantage when starting school, as is suggested in the research of Wells (1987) and Fox (1993). However, there might be erosion of their own culture and in turn of their own identity if they do not have equal access to stories from their own cultures. The school was aware of the problems of resourcing for the cultural needs of the children and had allocated money in its budget requirements to be spent on providing more books that reflected its cultural diversity. It was thus committed to developing a more culturally relevant curriculum, which should, where resources are used correctly, provide for a more child-meaningful learning environment.

Suggestions

- Look for stories with repetition and strong prediction included so that children can practise patterns of language – for example, *Chicken Licken, The Gingerbread Man, The Elephant and the Bad Baby* and some of the books from the 'Story Chest' series.

- Practise songs and jingles with children, for example, jingles heard on television, again emphasising the practice of repeatable patterns of language.

- Look for poetry and action rhymes with which the children can join in and link actions to words. Poetry can have a strong rhythm that is predictable. It can provide patterns, not just in its words but in its sentence structure. It can also enable children to play with language.

- Children in groups or as a class can make a series of books with you over a period of time which provide for repeated patterns of language connected with things which are familiar to them, for example 'My mum is ...', ' My dad is ... ', 'I went to the church', 'I went to the mosque', as part of the process of learning 'chunks' of language. These books could be placed in the class library for children to return to and read. For an interesting project celebrating multilingual skills through story-making using a variety of media, see Khela and Deb (1993).

- Using puppets as an aid in group or class language work can help children to focus on what is being said by the puppet and provide models of language for children to hear. Puppets also give children courage to share their use of language and express themselves if they are lacking in confidence with the teacher. Again, the puppets should be examples of the cultures represented in the classroom.

- Choose examples of children's literature which model particular forms of language, such as words of position, for example *Rosie's Walk* and *Bears in the Night*. Such books can be used also as models for the children to make their own books with you, for example 'Attia's walk round the school'. Other ideas can be found in books such as *Not Now Bernard* and *We're Going on a Bear Hunt*.

- Look carefully at the choice of books available to the children. Do they extend the children's imagination? Do they allow identification with the characters? What are the models of language presented? Are some of them about children whose cultures are represented in the classroom? Are some of the books in community languages? Do they draw on children's knowledge of their own cultures? All these factors enable the children to identify with the stories and their languages.

- Provide for a variety of print around the classroom including some in community languages.

- Look at resourcing in the house, cooking and dressing-up areas, which should reflect the cultures represented in the classroom. This enables children in their talk with their peers and adults to call on what is familiar and known to them in their speech.

- Explore with parents and children the latter's reading practices and learning strategies at home. Gregory and Mace (1996: 2) argue that such research 'could provide teachers with a valuable yet hitherto untapped resource and promote effective literacy teaching'.

The following is a selection of children's picture- and poetry-books which you may find useful. We have included examples of poetry and stories from different cultures, including, where available, books that are dual-text.

Aardema, V. (1977) *Who's in Rabbit's House?* London: Bodley Head.
Aardema, V. (1985) *Bimwili and the Zimwi.* London: Macmillan Children's Books.
Aardema, V. (1985) *Oh Kojo! How Could You!* London: Hamish Hamilton.
Agard, J. (1981) *Dig Away Two-Hole Tim.* London: Bodley Head.
Agard, J. (1991) *I Din Do 'Nuttin'.* London: Little Mammoth.
Agard, J. and Nichols, G. (1991) *No Hickory, No Dickory, No Dock.* Harmondsworth: Puffin Books.
Bennett, J. (ed.) (1980) *Roger was a Razor Fish, and Other Poems.* London: Hippo Books.
Berenstain, S. and Berenstain, J. (1971) *Bears in the Night.* London: Collins and Harvill.
Bond, R. (1982) *Tales and Legends from India.* London: Julia MacRae Books.
Bond, R. (1994) *Tiger Roars, Eagle Soars.* London: Walker Books.
Burningham, J. (1978) *Would You Rather?* London: Jonathan Cape.
Carle, E. (1969) *The Very Hungry Caterpillar.* Harmonsworth: Puffin Books.
Charles, F. (ed.) (1991) *The Kiskadee Queen.* Harmondsworth: Puffin Books.
Dhami, N. (1990) *A Medal for Malina.* Harmondsworth: Puffin Books.
Foreman, M. (1974) *Dinosaurs and All That Rubbish.* Harmondsworth: Puffin Books.
Gandhi, N. (1990) *Sari Games.* London: Andre Deutsch.
Gregory, E. and Walker, D. (1987) *The Hen and the Mice: A Tale of Laziness.* London: Hodder and Stoughton (dual-language texts available in Bengali, Gujarati, Panjabi, Urdu).
Gregory, E., Walker, D. and Matharu, M.K. (1987) *Gangli Gauri: A Tale of Foolishness.* London: Hodder and Stoughton (in dual-language text).
Grifalconi, A. (1990) *Osa's Pride.* Canada: Little, Brown and Company.
Hadley, E. and Hadley, T. (1983) *Legends of the Sun and Moon.* Cambridge: Cambridge University Press.
Haley, G.E. (1972) *A Story, a Story.* London: Methuen.
Hersom, K. (1981) *Maybe It's a Tiger.* London: Macmillan.
Hester, H. (1983) The six blind men and the elephant. In *Stories in the Multilingual Classroom.* London: ILEA.
Hewett, A. (1970) *Mrs Mopple's Washing Line.* Harmondsworth: Puffin Books.
Hoffman, M. (1991) *Amazing Grace.* London: Frances Lincoln.
Hunt, R. (1996) *Rockpool Rap.* Oxford 'Reading Tree' Series. Oxford University Press.
Hutchins, P. (1968) *Rosie's Walk.* London: Bodley Head.
Hutchins, P. (1975) *Goodnight Owl.* Harmondsworth: Puffin Books.
Jayal, A. (1974) *Bhondoo the Monkey* series. India: Thomson Press.
Jones, J. (1986) *Kausar at Home.* London: Blackie.
Kamal, A. (1989) *The Bird Who Was an Elephant.* Cambridge: Cambridge University Press.
Lloyd, E. (1988) *Sasha and the Bicycle Thieves.* London: Mammoth Books.
Lobel, A. (1971) *The Frog and Toad Stories.* Tadworth, London: World's Work.
Lobel, A. (1976) *Owl at Home.* Tadworth, London: World's Work.
McKee, D. (1987) *Not Now Bernard.* London: Arrow, Random Century.
Minarik, E.H. (1983) *Little Bear.* Harmondsworth: Puffin Books.

Murphy, M. (1997) *I Like It When*. London: Methuen.

Oxenbury, H. (1981) *Tiny Tim: Verses for Children*. London: Heinemann.   •

Oxford University Press (1982) *A Packet of Poems*.

Rosen, M. (1989) *We're Going on a Bear Hunt*. London: Walker Books.

Hairy Bear. Storychest Series. Ashton: Scholastic.

Mrs Wishy-Washy. Storychest Series. Ashton: Scholastic.

Sing a Song. Storychest Series. Ashton: Scholastic.

Smarty Pants. Storychest Series. Ashton: Scholastic.

The Hungry Giant. Storychest Series. Ashton: Scholastic.

Styles, M. (ed.) (1984) *I Like That Stuff: Poems from Many Cultures*. Cambridge: Cambridge University Press.

Thompson, B. (1980) *The Story of Prince Rama*. Harmondsworth: Kestrel Books.

Topiwalo the Hatmaker. Stanmore: Harmony

Vipont, E. (1969) *The Elephant and the Bad Baby*. London: Hamish Hamilton.

Chapter 5

Bilingual Children in Transition

Introduction

We turn in the next three chapters to the children, attempting to see their experiences and perspectives from their own point of view. Starting school, the subject of this chapter, is one of the great status passages in life, having profound repercussions for identity. Before starting school, children already have multiple identities. They are a son or daughter; brother, sister, only child or particular-placed sibling; Pakistani, Indian, Bengali, African Caribbean or English; friend of someone; and a young child. On starting school they acquire another identity, that of 'pupil' (Edwards & Knight, 1994). For many children, this is their first step towards secondary socialisation (Berger & Luckmann, 1967). It is their first major break in the day-to-day regularity of family life where the primary care-givers are the focus of their world 'and what is mediated through the family is the only reality that is known' (Woods, 1990: 145).

Secondary socialisation involves children's first regular experience of institutional life and the internalisation of specific roles. The first of these is that of pupil. The shaping of this new role is not a negotiated one, but very much dependent on the teacher image of the 'good pupil' (Waterhouse, 1991). Burns (1992: 155) argues: 'All organisations seek to impose an identity on their members, allocating to each of them a character and a conception of self which is consonant with the organisation's values, requirements, and expectations.' This involves 'a thoroughly embracing conception of the member – and not merely a conception of him [sic] qua member, but behind this a conception of him qua human being' (Goffman, 1961: 179). In school the notion of the 'good' or 'ideal' pupil is a 'construction which is drawn primarily from the lifestyle and culture of the teacher concerned' (Wright, 1993: 28).

'Culture' is a crucial concept here. Tyler (1971) defines it as 'that complete whole which includes knowledge, beliefs, art, morals, law, customs and any other capabilities acquired by man as a member of society'. Yet any one society might be made up of several different cultural bases. For example, though we might refer to a British culture, it has within its basic make-up distinct Scottish, Welsh and English cultures, and within each of those cultures there are distinctions between regional and local areas. Therefore culture acts at different levels and for different reasons.

The function of education in relation to culture was considered by Chinoy (1967) as one of the principal ways in which the preservation of culture is transmitted to society as a whole. Durkheim (1956) observed that education was a primary method of enabling society to perpetually recreate itself. Singh (1993: 35) comments that:

> By passing on from one generation to another established beliefs, knowledge, values, and skills, education contributes to continuity and the development of an organised social life. Thus 'culture' and 'education' are inter-related processes of social organisation and social structure within society.

Yet in a multicultural society there must be questions about *whose* culture is being transmitted from generation to generation – as in Chapter 4 it might be asked *whose* stories are being told, encouraged and made available. While there are those who contend that schools should develop in their pupils a sense of cultural heritage and national identity which is essentially (and traditionally) 'British' (see Tate in Pyke, 1997), others believe that it is important to show recognition of other cultures (Taylor, 1992). The provision of such recognition through educational processes will give children the opportunity to operate from a wide range of cultural bases (Verma, 1984).

Where other cultural forms are not taken into account, the child from a minority ethnic group may find the difficulties of transition to school compounded (Wright, 1993), for it will involve another transition, one from their own ethnic culture to a dominant culture. There are further problems associated with having to learn at school via a second language whilst maintaining a mother tongue (Rex, 1986). Such children stand to experience all the bewilderment and confusion of Schutz's (1971: 30) 'stranger', for whom 'the whole hitherto unquestioned scheme of interpretation current within the home group becomes invalidated'.

In many schools the experience of transition at this stage is unalleviated by 'in-between' phases. The reception class used to be considered a bridge between nursery and school, but has increasingly become the point at which children start their studies of the National Curriculum. Blenkin and Kelly (1994: 3) see this as having 'destroyed the concept of infancy', and failing to differentiate between the educational requirements of children from five to seven years of age and those of 16–year-olds. The transition is thus starker, and the National Curriculum has become part of the problem, rather than, as embodied in its rationale, an aid to its resolution. This is even more the case for bilingual learners, since the National Curriculum is distinctly mono-ethnic as far as these children are concerned (see Chapter 2).

In this chapter we discuss the induction of our groups of bilingual/bicultural children into the world of school and into the role of pupil. All children face certain problems in transferring from home to school, some of them recounted here. However, we argue here that the concept of 'normal pupil' implicitly embraced by the school is in fact embodied within a traditionally English model, leaning toward anglocentrism, which has profound implications for the sense of identity of children from minority ethnic groups.

We draw on our observations of two groups of children, one from the nursery unit and one from the lower school. Children entered Westside Nursery Unit at the beginning of the term after they had reached their third birthday, provided there were places available; otherwise when there was a vacancy. Entry was staggered at the beginning of each term, with a maximum of two children starting on any one day. They transferred to the school's Reception class as a group at the beginning of the term following their fifth birthday. The seven children studied in the nursery unit started at different times during the research: one in the autumn term of 1994, three in the summer term of 1995, two in the spring term of 1996 and one in the summer term of 1996. All of them had been born in this country. They were used to speaking their community languages at home and used English with varying degrees of confidence. Five of the children's families were originally from Pakistan, and two from Bangladesh, although a number of parents had been born and educated in this country. The staff in the unit consisted of one qualified teacher, two full-time nursery nurses and one part-time Section 11 bilingual Panjabi- and Urdu-speaking nursery nurse.

The lower school also had a staggered entry system, whereby groups of children started at the beginning of each new term depending on whether they had reached their fifth birthday by its first day. In the autumn term of 1994, when the research began, a group of 17 children started school as Year 1 children (meaning that these children, by law, had to follow the National Curriculum). In the spring term a further ten children joined the class, and two started later in the term when they returned from extended stays in Pakistan. This second cohort was deemed Reception class, the children having turned five after 1st September. Much of the data reported here was collected at the beginning of this spring term. All of the children in the class had been born in England, though proficiency in English varied from child to child. All of them, with one exception, had attended the nursery unit attached to the school, and we draw on the nursery research to illustrate continuities and changes in their experiences of transitions. There were two class teachers for the mixed Reception/Year 1 class at the school: Elaine, who taught in the morning, and Chris (the headteacher), who taught in the afternoon. In addition, Hardip, a non-teaching assistant fluent in Urdu and Panjabi as well as some Bengali, was available during the morning sessions.

Marking New Identities

Establishing the identity of 'pupil' entails demarcating it as different from that of 'child'. One way of doing this is to separate child from parent. This process began in the nursery unit. For a short while the children would come into the unit with their parents, who helped them to hang up their coats. This provided parents with an opportunity to talk with the nursery staff about their children and was all very informal. The children would then have free choice over which activity they wanted to do. Individual parents were encouraged to stay in the nursery for a period of time each day if their child was having difficulty settling into the new environment. Generally the educators in these cases would encourage parents gradually to leave their children so that over a period of days support could be transferred to the unit's staff.

This process continued *a fortiori* at the school. Parents, though at first encouraged to bring children into the building to meet their teacher and settle them, were asked to leave them in the playground before school started once they had become used to the start of the school day. The apparent reason for this was a practical one, the main entrance to the school being too small to cope with parents and children all coming in at once – something which also cut down on the amount of contact between parents and teachers. So the school design, intentionally or unintentionally, helped to separate out children from parents, and aided the transition to the school's concept of pupil.

By the start of the spring term at the school the new children had become quite used to the 'separation' routine. They had even begun to reinforce it themselves. One mother appeared to be having more difficulty adjusting to starting school than her son, Adam, reminding us that this is a key transition for mothers as well as their children (see Chapter 8). She continued to deliver her son to the classroom door, despite his obvious embarrassment. He would rush to take his coat off as quickly as possible and then jump on to the mat to be with his peers, rather than stay with his mother. Eventually the class teacher asked Adam's mother if she could simply leave him in the playground with his friends at the start of the day. She did this, but then began turning up at dinner-time to give him his packed lunch. Adam seemed very uncomfortable with this. He would collect his dinner quickly and run off to be with his friends, rather than stay to talk to his mother. As time went on her visits became less frequent.

Having achieved separation, the pupil's identity became designated in the ritual of 'registration'. Bernstein (1977: 54) has described the symbolic function of ritual as relating the individual to a social order, 'to heighten respect for that order, to revivify that order within the individual and, in particular, to deepen acceptance of the procedures which are used to maintain continuity, order and boundary and which control ambivalence towards the social order'. Registration, which might be seen as operating in this way, is an essential part of becoming and being a pupil. It is a check on one's being present; it marks the child's identity as one of a number of pupils who are all the same in that respect; it is a reminder of this at the start of every session; and it establishes an underlying formality to proceedings.

At the lower school, unlike the nursery, registration was the first requirement of the day. The children sat on the carpet and awaited the register. For some of the new entrants this caused confusion. Their mode of coping with the situation was to sit very quietly, mainly near the back of the carpet, and to listen to and observe what the older children said and did. The new children were at first prompted by the class teacher, and later by their peers, when it came to their turn to answer to their name for the register. It was an indication of the way in which they needed to become quickly accustomed to how they would now be addressed at school, compared with how staff at the nursery or their parents at home might speak to them. The teachers were careful to try to pronounce children's names correctly, but avoided the sort of pet names or nicknames that might be used at home. This puzzled some children, as they were unaccustomed to being referred to in this manner. Guvinder, for example, who was used to being called 'Guvi' at home appeared a little perplexed by being given his full name on his first day at school. Similarly two of the boys had the same first names, Ahmed. To make the distinction, therefore, they were always referred to by their full names – Ahmed S. and Ahmed H. The latter child was particularly confused by this and during registration on the first few days other children around him would give him a slight nudge when it was his turn to answer. The children also had difficulty in pronouncing their teachers' names.

Many of the children incorporated 'taking the register' into their play, thus internalising this part of the role and their relationship with the teacher. One of the children would take on the role of teacher, sitting in the teacher's chair and using an old red diary that had been provided. Names would be called out and 'marks' given. On the odd occasion when Mari took the register, the children insisted on her carrying out the activity in the correct manner:

Damian: *[to Mari]* It's Ali first, then me.

Sofia: Ali first.

Damian: *[to Mari]* Can you do surnames?

Mari: OK, I'll do surnames. Damian asked me to do surnames.

Sofia: Ali first.

[Children begin talking with each other, but eventually settle down.]

Mari: Right, Ali Iqbal.

Ali: No!

Children: *[several arguing about the right way to do this]* Yes/No, it's 'Master'!

Mari: Master Iqbal, sorry.

Damian: Everybody's 'Master'.

Ali: Yes Miss Boyle.

Sofia: And the girls are 'Mrs'.

This is a very English format for addressing people – 'Master', 'Miss' and 'Mrs'. The children also often replied 'Good morning' or 'Good afternoon', rather than, for example, 'As-salamu-alaykum [peace be upon you]', which many of the Muslim children were accustomed to use. But it was important to get things right. The children knew what colour pens should be used, and as soon as the register had been taken hands were raised in the hopes of being chosen to guess how many were present in class, all vying for the opportunity to write the number on the easel board. They all, including the newer ones, knew the routine well and giggled at Mari's mistakes with names.

The daily repetition, and children's use of 'storying' (see Chapter 4), reinforced the children's new identities as proper pupils within the existing framework of things. There were few concessions to their own cultural forms. Status accrued to pupils with mastery of the rituals, as illustrated by the comparison between them and the neophyte researcher in the episode with the register above.

Children Play, Pupils Work

The new identity was consolidated in the process and structure of activities, and in divisions of space and time. We discussed in Chapter 3 the significance of play for bilingual children. However, one of the most conspicuous changes for the 'new starter' at school came with the marked separation between 'work' and 'play', which privileged the former against the latter. Play was an important feature in the nursery, whether as free play or as what the unit's policy called 'structured play activities'. The latter were those which were planned on a daily and weekly basis by Jenni and her nursery nurses in connection with the school's termly topic or for special occasions such as the celebration of festivals. These activities took one of two forms. There were sessions of experimentation where the teacher would demonstrate a particular activity, for example cooking, to a group of children and the children would join in with it or repeat it. Alternatively children would, individually or in a group, carry out specific tasks such as painting or sticking as part of the preparation for displays of work in the unit.

Jenni carried out additional activities with the group of children who were to move to the Reception/Year 1 class the following term. These consisted of structured language and mathematics work and reflected the obligation felt by the educators in the unit to prepare the children to be pupils in the context of the academic demands of the main school, as Jenni herself acknowledged:

> Obviously you're preparing them for school inasmuch as you want them to be able to sit down and concentrate, but as far as National Curriculum goes I don't particularly say, 'Oh yes, we ought to do a bit on magnets or weather-watching because that's going to come up.' I don't want it to be prescriptive. What I would consider for my specific group is not more formal but more of the pre-reading ones or develop speaking and listening skills with a Lotto game on the tape or something like that.

In the lower school work and play were differentiated in three main ways. Firstly, the classroom was divided into two main areas: the carpeted area, reserved for whole-class activities (including registration and story-time) and play, and the tables where the children sat to complete specified curricular work. The area in which the children were allowed to play was considerably smaller than that designated for work. Secondly, though our teachers proclaimed a basic belief in child-centredness, and occasionally acted on it, work activities remained largely teacher-directed in order to accommodate the National Curriculum. Play, on the other hand, was child-directed, children being given free choice, within the limits of the materials available to them, to develop interest and learning in whatever direction they chose. Thirdly, work in most instances had to be completed before the children could play. Play thus became a marginalised activity and work began to dominate more and more of the school day. The diminution of opportunities for play at school meant a corresponding reduction in their ability to bring their cultural and linguistic knowledge to bear on the activities in which they were involved there, making these potentially less relevant for them. For example, children playing in the home corner would role-play their home experiences and appear more comfortable using their mother tongue than they did during most work-related activity.

By the summer term of the first year the dominance of work and its relationship to time were exemplified through the topic of 'time lines', introduced by the teacher as part of the history curriculum. As an example, the teacher used the school day. On a line that spanned the classroom were the divisions of the day:

register/work/playtime/work/dinner-time/register/work/
assembly/story-time

An article was placed with each section to symbolise the activity, and for the work sections maths and writing-books were used. Although the time line was created to develop the children's historical skills, it served also to reinforce the centrality of work and the appropriate divisions of time and space in the school life of the 'normal' pupil.

Side by side with this activity, another was being constructed for the Muslim children at the mosque, which they attended between three and six evenings a week. Teaching methods here showed a marked contrast with those of the school. The sole aim of the lessons was to teach children to read the Qur'an. The teaching methods employed were not observed by the researchers, though from talking with both the children and the parents they seemed to reflect very much the pattern of 'listen, repeat, practise, test', noted in Qur'anic classes in many countries (Wagner, 1993; Gregory & Mace, 1996). Mobeen, one of the children, explained:

> You learn to read something by heart ... First, you read your holy book, then you read another thing it's got in the mosque and you have to read it on the day and you have to read that by heart ... to the person that is the mosque man.

Mobeen explained that the children must first learn to read Arabic and then Urdu, though many of the Pakistani Muslims at the school spoke Panjabi as a mother tongue (it should be noted that Urdu and Panjabi are mutually comprehensible languages, and written Urdu is based on the Arabic script). The children therefore had to learn what the cultural expectations of themselves as pupils were both in their native culture and in the dominant English state school culture. They commented on the expectations inherent in rituals at the mosque, the need to take off their shoes, cover their heads, wash their hands, feet and faces before beginning their lessons, and the separate tuition for boys and girls. We were unable to compare how far one expectation of pupilhood impacted upon the other, though one parent at least commented that she and her children were able to maintain both identities without difficulty:

> I'm Pakistani, but I live in Britain, and a lot of my way of life is the way most British people live it. But then again I've got my own separate life as well. And for example the children at school, that's totally different, and they go home and it's totally different for them. But it's so easy for them to be in the two situations and it's because it comes naturally to them because it's not been any different from the day they were born. So they just accept it.

This separation of identities depending on context is perhaps one way of maintaining a strong Pakistani identity distinct from a British identity. But the complete separation suggests bifurcation rather than mutual enrichment, and a problem of ambivalence for bilingual children.

Appearance and Identity

Stone (1962) has pointed to the importance of appearance in the establishment, maintenance and alteration of the self. Hence the importance of school uniform in some schools – it is a prominent feature in the discourse of normal pupils. Our school did not have any uniform, children being allowed to wear whatever they (or their parents) chose, though many of them wore new clothes or new shoes bought specially for their first day of school, the new clothing acting as a material symbol of the new status. The children (or perhaps their parents) wanted to look smart and tidy for their first day, and for some of them age-labels on jumpers or an increase in shoe-size indicated that they were growing up. Whilst dressing and undressing for Physical Education (PE) a number of the children would comment that their jumpers had labels on them marked 'age 5–6 years', or that they were now wearing a size nine shoe.

Yet though there was no official school uniform there were peer pressures, among the boys at least, to wear Westernised forms of dress. Thus Shiraz, a boy who liked to wear shalwar kameez – a common form of dress in India and Pakistan and an accepted style of fashion, for the girls in particular – was sometimes teased by his fellow male pupils, as his mother pointed out:

> He gets very easily upset, like just now as we were walking in this morning he decided himself that he was going to wear his shalwar kameez, which is what he wears at home at the weekends, especially when it's hot, he doesn't like wearing trousers when it's hot, and he's often said that some of the children take the mickey, and I'm always saying to him that as long as you know who you are, and you know that is part of being you, and if people want to take the mickey then that's fine, let them as long as you don't let it get to you.

Shiraz was asserting his cultural identity in spite of peer pressure that he should dress in more Western styles, in jumpers, tee shirts and trousers as many of the boys did. In an exercise based on 'my special clothes' a number of children mentioned new Eid clothes they had been bought – often shalwar kameez, but also jeans, Batman clothes, Power Rangers tee-shirts and pullovers. The latter, however, were mainly for the boys, as they were more easily able to wear Western-style clothing than the girls, who even in Western-style dresses would still keep pyjamas or leggings on to cover their legs.

Equal, if not more significance, attached to undressing. This was another new experience for the Reception group and is a good illustration of the ambivalence thrust upon them, for they felt both shame and pride – the former a product of their own cultural experiences, the latter coming from mastery of skills involved in induction into the new culture, as our researcher's fieldnotes show:

> 10.05: Children got changed for PE; some of the younger children needed a lot of help with undressing. The children were asked to put their clothes neatly next to their name labels. The teacher mixed the children so that the newer children were placed next to an older child so that they could follow what they should do. This was the second PE lesson the children have had this term, and most of the newer children seemed happy enough to take off their clothes,

though Guvinder and Ahmed H. needed more encouragement, and Ahmed H. particularly needed help getting undressed. Because of the time taken to get undressed the PE lesson was very short, about 10 minutes. (11 January 1995)

Before children start school their parents are advised to dress them in clothes that they can easily take off and put on themselves. Clearly this was a skill that some of those in our study had not mastered when they started. But there was also a cultural significance for them in undressing for PE, as many of them were Muslim or Sikh. Communal undressing is generally considered unacceptable, particularly for Muslims, and more especially for girls (Sawar, 1994). Yet difficulties with undressing for PE lessons are more often thought to be associated with secondary schooling. Even some of the parents interviewed for our research felt that at five it was not so important because, as one father commented, 'they're too little'. A mother thought it 'not a problem' for the moment, but that when they were older she would 'certainly be happier if they have all-girls' swimming sessions; PE and stuff doesn't really bother me, but swimming I wouldn't be too happy with it'.

However, by the time the children had moved into their second year at school both boys and girls were hiding behind bookshelves and tables to gain a little privacy. Most now brought shorts and tee-shirts to change into, where they had previously only worn vests and knickers (see also Wright, 1993). During the summer term of their second year the embarrassment factor rose further, as they went swimming and therefore had to strip completely. It was noted that children frequently 'nipped' into the toilets to change rather than have to undress in front of their peers. Wilkins (1986) argues that there is potential harm for all children, regardless of religious or cultural background, from enforced communal changing: 'Compulsory group nakedness constitutes a gross infringement upon the civil liberties of a child and is a prospect no adult would willingly contemplate' (Wilkins cited in Sawar, 1994: 13). Wilkins calls this the 'quintessential humiliation for the pubescent child', but in fact it would appear that even younger children are experiencing some humiliation. In some ways, therefore, such an induction into PE could be creating problems for both teachers and pupils in their later school careers.

Being forced to undress is a well-known technique of 'mortification' (Goffman, 1968: 24). 'Stripping people of their clothes strips them of part of their selves' (Woods, 1979: 152) and, in this case, represents another device for preparing them for their new identity of 'pupil'. Yet the induction at Westside was certainly very successful, and worked through status acquisition rather than degradation. As with registration, the children soon became skilled at getting dressed and undressed for PE and requested far less help when dealing with the intricacies of buttons, bows and inside-out jumpers. For many of them the ability to dress and undress seemed to signify another mark of accumulating status, a sense of achievement, a growth in independence, and competitions quickly developed to see who could be ready first. In this way personal shame was mingled with pride in becoming a proper pupil.

Learning the Rules

Part of becoming a pupil is understanding school rules, many of them implicit (Woods, 1996b). Much use was made of older Year I children to familiarise the new recruits with the rules. To the latter, Year 1 children had the authority of time served, yet were sufficiently close to them in both age and ethnicity to help them steer a way through the introduction to school and bridge the gap between the two cultures of school and home.

This is illustrated in the way the children learnt how to move around the school. It was a crucial issue, since they were expected to move frequently from room to room, from the classroom to the hall for PE, dinners and assembly, from the classroom to the library, from the classroom to the playground, from the main teaching area to a second teaching area and from their classroom to other teachers' classrooms to convey messages. Both teachers relied on the Year 1 children to show the Reception children about the school. They paired children off to go and collect the register from the office or to take messages to other classes, and placed Year 1 children as the leaders of the line when the class went as a whole to other parts of the school. In this way the teachers and Year 1 children were able to lessen any anxieties the new children might have had about getting lost.

Three weeks into the new term the class teacher asked Ahmed H. (a child identified as having special educational needs), one of the new entrants, if he could collect the register from the office. Asked if he wanted anyone to go with him, he shook his head and enthusiastically sped off in the right direction. After some minutes the teacher became concerned as to where he was and was about to send another child to look for him when he returned, a triumphant smile on his face, waving the register. He had been successful. Later the researcher found out from the secretary that although he had found the office correctly, he was not sure which register was for his class and had to wait to be shown. On previous occasions when he had been to the office with one of the older children it had been the other child who had picked up the correct register, and though Ahmed H. was confident of finding his way he still needed some help once he arrived. Similar problems were encountered when the new children were asked to take messages to other teachers in the school. Although they could find their way around the school, having been shown on previous occasions by the older group, once there, messages became confused. On one occasion one of the children was brought back by a pupil from another class so that the older pupil could find out what the message had been.

Teachers also used older children in the class to make a point about acceptable pupil behaviour. For example, the Year 1 children were often told to put their hands up when answering questions, followed by 'you should know that by now', or were expected to behave 'more sensibly' because they had been at school longer than the Reception children. When Year 1 children were creating too much noise, especially when teachers were working with the Reception group, they were reminded that 'you know how to work quietly'. In this way the teacher often reinforced the rules of the classroom with the Year 1 children, whilst at the same time providing a model for the Reception group. For the latter, on the other hand, this created an opportunity for 'sussing out' the teacher (Beynon, 1985: 37), something which involves detecting 'each [teacher's] managerial expertise and a clear definition and demonstration of the parameters of the control s/he seeks to establish'.

The presence of the Reception children also raised the status of the Year 1 group. They were given more responsibility in class, and more independence, too, as they were frequently allowed to simply 'get on' with their work whilst the teacher concentrated on developing work with the younger children. Meanwhile for any Reception children whose English made understanding what was expected of them in the classroom difficult, modelling themselves on the Year 1 children became one way of coping with the new expectations of themselves as pupils. Simera, for example, spoke very little English. She was frequently observed waiting, before she would join in, to see what other children were doing – lining up, or going to their tables to start work, or putting their hands up in response to teachers' questions. She soon worked out why they were doing this and followed suit, but when she was asked for answers her face would immediately redden, her eyes drop to the floor and her hand cover her mouth. For a time she stopped raising her hand to answer questions and positioned herself as far from the teacher as she could get. It was not until her second term at school that her confidence in these situations became such that she began to raise her hand once more, though if asked for an answer she would still cover her mouth with her hand and speak in a quiet voice.

In these ways children acquired the cultural resources to fulfil what was expected of a 'normal pupil' (See also Holt, 1969; Hammersley, 1977; Tuckwell, 1982). The concept of 'normal' or 'good' pupil was reinforced periodically throughout the two years of this study, often in quite an overt fashion. In the summer term of the children's first year at school one of the boys in the class, Ahmed S., broke his leg on the school playing field. Following this incident the headteacher conducted a special school assembly to discuss rules for safety in the playground. In class the teacher then discussed with the children rules for class behaviour. The children made many of the suggestions and the teacher drew up a list for which the children provided illustrations. The list was then displayed on the wall by one of the classroom doors, where the children lined up at least twice a day. It consisted of the following rules:

- No kicking.

- No pushing.

- No hitting.

- Don't pull hair.

- Be kind.

- Share.

- Do your work quietly.

- Put your hand up.

- Be helpful.

- Play together.

- Put things back where they belong.

- Don't run in school.

- Push your chair in.

These rules covered the various behavioural aspects of the 'good' pupil. The first four reflected very much the complaints the children voiced regarding playtime. 'Be kind, Share, Be helpful' epitomised the caring ethos promoted in the school, particularly by the headteacher (see Boyle & Woods, 1996; Woods, Boyle & Hubbard, 1997). Such caring behaviour was also frequently rewarded by teachers placing children's names in the Golden Book, a special book for recording good work. The names were read out in a special assembly each week and the children awarded certificates of merit. Other rules related to the manner in which the pupil should work.

Adapting to New Cultures

Whilst establishing its own basic anglicised framework the school also incorporated many of the cultural differences of the children into everyday aspects of school life. We have seen how this applied to dress. Options were provided in school dinners for Muslim children who ate only halal meats, Hindu children who refrained from beef and children who had vegetarian diets. Like choice of clothing, diet was not considered a problem, though some aspects of mealtimes linked to religious practices had caused problems in the past. One parent, for example, reported her child's confusion when she was required to hold her fork in her left hand, when at home they only ever used the right hand. This issue was quickly resolved when pointed out to the headteacher.

Such questions can cause major problems for some children (see Siraj-Blatchford, 1992). The school sought to accommodate as much of the children's culture and tradition as possible, but many areas of their lives were influenced by the wider English society in which they were growing up. For example, in their second year the children did some written work on their favourite foods. Popular repasts were 'Easter egg and jelly and grapes'; 'hamburger and chips'; 'chips and beans'; and 'pizza'.

The school celebrated all the major religious festivals of the children, including Christmas and Easter, which the children talked about though at a purely secular level, and the gift-giving traditions of these festivals were clearly noted. As Christmas loomed, cards were exchanged, visits to Santa arranged and who was getting what on Christmas morning was eagerly discussed. Similarly at Easter there was animated talk around the variety of Easter eggs available in the shops. Eid and Diwali were also talked about by the children, but limited within their own religious groups indicating that there was less cross-cultural celebration in the Islamic and Sikh traditions by comparison with the Christian.

As we saw in Chapter 4, the children's reading habits encouraged further anglicisation. Few of them chose library books which told Asian stories or were linked with Pakistan, India or Bangladesh and, as the examples of Imran and Azmat in the Introduction illustrated, many of the children considered themselves and their families to be exclusively English-speaking (see also Chapter 7).

We might consider many examples of such anglicisation as almost inevitable – choice of food, clothing, the celebration of festivals, television, film and other media, all of these would be difficult to avoid. Indeed aspects such as book-reading might be viewed very positively. Fox (1993) and Wells (1987) emphasise how beneficial it is for children to have a literature-rich world before starting school. Nevertheless, it was found that many of the parents at Westside were cautious and uneasy about the extent to which the Western culture dominant there influenced their children. In the lower school the greatest impact of anglicisation appeared to be on the children's use of mother tongue. In the nursery unit their use of their community languages with each other and with the bilingual nursery nurse, who was present each afternoon, was viewed positively by the educators. For example, Jenni recognised the linguistic significance of the children's use of their community languages:

> I think I've probably read and I've always thought that if you're fluent in one language you're more quickly fluent in this language and if you're having problems with one, you'll have problems with the other so really you shouldn't inhibit them using the language they're not having problems with.

Linda also considered that encouraging community languages in the nursery had an educational value:

Some of the children obviously don't speak as good English anyway so it's good for them to be able to mix and socialise and it obviously helps them when they switch from one to the other anyway, so I do think it has learning purposes.

Because the majority of the educators did not speak community languages, however, English obviously predominated in the curriculum. The resultant use of and increasing confidence in English manifested by the children over a period of time was noted by many of the parents, sometimes in terms of satisfaction but sometimes as a concern in relation to the maintenance of mother tongue. For example, one of the parents of this focus group was worried about her son's lessening use of Panjabi:

Shiraz does [speak Panjabi], but he doesn't speak it as well as he used to, 'cos it's a lot easier for him to express himself in English, which I'm not quite so happy about ... With me it's fine, I speak English so they can say whatever they want, but they need to be able to communicate with their friends and all their relatives who don't speak English ... I think that's *very* important, because they're not always going to be with somebody who speaks English, and they really do need to, because that's a big communication barrier between grandparents and the children, or maybe there's even aunts and uncles or any other member of the family.

A parent of a nursery unit child commented:

That's our identity, that's our inheritance, otherwise if we didn't have the culture, the language, what are we then? We'll be deprived of everything, we're not going to have anything, we're not going to have our identity. So our identity is very important to us – the way you dress, the way you live your daily life ... it's very, very important.

But parents differed in their views on language. Guvinder's mother, who had been born in England, believed that the mother-tongue language would automatically be 'caught', as her children were surrounded by it every day outside school. To her, it was learning English well that was of paramount importance:

Me and my husband we sort of argue, because I'm not talking Panjabi to them ... I didn't prefer them to learn that language anyway, because they gonna talk it any way, catch it from us, but the base thing is English, 'cos then they can go off and study, and learn.

Guvinder's mother was confident of her children's ability to speak Panjabi. She felt they spoke it better than many of the other children from the area, and was very impressed by the way they had picked up the correct accent – 'I think they come from abroad [*laugh*], the way they talk Panjabi'. She articulated some of the problems of young bilingual children and their parents. In Guvinder's case it appeared that he was making the most of his bilingualism and biculturalism – though his father, whom we were not able to interview, might not have agreed. It might, of course, be argued that parents are simply being inducted into an anglicised model of parent-hood; equally, that they are just being realistic about their children's life-chances.

Yet there were children in the Reception group for whom English still provided many instances of misunderstanding, both in their trying to understand the teacher and in the teacher trying to understand them. We have illustrated how Simera, for example, learned to cope with much of what she did not understand by simply copying her peers. Other children such as Asria and Ahmed H. were more willing to make use of the little English they had in order to be understood. Where this failed they would often rely on Hardip, the bilingual non-teaching assistant, for transla-tion. Hardip was an invaluable asset in the classroom, though more in support of the anglicised model than of the children's own cultures. We noted that while the school was happy for children to use their mother tongue in class, this was not actively promoted. The language-rich environment the children were part of was not fully exploited and English became the common language of the classroom. In this way the discourse of the 'normal' pupil was allowed to fuel its own develop-ment. It is not surprising, therefore, that Shiraz's mum noticed her son's declining use of Panjabi at home. Clearly, merely tolerating children's use of home languages in school is not an effective method of mother-tongue and cultural maintenance, and much of the children's ethnic cultural identity was consequently being chal-lenged by the task they faced of constructing a culture-specific pupil role and discourse, all articulated in English. This stood in sharp contrast to their daily expe-riences in their community through their attendance at mosque and temple and their interaction with parents and extended families.

Conclusion

Starting school represents a radical move for all children from 'child' to 'pupil'. But for bilingual children it additionally involves internalising rules and rituals as defined within a traditional English society. To some degree it is essential for them to do this, though ideally if their parents' ambivalence and fears of identity diminu-tion (see Chapter 8) are to be allayed, a balanced framework appears preferable, one that celebrates the strengths of both cultures. This was in fact the case to some extent in our study, at least on the surface. The induction was not confrontational, as in the school of Wright's (1993) research, where 'the Asian pupils (particularly the younger ones) were perceived as a problem to teachers because of their limited cognitive skills, poor English language and poor social skills and their inability to socialise with other pupil groups in the classroom' (p.52), and teachers showed 'open disapproval of their customs and traditions' (p.28). Such disapproval was emphatically not evident at our school. The teachers were sensitive and caring, they celebrated the children's cultural traditions in assemblies and on special occasions, and sought to make their teaching relevant to the children's own constructions of meaning. At the level of conscious interaction they engaged with the issues in committed fashion. At a deeper level, however, the children's own culture and language were becoming marginalised by default, as teachers were being constrained to 'make pupils' according to culturally specific role-models derived from tradition, institutionalisation, the demands of the National Curriculum and assessment. Even the notably caring ethos of the school was ethnically specific; for while it might in itself have been beneficial for all pupils (Noddings, 1992), yet it involved, as discussed in Chapter 1, a deficit model of the home environment, which inhibited teachers from taking full advantage of the children's backgrounds. The children's immediate launch into the National Curriculum and the implicit bias in favour of the English language, as opposed to mother tongues, gave further structure to the passage into anglicised cultural norms.

The process of these children starting school may seem smooth enough on the surface, but underneath there are a number of levels. The children are having to deal not only with the transitions from family to school, and from primary to secondary socialisation, but also in certain respects from their own ethnic culture to English culture. This is by no means a complete picture. The situation is complex: there is a mix of cultures, individuals differ, and lives are lived out at different levels. Nor are the teachers clearly seen to be doing anything wrong. In many respects they are achieving high standards against unreasonable pressures and inadequate resources. They received an excellent report from their OFSTED inspection – though the fact that these inspections are conducted within an anglicised, managerialist framework only emphasises the point being made here (see Jeffrey & Woods, 1998; Woods *et al.*, 1997).

A course of action more consonant with a culturally diverse society involves the positive encouragement of cultural diversity within schools in such a way as to reflect the equal status of all the cultures that support pupils' identities. If this is not done at the launch of pupils' careers, and sustained thereafter, monoculturalism becomes fixed and identities diminished. To create the opposite situation, that of a truly multicultural society in which every culture is to be maintained with equal status, we have to review models of childhood and pupilhood that have become ingrained within the system. This is not just the teachers' responsibility, but concerns all those who devise and enforce policies within which teachers have to work.

Suggestions

(1) Gaining a detailed knowledge of your children before they enter nursery or school is obviously important. The following suggestions might help you in examining the issue:

- Does your profile system enable information about the child to be gained directly from the parents? This information could be obtained by a parent interview or a profile the parent could complete that included what the child likes to do at home.

- Westside had a system of pre-entry home visiting in the nursery unit and regular home visits in the primary part of the school. Have you considered starting such an initiative? In Chapter 8 we suggest this also as a way of creating meaningful links with parents and their families. It could be used as an important means of obtaining information about children in order to ease their induction into the school setting.

- On behalf of those children for whom English is an additional language important cultural information can be obtained from members of the community, including bilingual educators, governors and religious and community leaders. This can also give you important information about the cultural aspects of your children's 'prior knowledge' on entry to school. See also Riley (1996) for further profiling ideas.

(2) Do you have regular links with your feeder schools, either as a nursery school or unit feeding into your local schools or as a primary school receiving children from your local nurseries? If not these links could take several practical forms, enabling both children and teachers to become familiar with each other and to smooth the way for the children's entry to their primary school. For example:

- Nursery children could visit their new schools and meet their reception class teacher towards the end of the term before they move to their new school.

- There could be visits from the respective teachers in order to get to know each other's school and to look at first hand at the teaching methods.

- These visits could also be extended to provide opportunities for teachers to 'exchange', working for a short time in each other's schools. This would give both nursery and reception class teachers practical experience of the methods used in the other educational phase.

(3) If you do not speak any of the children's community languages there are nevertheless ways in which you can encourage them to use their knowledge and skills in this respect. This chapter has highlighted how important it can be for children learning English as an additional language to have bilingual support in the classroom. Consider ways of making bilingual support more effective. Are there opportunities for bilingual support staff to teach in mother tongue, rather than using it simply for translation or as a last resort in 'emergency' situations because children do not understand English instruction? In Chapter 2 we

suggest some ways in which you could encourage your bilingual children to use their first language or languages.

(4) In school, routines and 'rituals' are an important part of maintaining a sense of community as well as giving children a feeling of security, established by the expectation of recognised and habitual practices. Do the routines and practices in your school serve this purpose? Or are they merely traditional ways of doing things? For example:

- The completion of the daily class register is a statutory requirement in schools. Are there less formal ways in which it could be completed in your school, involving children actively in the process rather than passively?

- Do the children in your class and school have opportunities to talk about school rules? Are they able to take an active part in formulating them? You could start in your own classroom by discussing and establishing with the children what constitutes acceptable behaviour. The children could display these rules either in written or in picture form. They could review them regularly to assess their effectiveness.

- Are the names you use for children their preferred names? Are you pronouncing the names of your bilingual children correctly?

(5) Changing for PE and swimming in school is treated as a normal part of the curriculum routines. Individual schools usually establish conventions for this, for example wearing tee shirts and shorts or just knickers and vests for PE. Have you consulted your ethnic minority parents about their views on this? Misunderstandings and resentments could be avoided by such a process.

(6) Sometimes although you may be aware of the dietary requirements of your children you may not be able to satisfy them. For example, not all local authority or private school caterers provide halal meat for Muslim children, who usually in these circumstances have to eat vegetarian food as a substitute. Have you made your families aware of the fact that you understand the difficulties that can arise? Perhaps this could be a regular topic in newsletters home or at parent consultation meetings. This would help to emphasise to parents that you do appreciate their children's needs, even if, for reasons beyond your control, you are not always able to satisfy them.

Chapter 6
Opportunities for Learning

Introduction

In this chapter we examine the ways in which the children in our study were given opportunities to develop creative learning. The term 'opportunity' is used here for a particular reason. The ability of children to gain control of their learning depends on the opportunities which they have to engage with their environment and with those others who can aid them in their learning. As Woods and Jeffrey (1996: 5), following Eisner (1979: 160), emphasise:

> Exploration involves freedom to try out new ways, new activities and different solutions, some of which will inevitably fail. It is important that education provides that kind of opportunity and disposition to play and to take it to the limit, for 'to be able to play with ideas is to feel free to throw them into new combinations, to experiment, and even "to fail"'.

Creative learning possesses also the quality of innovation. The possession by children of control over their learning enables them to act in new ways, leading to personal development and the growth of adaptive skills – a matter of critical importance in the modern age. Kress (1995: 3) suggests that the immense technological changes which are taking place, coupled with the growth of 'globalisation and its corrosive effects on the nation-state', resulting in a 'multicultural, multilingual society', have created the necessity within education of the development of a 'culture of innovation':

> Everything in the new curriculum will need to be judged in terms of its effect in giving young people certain dispositions: confident in the face of difference – cultural, linguistic, ethnic, ethical – and confident in the everyday experience of change.

Central to this project is the development of an innovative approach to the challenges that any individual is likely to face:

> The curriculum should envisage, project, and aim to produce an individual who is at ease with difference and change, whose fundamental being values innovation and is therefore able to question, to challenge, and above all to propose alternatives, constructively. (Kress, 1995: 29)

We organise our discussion around the examination of the opportunities that existed in our schools for making learning relevant to the child; the child's owner-ship of knowledge; the child's control of learning; and innovative learning.

Opportunities for Relevance

Relevance and the child

Within the structure of both nurseries there were opportunities for children to select their own activities, to move from activity to activity, and to experiment and seek out what interested them. Iqbal demonstrated the value of such opportunities on his first day in the nursery, as our researcher's fieldnotes show:

> Iqbal spent a lot of the first part of the morning just flitting. He was not bemused by the variety of activities, but he seemed to want to experience them all in very quick succession. He went first to the jigsaw puzzles, not really doing any but taking the puzzles to bits. He was also fascinated by the trays in which construc-tion activities were kept and at one point moved bits and pieces to other parts of the unit. He also wanted to play with the workbench that had been put out for the first time that morning. He did not recognise the need to wait his turn and merely moved in and wanted to use the hammer and nails. He also played on the computer and was thrilled when a picture with his name at the top was printed out. He kept wanting to tear it out of the printer before it was com-pletely finished.

Iqbal's exploration was concerned with identifying what was available to him as part of gaining an overall picture of his new world. Secondly, he was seeking out those activities and experiences in which he could be interested and to which he could return. The process of moving between activities could continue for some time as the child on any particular occasion sought out what and who was of interest on that day. Thus Attia came into the nursery one morning and started playing with the small coloured blocks. Then she wandered around the nursery looking at other activities before returning to the blocks. Before long she went outside where her activities consisted of riding on one of the unit's tricycles for a short time, pedalling between groups of children to observe what they were doing. After playing with different pieces of the climbing frames she returned to the large plastic tube she had climbed through and concentrated on playing with that for some minutes. This experience of moving from activity to activity forms a stage in a process in which children 'launch' (Bruce, 1991) themselves into play during the first months of nursery experience in such a way that personal agendas become predominant. The process of wandering and watching forms part of the exploration of and experimen-tation with different activities through which children can explore the potential for their interest. From this process of continuous familiarisation they can begin to develop deeper and more sustained ways of playing with activities.

The opportunity to spend time watching others at play represented an important means by which children could assess what would be likely to interest them as well. It was also a means of developing understanding and skills at second hand, which then enabled them to interact with those activities with some level of familiarity. Thus Naveen spent much of his time watching other children involved in activities, whether on their own or with others. On one occasion he was watching two girls playing with the smaller wooden blocks. After a time he collected some of his own and imitated what they were doing. At one point he even tried to take some of their blocks away, but they took them back. After a few minutes the girls moved on to other activities and Naveen was left to play on his own. He then became absorbed with the blocks for almost half an hour.

Watching others could occur from within an activity, as a child looked for clues and signals to lead her on to the next stage and to help her understand the possibilities implicit in the activity itself. One morning Aditya joined a group of girls in looking at a story on the computer. It was a story where the children could interact with the pictures and turn the pages when they were ready. Aditya watched carefully for some time as the other girls took turns in using the mouse to execute instructions for the story. At last she took the mouse from Kieran, asking her at the same time, 'Do you turn the page?' She then used the mouse to switch to the next page.

In the lower school the children had fewer opportunities to choose their own activities, which meant that much of their time was directed by their class teacher. Bennett's (1976) study of 'time on task' indicated that this was a crucial factor in pupil attainment. Sylva *et al.*'s research (1980) of nursery children went beyond Bennett's observations and noted that it was the sustained engagement with a task that was the central key to children's learning. It was observed within the lower school that pupils' engagement with an activity was a significant factor in their learning, as illustrated in the following example.

Shareen had been observed on various occasions avoiding completing work. On one particular occasion during her second year at school she was among a group of children to whom the teacher gave out work cards. Each work card had a set of sentences with words missing, and a choice of words at the top of the card for filling in the spaces. Shareen's card was:

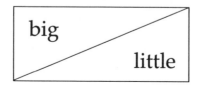

1. A mouse is _____ .

2. An elephant is _____ .

3. A house is _____ .

4. A pin is _____ .

5. A horse is _____ .

6. A bee is _____ .

7. A cow is _____ .

8. A chicken is _____ .

9. An egg is _____ .

10. A school is _____ .

11. A finger is _____ .

12. A bus is _____ .

The teacher had started the lesson by impressing upon the children that the main aspect of this exercise was that it was 'a handwriting practice, that's the time when you should be making your writing the very, very best you can make'. The following observations are taken from Mari's fieldnotes:

As I watched Shareen, her first task was to write the date on her paper. She would write the date, and then rub it out, write it again and rub it out yet again, then get up to sharpen her pencil, come back to her seat and start to write once more. After fifteen minutes she had written 'Thursday 21st March'. As I continued to watch she began to write, and then rub out, write and rub out and so on. She then began to complain that her hand hurt, though no one around her paid very much attention as they were busy with their own work. At one point she sat with her head in her hands and looked out of the corner of her eye to see if I was looking, to see if I would give her sympathy and come and help her or not. As I didn't she went on with her work, frequently stopping, looking around, getting up to sharpen her pencil, rubbing things out on her page (despite the fact that what she was doing was correct). After an hour Shareen had finished three sentences. Most of the other children had finished and moved on to something else, many were now playing on the mat. When the teacher checked her work she promptly moved Shareen away from the other children, close to her so she could check what she was doing. At this point the bell for dinner-time went. During dinner-time Shareen was kept in to do some more of the work card. By the end of dinner-time she had finished question six and her writing had got progressively bigger and bigger down the page. As the other children came in the class teacher insisted Shareen continue with the work. The teacher, having completed the register, then went on to share a poem with the children. Shareen again sat playing with the rubber, and tried listening to the poem. Eventually she was allowed to sit with the rest of the class to find out what they were going to do for the afternoon. In the end she had just begun the eighth sentence.

Shareen was one pupil her teacher, Theresa, felt she had had little success in reaching over the year. Shareen had done very little work during the week and Theresa had become frustrated by her attitude, hence the attempt to get her to complete at least one exercise. However, Shareen seemed very adept at avoiding this. The reason might lie in her attitude toward writing. When asked about the things at school she enjoyed most she talked about painting and playing on the computer. When asked about the things at school she was 'not good at doing' she replied, 'It's getting some work and books, and doing "e".' She felt she was not a 'good' writer, partly because 'my hand gets sore ... [my] hand gets tired', though she admitted that her hand did not get tired when painting or working on the computer. The physical effort which went into writing may account for some of her dislike of this type of activity, but the type of exercise she associated with writing had perhaps more influence on her view of her ability as a writer.

There were times when Shareen enjoyed writing. We have already seen the educational value of stories, and that is endorsed here. In the term after this incident, one of the topics the teacher was covering was story. The work included the children listening to a traditional story, and then writing their own version of it. In this instance the story was *The Pied Piper of Hamelin*. After listening to it Shareen sat down and wrote four and a half sides of A3 paper. Rewriting the story of the Pied Piper was apparently more meaningful to her. She enjoyed stories and was regularly read them at home by her cousin Javeria. She also enjoyed watching videos of fairy-tales such as Disney's *Snow White*. *The Pied Piper* fitted into this genre of fairy-tale, providing a sense of personal motivation and an encouragement to Shareen's imaginative sense that was lacking in the 'big/little' exercise (see also Chapter 4 for the benefits of story for bilingual children).

Motivation could be extrinsic, deriving from the children's desire to please their teacher. This was very much the case for a number of the girls, in particular. Axia, for example, associated achievement with teacher acknowledgement: '[The work] was hard, yeah, an' when I done maths, yeah, miss I worked very hard yeah, an' miss, that's why miss chose me to em, er, line up first, with the others, 'cos me an' Mosem worked very hard, that's why.' Other girls felt that if they produced good work the teacher would reward them in other ways. Sabida A. commented that 'the girls do [their work] more properly so that girls go in the Golden Book the most.' Fouzia and Semina R. talked about getting stars on their work, or being placed in the Golden Book which was strongly associated with their feeling of having achieved success. Although the class teachers did not overtly say to the children that their hard work would be rewarded by being allowed to line up first, or being chosen to do certain things, the children were frequently rewarded for good work by such acts. Thus working hard in class became a meaningful activity because by so doing the children enjoyed their teacher's favour.

A response to these same types of activities which was particularly true of the boys was to use strategies to complete work as quickly as possible in order to pursue their own interests in play. It was a strategy recognised by some of the girls:

Sabida: ... if we're playing you have to put the toys on the floor.

Mari: And do you get to play that, or is it always just the boys?

Mobeen: Normally the boys.

Sabida: Yeah, because the boys finish [their work] first.

Mobeen: They just do a short story.

Sabida: Yeah, they just rush like, they just fill up ... [*Sabida then went and drew very large writing on the chalkboard to show how the boys write in large lettering to fill up their paper so that they can finish their work quickly in order to play.*] And boys' writing is all joined up [*i.e. has no spaces between the words*], you can't see it ... Mosem does it like that.

Sabida and Mobeen's observations were in part confirmed by Peter and Ravinder:

Mari: What's it like to go to school?

Peter: It's boring man, you never get time to play.

Mari: Somebody told me that the boys try and do their work dead quick so they can end up playing. Is that true?

Ravinder: Yeah that's what we do!

Peter: Yeah, but when we try we always get it wrong don't we?

Ravinder: Yeah.

Peter acknowledged that this ploy was not always successful and their class teacher when marking work would often send children back to redo it if it was not up to the required standard. Interestingly, Peter's comment that 'you never get time to play' indicated the importance of play to the children. It was found again and again that the children in the lower school commented throughout the two years of research how much they enjoyed 'choosing time'.

There were also opportunities within the curriculum for the children to make connections between school and home. This formed an important means by which the bilingual children could make significant bridges between their 'prior knowledge' (Woods & Jeffrey, 1996: 118) gained at home and in their communities and their lives at school. These bridges provided a means by which established knowledge could be applied to their school activities. We have seen some examples of 'bridging' in the nurseries in Chapter 4. In the lower school an interesting example occurred during the children's second year, when one of the topics for the first term was poetry.

The teacher had introduced different poems to the class and it was noticeable, particularly at reading-time, that many of the children took the opportunity to look through the poetry books on the shelves and find the poems the teacher had been sharing. Some of the children would even pick poems and ask if they could read them to the rest of the class, which the teacher encouraged. On one particular morning the teacher read out two poems to the children, 'Don't' by Michael Rosen, and 'Never' by Rebecca Halliday (aged 8). The children listened and laughed, as both of the poems were humorous, and the teacher read them out again, and a number of the children attempted to join in. At this point the teacher began to ask the children what type of things they were told not to do. Immediately a flurry of hands went up into the air to offer things they were told not to do at home. The teacher then asked the children about things they were not allowed to do at school. Next she explained that she wanted the children to write their own 'Don't' or 'Never' poems, and initially gave them an outline to follow: 'My mum/teacher/ dad says don't/never ...' This outline immediately provided an opportunity to make the poems relevant to each of the children. The teacher scaffolded the activity by providing a framework for them to use. This supported a number of them, particularly those who were less confident in their use of English and who now had something on which to base their poems, for example Asria who wrote:

> My dad says don't do fighting.
> My dad says don't throw the door.
> My mum says don't go on the road.

Ahmed Shambreez also took advantage of the structure:

> My mum says never swear.
> My brother says never kick.
> My auntie says never shout.

However other children adopted their own style, as the next two poems show:

Don't

My mum says
Don't do that.
Why don't I do that?
My mum says
I don't do that.
My brother says
Don't do that.
Why don't I do that?
Don't break toys,
My mum says.
Why don't I do that?

Fouzia

Never

I say never steal.
My mum says never jump on the bed otherwise it is going to break.
My dad says never go out at night.
My dad is right.

Mobeen

As the children were writing their poems there was a great deal of talk going on around the tables. Even children such as Ahmed Shambreez, who on most occasions tried to write as little as possible, was eager to put his thoughts down on paper. The children were told not to worry about spelling or handwriting on this occasion. What the teacher wanted was their ideas, so the very nature of the activity became personal to every child, as the poem was to be about what people said to them. It was noticeable also that although certain themes were repeated, no poem was very similar to any other, despite the fact that the children were sitting in friendship groups.

Cultural and linguistic relevance

As noted in Chapter 1, teachers expressed their belief that their schools should reflect the linguistic and cultural heritage of the children, although this was not easily put into practice. However, both in the nurseries and the lower school the children sought ways of using their prior knowledge to make meaning from their experiences at school. Most frequently this was in their use and understanding of language, especially during their play (see Chapter 3). In the nurseries the children used their community languages to find common ground together and establish bonds, revealing a flexible set of skills that they used quite naturally as part of their cultural repertoire. This knowledge about language was a common feature manifested by even the youngest bilingual children in the nurseries. Thus Attia and Rabeela always spoke in English together because Attia's community language was Bengali and Rabeela's Panjabi. Within the lower school it was noted that several of the children talked with their friends in mother tongue. Asria for example was very proud of her ability to speak Panjabi, commenting during an interview with Mari, 'I'm good at Pakistan, always'. During this interview Asria also illustrated her developing bilingualism:

Asria:	First I am nursery, then I em, when I will come back, back an' em Pakistan, an' then I come back to school. *[Asria had been in Pakistan for an extended visit shortly before she started at the lower school.]*
Mari:	And then you come back to school. And when you were in Pakistan, did you speak in Pakistani?
Asria:	Yeah.
Mari:	Yeah, all the time?
Asria:	Yeah.
Mari:	Because sometimes in school you speak Pakistani don't you?
Asria:	Yeah, an my friends.
Mari:	With your friends. And sometimes when you're in class as well you speak ...
Asria:	[Axia's] my friend.
Mari:	Axia's your friend isn't she, and you speak Pakistani with Axia.
Asria:	Yeah. Sometime English, sometime Pakistani yeah.
Mari:	Sometimes English, sometimes Pakistani. When do you speak English mostly?
Asria:	Er, I can talk English little bit.

Within the lower school it was noticeable that the children spoke in their community languages more frequently during play than at any other time. Yet even home languages were sometimes used in specific contexts during play. For example, on one particular morning, Mari observed Ahmed S. and Mosem playing in the shop area of their classroom. When talking to each other and to other children they spoke mainly in English, yet when either of the children pretended to speak on the phone they immediately began to switch their language to Panjabi. This may have been due to their experience of using a telephone at home to speak to relatives and friends in the local area and to members of the family in Pakistan.

Where children developed friendships with others who did not share their mother tongue they communicated through English; for example Attia and Rabeela always spoke in English together because Attia's community language was Bengali and Rabeela's Panjabi. So did Riad and Hasanan in the lower school, who were observed playing together making a car from Lego. Riad's first language was Bengali whilst Hasanan's was Panjabi, so in sorting out any dispute or creative difference the children had to communicate in English. Both were thus using and developing their English through practical activity. During the same free choice session, Azmat (an Iraqi girl) and Parminder (an Indian girl) were playing with a set of construction straws. Azmat became bored with this activity and Mari suggested they share a story in the reading corner. Azmat recited some poems she knew by heart and Parminder joined in. From the poems researcher and children moved on to talk about different languages, words that were similar in English, Panjabi and Arabic, and Mari mentioned some words she knew in Japanese. For example 'hey' in Panjabi and in Arabic is equivalent to saying 'yeah' in English, and was frequently used by the children. Mari pointed out to Parminder and Azmat that in Japanese 'yes' is 'hai'. In this way they shared their knowledge of different languages. In such a context learning became relevant, with the children in control; in fact roles were reversed – Mari was not, as an adult, the one automatically in possession of all the knowledge.

In the lower school role-play provided a means by which even children who had limited English were still able to play together. This was evident in the children's first year at school, when the girls in particular were fond of playing 'school'. Playing 'school' frequently involved taking the register. In Chapter 5 we showed how taking the register could contribute to anglicisation and that it had a particular significance in the process of inducting children into school. But it also resulted in real educational gains for the children, as shown in the following example. The teacher had provided an old red diary that the children used as the register. Someone took the role of the teacher, sat in the teacher's chair and used the teacher's pens, whilst the other children answered to their names, often including children who were not necessarily playing the game. It was a very enjoyable piece of role-play, as Raya explained to Mari when they were talking about who told her stories. Raya began to tell Mari about playing 'school':

Raya: Asria's the teacher. And we are, we are children.

Mari: Oh I see, when Asria pretends that she's the teacher and you are the children and then she, does she read to you?

Raya: No.

Mari: Oh, she tells you a story?

Raya: No. He said 'Raya', I say 'Mrs B, yes Mrs B' and he's not, Naeem is not here.

Mari: And he's not here?

Raya: And Ahmed Hussain not here, and Simera and Nazneen.

Mari: Oh right.

Raya: And Shareen.

Mari: And Shareen and when do you, when do you hear stories?

Raya: Why 'Here' I say, em Asria said 'Raya'. This girl she was somebody, Azmat somebody and I say 'Yes'. And then 'There', I said to Azmat, 'er Azmat, all right, c'mon Azmat get the tresher' [the register] and we go with Azmat.

Raya was one of the few children in the school for whom Arabic was her first language. She was playing school with Asria whose first language was Panjabi, as it was for Naeem, Simera, Nazneen and Shareen. Ahmed Hussain's mother tongue was Bengali, and though Azmat had a strong identity as an Iraqi, her preferred language was English. Despite the variance in language, the children were able to do this particular role-play through the strong language model they had from the teacher who took the register every morning and afternoon. The children also incorporated the use of the easel board, frequently used by the teacher to illustrate letter and number formations, another activity which they copied. Play activities highlighted the influence of adults by providing these bilingual learners with appropriate language models in their second language.

Ervin-Tripp (1986: 356) argues that play activities:

> ... not only make possible the child's display of language knowledge, but create some conditions for the child to learn, to understand new words and new constructions, to imitate, to recall, and to try to extend what is known. Learning derives not just from speaking but from hearing language used in a context where the meaning is obvious and where the learner is interested enough in what is going on to pay close attention. That is why play contexts are so much more efficient than traditional classrooms.

The children's knowledge of their languages and cultures arose from their understanding that language was a central aspect of their cultural identity (see Chapter 7). Although, as we have indicated in Chapters 2, 3 and 4, our teachers attempted to create a school environment which reflected the cultural and linguistic diversity of the children, the reality in the two schools was that the predominant use of English by teachers meant that community languages were of inferior status. Also, speaking one's own first language became less than overt.

Opportunities for Ownership

The development of children's ownership of knowledge can arise from the process of interaction with adults, or as part of the provision of opportunities for children to explore their environment on the basis of what interests them. Ownership involves 'internalisation', in which 'the natural end-product of the learning process is a competent individual who has become able to perform alone, or in new contexts, activities and conceptualisations which could earlier be achieved only with the teacher's help' (Edwards & Mercer, 1987: 86). This idea echoes the notion of 'handover' (Bruner 1983), in which the child, after help from an adult with a particular task, is able to take personal control of the task and carry it out for herself (Edwards & Mercer, 1987:23).

An example of the process of 'handover' was observed at Bridge. Kate, the deputy head, was making green chutney with the children. The children were all three-year-olds and Kate had purposely invited a particular girl, Athalia, to join in because she was not speaking at present and Kate hoped that including her would encourage her to join in with the others. Kate developed the activity by showing the children actual tomato plants and talking to them about tomatoes going red, pointing out on the plants both green and red tomatoes. She then demonstrated how to cut up a tomato, and the children repeated this with a small supply of their own. During this part of the activity Kate encouraged the children to taste the tomatoes, and Simeon sorted his into a row by size before he attempted to cut any of them up. The children then cut the apples into small pieces. Kate showed the children how to cut the onions and Thalia and Reece elected to do this. Their eyes stung and Kate discussed with the children why this was. Athalia cut open the bag of sugar for the chutney and the children weighed the ingredients one by one, Kate showing them initially how the scales worked. Simeon then measured out the vinegar into a jug while the children watched. After this they took it in turns to put the ingredients in the pan and then went with Kate to the kitchen to cook the chutney.

Kate's mode of interaction with the children had been in the main by means of instructions and questions. However, with her presence and help they had not only been able to practise a variety of manipulative skills, while being encouraged to engage with her both practically and linguistically; they had also, almost incidentally, been introduced to many other new concepts such as number, measurement, capacity and science, including biology. Though we might expect that they would need to be introduced to many of these concepts again and again, the process of handover had begun. Some of their new skills, such as using a knife to cut up tomatoes, might even have been mastered, and they were perhaps able to indicate their proficiency at the next opportunity they had of working in the cookery area.

The following example from the lower school illustrates both the linguistic and learning problems which can arise in a situation where attempts to scaffold children's learning do not provide them with a sense of ownership firmly rooted in an understanding of the knowledge they are being required to develop. The session was based on the Letter Land phonic scheme. We have already examined in Chapter 4 some problems bilingual children may encounter in connection with this approach to teaching and learning. On this particular occasion the letter and phonic sound being introduced was 'n', introduced by the character 'Naughty Nick', and the teacher used the finger-puppet to capture the children's attention. The teacher then introduced a worksheet to the class, explaining precisely what they needed to do and actually giving them the 'answer' before they went off to complete it.

The worksheet had a variety of pictures on it – a (fishing) net, numbers, a nest, nuts, nails, a nose and an insect, and in the centre was a picture of Naughty Nick. The object of the exercise was to find the picture that did not begin with an 'n' sound, mark it with a cross, and then tick and colour the pictures that did begin with 'n' (ticks and crosses already symbolising right and wrong answers). The teacher went through each picture asking what it was, and once given the correct answer, would then heavily emphasise the initial sound of the word, encouraging the children to join in, for example, 'n-n-n-n-nest: n-n-n-n-nail: i-i-i-i-insect'. She repeated this several times, and the children joined in and as a whole class they identified the odd one out. Instructions were again repeated carefully and the children were then sent off to work at a table, collecting the materials they would need to complete the exercise. Up to this point they seemed to understand what the exercise was about. However, when Mari sat with one group who all carried out correctly the instructions they were given, she found that one child, Sidra, was simply mirroring the teacher's actions. When Mari asked Sidra what the objects on the sheet were her answers bore little relation to the teacher's descriptions. With regard to the net she had no idea; the nuts she said were onions (this may have been because of the picture clue), and the nose she said was a face (again, the picture clue). There was a difference here between the objective of the teacher, which was to develop phonic work, and the objective of the child, to complete the worksheet.

Another example of this same problem was illustrated during the second term at school during a similar activity with another group of children – Simera, Raya, Allan and Asria – who had difficulty with identifying various items beginning with the sound 's'. Again the children were to put a cross through the picture which did not start with the letter 's', and tick and colour the other pictures. Almost before the children had sat down Raya announced in a loud voice, 'And this cross, cross', pointing to the tree as being the item to cross out, though she was unable to tell Mari why. She quickly ticked and coloured in the other pictures: a starfish, a pair of socks, a ball of string, a square, a strawberry, a stamp and a flight of stairs. The other children were equally quick to point out which picture should be crossed out and which should be ticked and coloured. However, when they were asked the names of the other objects there seemed to be considerable confusion. Simera, for example, when asked what the strawberry was simply replied 'mmm', indicating it was something to eat; the stamp and the square she described as a photo, and the stairs as 'go up and go down and go up and go to sleep'. The other children also had problems identifying some of the pictures, and yet all completed the worksheet correctly, and in this sense were simply in the process of 'getting done' (Apple, 1986). Holt (1969: 37), observing children in a similar situation, felt this was in fact an important survival technique: 'For children the central business of school is not learning, whatever this vague word means, it is getting these daily tasks done, or at least out of the way, with a minimum of effort and unpleasantness.' It could be argued that these types of exercise, unconnected as they were with the children's existing knowledge and interests, were more reflective of the paper and pencil tests which the children would be expected to do in the formative assessment of the Standard Assessment Tasks (SATs) (see Chapter 2).

As we have examined in Chapter 3, informal interactions between child and adult as the need arose in practical or play situations possessed more potential for children to acquire ownership of their learning than did structured activities. Children were observed in the lower school requesting help from their teacher with their work. What was noticeable was that the children often wanted help in their free choice activities, where the researchers often became the focus since the teachers were busy working with other children. An example of this in the nursery unit at Westside occurred one morning while Attia was at the paper-cutting table making a collage out of pieces of paper. She showed Nick how she was cutting the paper into shapes. 'Look at that,' she said. She waved the paper in front of Nick, saying a word that sounded like 'fly'. She then said 'No' and took him to the window, where she pointed at the yellow climbing frame in the outside area and said, 'Yellow. You climb up one end and then down the other.' Next she brought him back to the cutting table and told him to 'draw people'. He helped her draw a girl which she then cut out and stuck to the shape of the apparatus which she had already drawn. 'Look at that,' she said, 'I've done it.' She then proceeded to cut other shapes representing parts of the apparatus that she stuck on the collage to finish the picture.

In the lower school Mari became involved in board games, role-play, construction play, and was frequently the audience for children reading or showing her their writings and drawings. She often found herself in these situations giving children help, explaining the rules of a game more clearly, suggesting new ways of using the construction materials, extending their role-play and providing models for reading, writing and drawings. She did this only when invited; where children did not want her interference she refrained from involving herself. Yet what she observed was that play became a very strong medium for learning. It provided opportunities not only for extending learning, but also for practising skills and applying knowledge already developed through the more formal curriculum. The above examples emphasise the potential for development in the company of adults inherent in so much of the children's play, play that they themselves had initiated.

Opportunities for Control

Opportunities for control of the learning process depended on the way the schools approached their teaching. For example as we have seen in Chapter 4, learning through play was a major aspect of the teaching approaches of the nurseries by comparison with the lower school, where there was a noticeable divide between 'work' activities and play. This was an aspect of pupilhood to which the children were quickly introduced when they first started at the lower school (see Chapter 5). Their teachers divided the day into work and play on their behalf, and comments such as 'now we're going to do some work', 'you'll need your workbooks', 'when you've finished your work you can play on the mat', served to remind the children of this divide. Marginalising play in the classroom lessened the opportunities for the children at the lower school to take control of their own learning (see Bruce, 1987; David, 1996, Siraj-Blatchford, 1996a; and Chapter 4).

Control by the children of their own learning was a feature of a number of activities in both nurseries, although the degree of control could vary according to the ways in which activities were resourced. One of the aims of the pedagogy at Bridge, expressed in the written policy, was to enable children to 'take control of their own learning' by 'encouraging and developing children's abilities to make decisions and ... meaningful personal choices'. An example of this in practice was the way in which they were encouraged to explore and experiment with paint. Sonny was exploring the effect a roller had on the paint that he was using on paper. He covered a sheet of paper with brown paint, using the roller, and then turned the paper over and began to repeat the process on the other side, using careful short strokes and looking at the effect he was creating. After covering both sides he picked up the sheet, carried it to the painting rack and, collecting another sheet, began the process again with some fresh paint. The important aspect of this activity was that Sonny recognised that he possessed the freedom to experiment with the medium in the way which he considered was most appropriate to him, while exploring the ways in which colour and texture could be represented with his particular choice of tools. In this way he possessed control over the processes to the fullest extent of his interest.

This level of control depended, in Sonny's case, on his ability to have at his disposal the kind of resources with which he could experiment, based on his personal decision-making.

Resourcing for painting at Westside nursery was also designed to give children opportunities for engaging with a medium that interested them. Traditional painting resources were provided on a daily basis, consisting of paper attached to easels and pots of paint and paint brushes for each child. Children regularly chose this activity and were able to experiment freely with their painting, although their level of personal control was not as extensive as at Bridge because there was less diversity of resources available.

Opportunities for children to gain a measure of control over their learning could also arise from the way in which in certain circumstances routines forming part of the daily life of the nurseries could be adapted. At Westside there were occasions during the morning and afternoon sessions when teachers collected their own groups of children to have milk or water. This supplemented the additional routine in both nurseries of members of staff reading or telling stories to the same groups of children at the end of each session. Having milk in groups did provide potential opportunities for children to interact socially with each other and with their teacher. At Bridge, however, the milk was put out with mugs on a table in the centre of each classroom so that the children could help themselves. This was intended to provide opportunities for children to choose when they had their milk so that they were not interrupted if they had become engrossed in an activity. This was clearly intended to give them a substantial element of choice in and control over their activities. Again, at Westside children were allowed to use the outdoor area for approximately half an hour each session after they had finished their milk. The provision of climbing apparatus and games as well as scooters and bicycles provided opportunities for them to extend their play into that environment. At Bridge, by contrast, the outdoor area was available to the children throughout each session and was therefore regarded as a natural extension of the indoor provision, providing sources of experiential learning which complemented and, where appropriate, extended experimentation inside the classroom. The greater direct organisation of these routines at Westside reflected the significant influence of the same routines current in the lower school and the obligation felt by the nursery staff to introduce the children to aspects of them.

As children moved into the lower school the issue of control over their learning became more of a personal challenge, as the teachers' methodologies were now influenced by the demands of the National Curriculum. Teacher control became more noticeable, particularly with regard to time. Obviously timetables were necessary. It would not be possible for children to use the library, hall, and technology room or television room whenever they wished. Even more constraining, the

National Curriculum demanded that teachers spend a particular amount of time per year on each of the core and foundation subjects, and the school had to keep records on this, promoting a 'getting done' attitude (see Chapter 3).

At times, however, children were able to 'go with the flow' of a lesson (Woods & Jeffrey, 1996). On these occasions there was more of a personal approach to learning, something which frequently occurred during practical activities, of which the following is an example.

During Year 1 Ahmed Shambreez had spent a considerable amount of time absent from school due to a serious long-term illness. Because of this he had not settled into school well and did not enjoy the more formal aspects of work, such as writing, or number work in maths. When he did such work he would frequently complain of tiredness, although the fatigue often left when he was allowed to go and play. Much of his dislike of work may have been due to the fact that his friends were quite far ahead of him. By avoiding work he would avoid being shown up in front of his peers. During the first part of the summer term the teacher had given a group of children, including Ahmed, a patterning exercise to do. The children had initially been given some cards with patterns on them to copy, using interlocking cubes. Most of the children sat and copied the patterns on the cards, mainly using equal numbers of cubes. However, Ahmed began to add more and more to his pattern of yellow and red cubes. Eventually his pattern became too big for the table so he transferred it to the floor. The class teacher encouraged Ahmed to continue. He began to collect as many red and yellow cubes as he could, and once he ran out of red and yellow cubes he changed the pattern to orange and brown as they seemed the closest colours. As he continued, Taylor and Manjid asked if they could help. Ahmed allowed them, and then took on a supervisory role, telling Manjid and Taylor which colours to collect and how to continue the pattern. Where he saw the pattern was going wrong he was quick to make repairs, until eventually the cubes stretched almost the length of the carpet. At this stage the children stepped back from the pattern and were amazed at its length, commenting that it must be taller than them. The teacher suggested they find out, and so Ahmed, Taylor and Manjid lay down on the carpet head to toe to see if the pattern was longer than they were. Other children began to come round to admire the work. Ahmed was anxious that the pattern not be broken up yet as he wanted to show the headteacher, so the class teacher suggested he move it to another part of the classroom. He organised himself and his two helpers (and Mari) to move the pattern over to the window where he carefully reconstructed it. As dinner supervisors and other children began to wander through the classroom he acknowledged their glances over to him, and when the headteacher came to view his work he beamed with pride.

In all Ahmed had spent some 30 minutes creating his pattern, whilst prior to this often after ten minutes on any exercise he would have begun to complain about feeling tired or having a headache. He seemed particularly happy at being able to tell Taylor and Manjid what to do. This was *his* project. Equally he was pleased at the public recognition he received, not only from the teachers, but also from his peers, as in most instances he had difficulty in competing with them. Allowing him to 'go with the flow', to develop a sense of control of his own activity, seemed to spark off his self-motivation, enabling him to work at his own pace and his own level. We saw in Chapter 3 how teachers sought the 'teachable moment'; here is an example of how, on occasions, children sought the 'learning moment'.

Opportunities for Innovation

We saw in Chapter 3 some examples of innovative teaching, whereby teachers took advantage of the unexpected to promote learning. Children also came across such opportunities themselves. A particularly revealing example was provided in the nursery unit by Jabidul's exploration of containers in the water tray. This involved an activity consisting of filling and emptying containers and studying how the water flowed back into the tray. First Jabidul filled a small bucket with water from another container and then emptied it. He then picked up a short plastic hose and, after re-filling the bucket, put one end of the hose in the bucket, the other in his mouth and blew, watching the resultant bubbles in the water. After this experiment he returned to filling and emptying, first filling the bucket and emptying it, followed by filling it with a kettle, and lastly watching water flowing through a sieve. He then filled the kettle using the bucket and then a yoghurt pot, and repeated this sequence. His last activity consisted of filling another bucket that had a hole in its side. He filled this bucket with water and watched the water flowing out of the hole. He repeated this operation twelve times before moving away from the water tray in order to play nearby on his own with another activity. This particular example represented the way in which an ebb and flow of exploration and play could coexist within a single activity. Jabidul explored facets of the equipment, played with those facets, moved on to explore others and then played with them again in such a way that he moved beyond the straightforward use of the equipment.

An example of innovative learning in the lower school occurred in the final term of the children's second year when they were asked to make their own story-books. On this occasion they were given time over two weeks to work on their books from draft to final copy. They had control over their learning processes, choosing to write their own story, adapt one they knew already, or simply copy out a favourite rhyme. They also had to organise the layout of the book, decide which scenes from their stories would be best illustrated, and pick the paper colour that would complement both illustrations and writing. In addition they had to design the cover of the book, which involved a certain amount of research and observation. Some children had also noted aspects of the information usually printed on the back cover of books, and included bar-codes and prices on theirs. The creation of the books enabled the children to illustrate their personal knowledge of what constitutes a story-book, and to develop deeper understandings through this context. However, none of them was given the opportunity to write their book in their mother tongue, though some did include cultural references in their stories. Imran's story, for example, 'What's for Dinner?', went as follows:

> One day a boy came home from school. He said 'Mum, what's for dinner?' 'Fish, eggs and spaghetti.' The next day he came home from swimming. 'What's for dinner?' 'Chapattis and dahl.' The next day he went to play football. He said 'Mummy, what's for dinner?' 'Chips, fish fingers and beans.'

While in this form the story perhaps was a little basic, in the book itself, at the points at which the mother spoke Imran had created fridges and cupboards which opened to reveal the foods. It is a story that seems to reflect very much Imran's own experiences, and in his construction of it we can gauge his understanding and knowledge of book language and story. This example had the characteristics of a creative learning process, and was shared by all the children.

What have been illustrated here are the potential gains inherent in allowing children opportunities to become creative learners, where greater amounts of control and ownership by children allow a correspondingly greater sense of relevance and innovation within the curriculum.

Suggestions

(1) Observations of the ways in which children are using the resources in any activity can give you information about how far they are able to develop that activity and/or whether the resources provided need to be developed to enable them to experiment more widely with different materials and techniques.

(2) In Chapter 5 we discussed the importance of routines and 'rituals' in the life of the school. How do you treat some of these routines in the classroom? For example, do you have set times for children drinking their milk and playing in the outdoor area? The example given in this chapter of the treatment of these routines by Bridge Nursery School represents an interesting variation.

(3) The policy at Bridge included recognition of the need to provide adequate space and time for children to explore activities in which they are engrossed. Children also need to watch others, in order to pick up important information about the nature of activities being carried out by their peers. Within the busy classroom in which the requirements of the National Curriculum have to be sat-

isfied this is difficult, but you could review your organisation and planning to see if you could build flexibility into your routines.

(4) We have emphasised the importance of planning and resourcing for a curriculum that is relevant to children. Relevance can arise from the purposes for which you design activities in the classroom. Consider, for example, the purposes for which you might invite children to carry out written work. Is it merely to make a practical record of what they have done, or is it to develop the concept of writing for different purposes, to show them that language varies according to intention and audience? Writing for different purposes can include:

- Writing letters to teachers, parents, other children and adults. These can include letters giving news and information, asking for information, asking for help.

- Stories or poems written for personal enjoyment or to be shared with another or with a wider audience.

- Factual news about events at school or at home. With whom will this news be shared? The teacher, the class, all children at school in an assembly?

- Instructions for playing games that can be used by other children.

- After constructing a model, drawing and writing a set of instructions on how it was done. Other children could then be invited to use these instructions to build a similar model.

- Recording scientific observations made in the classroom. Again, who would be the audience for these written observations?

- Recording methods used to carry out mathematical procedures such as addition or subtraction.

Another way into relevance is to re-evaluate the curriculum to find ways of approaching subjects from alternative world views. For example introducing other systems of literacy and numeracy into the classroom may help children to understand more of their purpose. Consider Roman numerals, which illustrate a great deal about the concepts of counting, addition and subtraction.

(5) In our discussion of cultural and linguistic relevance we described ways in which bilingual children used their community languages and English in differing circumstances (see also Gravelle, 1996: 52). In connection with this the following ideas could be considered:

- To what extent do you set out in your planning and assessment to provide opportunities for bilingual children to work together co-operatively? Providing occasions for children to co-operate gives them opportunities for developing concepts of purpose and audience through the medium of their different languages. Creating opportunities for bilingual parents or volunteers to work with these groups might encourage children to use mother tongue in class more frequently.

- Providing occasions for children to interact orally enables them also to function independently at their own cognitive level of understanding.

- Creating opportunities for children to use spoken and written language for different purposes gives them greater ownership of and control over their learning, covering important aspects of the National Curriculum in the process.

- As suggested in this chapter, the provision of such occasions develops opportunities for more flexible and innovative approaches to activities and the learning resulting from them.

(6) In addition to the suggestions in this and other chapters the following reading will provide ideas for policy and practice:

Bearne, E. (1998) *Making Progress in English*. London: Routledge.
Gravelle, M. (1996) *Supporting Bilingual Learners in Schools*. Stoke-on-Trent: Trentham Books.
Gregory, E. (1996) *Making Sense of a New World: Learning to Read in a Second Language*. London: Paul Chapman.
Siraj-Blatchford, I. (1994) *The Early Years: Laying the Foundation for Racial Equality*. Stoke-on-Trent: Trentham Books.
Wray, D. and Lewis, M. (1997) *Extending Literacy: Children Reading and Writing Non-fiction*. London: Routledge.

Chapter 7
Children's Identities

Introduction

In this chapter we examine the social relationships of the children and their developing identities. Tajfel (1981: 225) argues that identity is 'that *part* of an individual's self-concept which derives from his membership of a social group (or groups) together with the value and emotional significance attached to that membership'. Tajfel illustrates two main influences exerted on the individual through group membership: first, that in-group membership identity is established in opposition to the ascribed identity of the out-group; secondly, that while this process of differentiation occurs between groups of similar natures, where there is a sharper contrast between groups comparisons will be greater and identities more clearly marked. This is particularly significant for the children of this research, whose social identities were multifarious, as was illustrated by the way in which they reproduced their social relationships. Martin and Stuart-Smith (1998: 250) argue that 'despite the strong assimilationist policy in English schools, the majority of young children from a substantial and established minority community choose a bilingual identity', and that they articulate this identity through constructs according to 'language, skin colour and religion' (p.249). Lloyd and Duveen (1992: 31) point out:

> Age, gender, social class, ethnicity and religious affiliation exert great influence on interpersonal relations and endow these groups and their social representations with salience. In addition, we expect that the more saliently marked social groups will be the first to be reconstructed by the young child.

Concentrating on our lower school sample, we examine the children's construction of social identities through their behaviour at school, their friendship choices and their experiences outside school.

Identities at school

Goffman (1963) identified three forms of identity: social identity, considered to be the interpretation of the individual in relation to cultural institutions; personal identity, which the individual negotiates through interaction with others; and ego or 'felt' identity, which reflects the individual's own interpretation of their 'self' identity. We have seen earlier how these three categories interrelate with regard to

...dren's identities as pupils and learners. In the first place their teachers identify children in certain ways, as good or bad pupils; able or poor learners. The children in our study were themselves able to identify their own classmates in the same way, and by comparing feedback from their teachers and their own knowledge of their classmates they were able to place themselves in a hierarchy of achievement, in terms of both behaviour and learning ability.

The following excerpts are taking from an informal interview Mari had with Parminder (aged 6) during her second year at school:

Mari: Do you like reading, Parminder?

Parminder: *[nods]*

Mari: Yeah. Are you a good reader?

Parminder: I have to go backwards, because I was on *Where is Jill*, an' Miss put me on here, *I can swim*, but I'm supposed to be on this one, then go on that one and that one and then that one *[pointing to the titles on the back cover of her current reading-book]*.

Mari: You're supposed to go that way round, are you?

Parminder: That way.

Adjmar: I gone past that one

Mari: So that one's, that one's the yellow books? And you're past that one?

Adjmar: I'm on the blue books.

Mari: You're on the blue books. So are the blue books, what does that mean?

Parminder: Blue books is more harder, but red books are really easy, these [yellow books] are nearly easy, but blue books are really hard, so are green books, innit? Green books are even more harder. Green books are.

Mosem: All these are. That's easy, that's easy, all of them is.

Mari: All of them are?

Parminder: Green books isn't.

Mosem: Yeah, green books are hard. I read that an' it's easy. Em, a easy book *[referring to Parminder's book]*.

We see here that Parminder is able to judge her reading ability based on her teacher's assessment of her reading progress, and in comparison to the level of book she is on in the reading scheme. She has interpreted her identity as a reader in relation to one of the products of the school system, the school reading scheme.

Later in the conversation Mobeen comes over with her reading-book to see what is happening. Parminder comments:

Parminder: Oh my gosh, she's beatin' me. She's gonna be on blue books after that. Let me show you look. She's on *Come for a swim*, there's nothing else. So that means she's gonna be on blue books.

Mari: So do you have to read all of the books on there?

Parminder: Yeah. 'Cos first you have to be on that one, then that one *[points to all the titles listed on the back cover of her book]*.

Mari: So, what do you do when you've read it?

Parminder: If you change it, if you're good at it, you can change it. The teacher told me to change it, so.

Again we can see the assessment of the teacher as being vitally important to Parminder's judgement of her own ability, but she is also able to place her ability in comparison with others in her class. Her view of her self as a competent reader is negotiated through interaction with others. Mari then asked Parminder again if she felt she was a good reader:

Mari: Are you good at reading?

Parminder: No, not that much.

Mari: Not that much.

Parminder: Some people are, but ... Because I went to India, yeah, I'm left behind. I'm left behind, so I have to catch up, yeah. I was on red books, and everyone was on blue books and these books innit, so I had to catch up. So I came on. That's why I, people are beating me, but some people aren't.

Mari: So do you think you'll catch up?

Parminder: Yeah.

We see here that while Parminder is able to judge her ability as a reader through interpreting her teacher's assessment of her progress and by comparison with other children around her, there is in addition her own 'felt' identity. She feels her current reading standard is not due to a lack of ability on her part but is more the result of her having missed school. Her assessment of herself is that she has the capacity as a learner to catch up with the other children in her class. In actuality Parminder believed herself to be an able pupil, particularly in relation to mathematics: 'I'm quite good at maths because, I don't know why, I'm just clever'. Parminder's perception of herself as being 'clever' was borne out in her Standard Assessment Tasks which she sat at the end of the year, and in which she achieved high levels in both maths and English.

The children's identities developed also through school experiences involving age, gender and ethnicity.

Group identities based on age

From the very beginning of their school careers age was used to differentiate the children, both by the teacher and by the children themselves. When the new starters began school in January the children were often divided into specific groupings, Year 1 pupils and Reception pupils, particularly for curricular activities such as language, maths and science work. From the teacher's point of view, differentiation in this way was necessary. First, the Year 1 children were already working within the framework of the National Curriculum, while the Reception group were only just starting, therefore desired learning outcomes were specific to each group. The class teacher felt she needed to give more of her time and input to the Reception children and hence initially set tasks for the Year 1 children which they could cope with either independently or with the aid of the non-teaching assistant. In activities such as drama, PE, music, story-times and some oral language and maths activities where the class worked together as a whole it was noticeable that the children organised themselves into age-groupings on the mat. The diagram below indicates this division during the start of a group session three weeks into the first term of the new Reception class children. The names in bold are those of the January intake of children, who sit closely together and nearer to the back of the mat area.

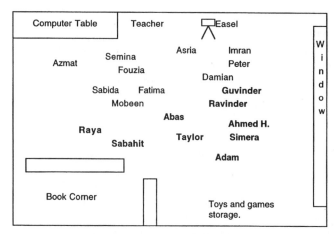

Figure 1   Age grouping among new reception class children, 30 January 1995

The Year 1 children have a greater amount of confidence than the new starters. Sitting closer to the teacher rather than hiding nearer to the back of the carpet is an indication of their status. These children have already developed a relationship with *their* class teacher, whilst the Reception children are still at a stage of 'getting to know' their teacher, as well as their new class. Even by the end of the spring term there is still a fairly noticeable division between the Year 1 children and the Reception children, although more of the Reception children are moving closer to the class teacher.

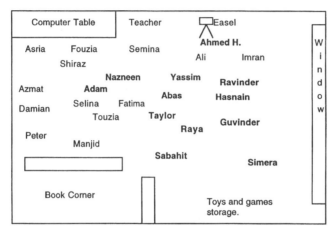

Figure 2   Age groupings among reception class children, 7 April 1995

This group identity was also exemplified in conversations with the children, mainly by the older group who would often refer to the new intake as 'the younger children'. On one particular occasion the children had been making collage pictures and mixing paint; the older group had mixed up purple paint and the younger children mixed green paint, as was explained to Mari by Shiraz (Year 1) who told her 'we made purple ones, the little ones made green'. Shiraz had picked up on his teacher's differentiation between the two age groups in the classroom, the 'older children', and the 'younger children'. Additionally he indicates a change in status. The previous term he may well himself have been considered one of the 'little ones' by teachers and other pupils in the school. By labelling other children in the class as 'the little ones' he establishes his own in-group membership (Tajfel, 1981) and his status in class. Changes in status are likely to be reflected in self-image and identity (Allan, 1989).

Negotiating one's membership was not always an easy task, as Taylor found. Technically Taylor was a Year 1 child, as he had reached his fifth birthday prior to 1st September. However, he had transferred to Westside from another school in the January and so was initially grouped with the Reception children until his teacher could get to know him and assess how much work he had already done. This problematised his position in class, because he had greater experience of school than those children who started with him at Westside, yet at the same time was separated from his fellow Year 1 classmates for much of the day. When he first started at Westside he was observed often playing on his own during free time for the Reception children, despite his overtures to play with other boys. In one free play session during his first week at school he was seen trying to join in with a group of boys who had formed their friendship in the nursery and were playing with the garage, but they ignored him completely. Eventually he found a Meccano set which he played with on his own. Later in the same week when he had the opportunity to mix more freely with the older children within the classroom he sought to ally himself with the Year 1 boys, in particular Peter and Damian who frequently played and worked together. During a maths session in which the teacher allowed the children to sit where they wanted, Taylor made his way toward a free chair between Damian and Peter. Damian placed his hand over the seat, indicating that it was taken, and asked the researcher to come and sit there, but Mari asked Damian to allow Taylor to sit next to him instead. Reluctantly he gave way, but like the Reception boys before him he ignored Taylor and talked mainly to Peter and the other Year 1 children at his table. On the same day the class teacher asked Taylor to collect the register and choose a friend to go with him. He immediately chose Peter and when they returned he sat next to him on the mat.

Taylor's difficulty in getting accepted went on for some time and even after four weeks at school there was evidence that he had still not gained membership of either age group, as illustrated in the following observation made by Mari of a PE lesson:

> The children came into the hall, and knew to find a space based on their experiences of earlier PE lessons. I mainly watched Taylor during this session. When he first came in he sat close to Peter, Damian and Ali (all Year 1 boys) at the far end of the room. The teacher started with some basic warm-up exercises which the children enjoy doing, judging by their smiles and giggles. The teacher then asked the children to sit on the floor while she got some hoops. These she spaced out around the room and asked the children not to go into them. The teacher explained that she was going to play some music. When she stopped the music the children were to go into a hoop, but there should no more than three children in each hoop. She repeated this exercise three times.

> The first time Taylor sought out Peter and stood in the same hoop as him. The second time, Taylor was closest to the hoop Mobeen (Year 1 girl) was in and stood with her. They were then joined by Adam (Reception boy). Taylor and Adam began giggling. The third time, Taylor was first to a hoop and was joined by Abas (Reception boy), who subsequently looked around and moved into an-

other hoop with Ahmed Hussain (Reception boy). The teacher told Abas to move back to the hoop with Taylor.

After this, the children were asked to come out of the hoops and sit next to them. The teacher then asked the children to find a partner and there was a great flurry of activity. Abas immediately went off to join Ahmed Hussain. Taylor was subsequently left by himself after all the other children had found partners, except for Ali who had gone to stand with Peter and Damian – possibly in the hope that there might be one left over and he could make a threesome. The teacher told Ali to go with Taylor, as Peter and Damian made it obvious they wanted to stay together by moving closer to each other. Initially Taylor and Ali did not talk with each other.

The teacher asked the children to find different ways of moving through the hoops, one was to hold the hoop, the other to move through. Ali immediately picked up the hoop, but when he realised it was more fun going through, gave the hoop to Taylor. After a short while Ali and Taylor began to talk and Ali let Taylor go through the hoop, raising the hoop every time he tried to go through. This was all in fun and both were laughing ...

The second task for the children was to skip with the hoop – this time Taylor got to the hoop first, and though Ali tried to take it off him, he wasn't giving in and got first go at skipping. (Fieldnotes, 25 January 1995)

There are a number of points here which highlight Taylor's efforts in seeking membership. Taylor is the one who seeks out children he wants to sit by; he is not chosen, and in fact Abas rejects him in favour of Ahmed Hussain, one of his friends. Ali is then removed from his own preferred group to be placed with Taylor who is the only child in the class without a partner. Ali is clearly unhappy at this move and tries to assert his status in the situation by taking initial control, though once the activity is considered to be fun he is willing to work co-operatively with Taylor. With the second activity Taylor is confident enough to assert his own interests with Ali and is not going to be manipulated by him. Taylor was actually bigger than Ali and this may account for Ali backing down. In standing up to Ali, Taylor may have raised his status with the Year 1 boys.

Taylor's initial problem of being somewhat on the perimeter of the social groupings in the class did not in fact appear to bother him. Rather than withdrawing or becoming disruptive, which might have been an indication that he was unhappy, he was active in class discussions and eager to participate in activities, talking freely with his teachers and other adults as well as his peers. It was noticeable that at playtimes Taylor tended to play football with his cousin and his cousin's friends who were in the year above him. This certainly gave him status in the playground. In this situation he became a gatekeeper, in that his association with the older boys meant that some of his classmates, in particular Jatinder and Hasnain, could also join in with the football.

During his second term at Westside Taylor was placed with the Year 1 children for his curriculum work, at which point he was frequently observed playing with Peter and Damian and established himself as a member of this particular group.

Group identities based on gender

The gender divide was quite noticeable in this class even in the first term of school. Using one of the diagrams from above showing the seating arrangements on the mat and dividing it purely into boy and girl, the split between the two groups is very obvious (the boys' names are in bold).

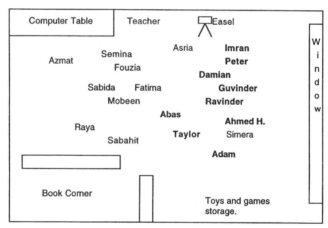

Figure 3   Gender divisions among reception class children

It has been found that children of very young ages are aware of gender stereotypes (Khun *et al.*, 1978) and tend to behave in accordance with them (Clarricoates, 1987, Fagot, 1974; Thomas, 1986). Paley (1984: ix) gives a vivid account of kindergarten life organised around the themes of superheroes and domesticity, and notes:

> Kindergarten is a triumph of sexual self-stereotyping. No amount of adult subterfuge or propaganda deflects the five-year-old's passion for segregation by sex. They think they have invented the differences between boys and girls and, as with any new invention, must prove that it works.

The children in our lower school similarly rejected teachers' attempts to mix girls and boys together. It was observed that, though children were frequently asked to work in mixed sex groups, around the same table the girls would all sit close together in one group and the boys close together in another. On occasions when teachers employed creative strategies for getting the children to line up, for example selecting children wearing particular coloured clothes, or with birthdays in particular months of the year, or able to answer a particular question, these children 'saved' places for their friends, who in the main were of the same sex.

In part the division of the class was reinforced by the school, which, for example, divided the register into boys' names and girls' names rather than having them in alphabetical order. Furthermore it was most frequently the boys who played with construction kits, trains and cars, while the girls took over the home corner or sat by the cutting and sticking table. Theresa was the only teacher observed who nominated days in her classroom when only the girls were allowed to play with the construction kits. This was an attempt to encourage the girls to become active in this kind of play, but because of their lack of experience in using Lego and Meccano sets their models were often just simple walls or towers, compared with the complex cars and machines the boys made. It was observed that only one of the girls, Semina, was able to make more complex models, and this may have been partly due to her close friendship with her male cousin Adjmar who was in the same class – they were frequently observed playing and working together.

Thus the boys in the Reception class dominated construction play, while the girls colonised the 'home corner'. Here there was a kitchen set up, baby dolls and stuffed animals in prams to be cared for, and a variety of dressing-up clothes. The girls reconstructed a stereotyped image of mother and housewife in their play, but none of the boys reconstructed a 'new man' identity in the home corner. Some of the dressing-up clothes were aimed at the boys, such as firemen's helmets, police caps and jackets, but the boys dressed up in these items and then played away from the home corner. Paley (1984) observed similarly how the five-year-old boys in her research set out to escape from home and domesticity, expanding their horizons through imaginative play, a choice the girls rarely undertook.

In the children's second year at school there was no 'home corner' and the creative play area was made into something different each term to reflect the school topic. This meant that both girls and boys played in the creative play area, though rarely together. However, even without such opportunities for the children to act out their stereotyped images of male and female roles, they reconstructed these identities in their stories. In a project in which they were asked to write their own stories, four in particular reflect their images of mothers and fathers (the first was discussed in a different context on p.154):

Imran   **What's for dinner?**
(boy):   One day a boy came home from school. He said 'Mum, what's for dinner?' 'Fish, eggs and spaghetti.' The next day he came home from swimming. 'What's for dinner?' 'Chapattis and dahl.' The next day he went to play football. He said 'Mummy, what's for dinner?' 'Chips, fish fingers and beans.'

Selina (girl):	**Where are you Mummy?** 'Where are you Mummy?' 'I am cooking the dinner for you and your daddy.' 'Where are you Mummy?' 'I am feeding the little baby boy.' 'Where are you Mummy?' 'I am taking you to school.' 'Where are you Mummy?' 'I am swimming.' 'Can I come please Mummy?' 'Yes you can swim.'
Shiraz (boy):	**Daddy where are you?** 'Will you play with me Daddy?' 'Not now, I'm having a bath.' 'Will you play with me now?' 'No not yet, I'm putting my clothes on.' 'Have you put your clothes on now?' 'Yes I have put my clothes on. First let me watch the news, then I'm going to play with you.' 'Have you finished watching the news now?' 'Yes I have finished watching the news. First let me have a glass of water. I've had a glass of water. I will play now.'
Touzia (girl):	**Daddy where are you?** 'Daddy where are you?' I am reading a book.' 'Daddy I can't see you.' 'I am washing my car.' 'Daddy, where are you?' 'I am writing.' 'Daddy, where are you?' 'I am making a cup of tea.' 'Daddy, where are you?' 'I am combing my hair.' 'Daddy, what are you doing?' 'I am bringing some bananas.'

These stories illustrate the kinds of image the children have of male and female, or more specifically mothers and fathers. Part of the role of mothers is to care for others, to cook, look after babies, take children to school. Mothers generally put others before themselves. Even in Selina's story where the mother goes swimming she immediately takes the daughter along with her. There are no delays of the sort shown by the father in Shiraz's story. Mothers are there to cater for the immediate needs of their family. This stereotype of mothering may well reflect the children's own felt experiences of their home life, but it may also be one which is reinforced by the teachers' belief in the caring nature of their profession (see Chapter 2). Conversely the fathers here are rather selfish. The boy in Shiraz's story who wants to play with his father is constantly 'put off' until the father is ready to play with him. Although the father in Touzia's story appears somewhat 'domesticated', being prepared to do some shopping and to make a cup of tea, the tea is for himself. Nor does he offer to read with or to his daughter. His actions seem to reflect his own interests.

There is a feeling of authenticity in what the children have written. The stories may or may not be an accurate reflection of their parents, but the children have created and recreated these images from their own experiences of the different ways in which men and women are treated in society. Lloyd and Duveen (1992: 10) suggest that, 'perhaps the most sexist persons in a Reception class are the children themselves'. It would seem that these attitudes remain with the children for some time.

Group identities based on ethnicity and religion

Ethnic and religious identities were not seen to be strengthened in the same way as age and gender, though Gay (1985) has argued that children's ethnic identity affects their whole development and learning. We have noted in other chapters that although the teachers supported in theory a multicultural curriculum and the children's use of home languages in school, this belief did not pervade the entire school philosophy, and links in the curriculum regarding ethnicity or religion in particular were often planned either within topics or as part of assemblies. In actuality the culture of the school appeared to reflect the culture of the teachers rather than that of the children. Lloyd and Duveen (1992: 13) noted in their research on gender identities in early years education that 'teachers rely upon their representations of such common social categories as age, gender, race, ethnicity and social class in their interactions with children and their organisation of classroom life'.

We have noted elsewhere that the main cultural representation within the curriculum and ethos of the school was dominated by an anglicised model of education, partly because of the nature of the National Curriculum, but also because the teachers themselves did not share the ethnicities of the children. In reality ethnicity was most frequently discussed through the celebration of religious festivals. In many other respects cultural differences between the children were either ignored, or at times children were even asked to believe that there were no differences between them, as shown in the following example, taken from their second year at school. Theresa, the class teacher, read out a poem written by a ten-year-old child entitled 'A Recipe for a Happy World' which subsequently sparked a discussion about war. Part of the discussion was about why wars begin, and one possible cause suggested by one of the children was that people do not like one another.

Teacher: Sometimes it's just because people don't like each other. You know it's a bit like in the playground. You know when we were talking about people being racist, yeah? D'you remember what Mrs M. said about that? They said, I'm not playing with you, because you're Pakistani, I don't like Pakistani people. That's being ...

Children: Racist.

Teacher: ... and some people start wars because of that, they say 'We don't like any of those people, they're not like us, so let's kill them, we don't like them.' And that's a bit like in fighting in the playground. Now we don't have that in our school, do we?

Pupil: No.

| Teacher: | We like everybody. We don't say, I'm not playing with you 'cos you're English. I'm not sitting next to you because you're an Indian, I'm not sharing my pencil with you because you're a Bangladeshi. We don't say that. We're all friends. |

Theresa raises the issue of racism in this discussion, only to close it immediately by asserting that 'we don't have that in our school' and 'we like everybody'. Such statements do not allow the children the opportunity to discuss their experiences of racism or their feelings about being Bangladeshi, Indian, Pakistani or white. As Short and Carrington (1996: 74) point out:

> Whilst we accept the importance of children learning about similarities, not least because of research showing that we are attracted to people who are like us (Byrne, 1971), we are mindful that negative perceptions of difference do not evaporate as a result of teachers choosing to ignore or underplay them.

Certainly the children seemed to be aware of differences between the cultural and religious groups in their class. Understanding these differences was one way of understanding one's own cultural identity. For the majority of the children their sense of identity in this respect was very clear. Curiously enough Peter, one of the few white children in the class, was one of the most unsure, certainly of any religious identity:

Mari:	... some of the children in your class are Muslim and some children are ...
Peter:	Sikhs
Mari:	And some children are ...
Peter:	Christians.
Mari:	Which one are you?
Peter:	Er ...
Mari:	Are you any of those or none?
Peter:	I don't know.
Mari:	D'you think you're a Muslim?
Peter:	No!
Mari:	D'you think you're a Sikh?
Peter:	No.
Mari:	D'you think you're a Christian?

Peter: Maybe.

Peter is very definite that he is neither a Muslim nor a Sikh, indicating that he has compared his own life experiences with those of his classmates and recognises that he is not a member of those religious groups. At the same time he indicates his uncertainty about Christianity. His family rarely went to church. Asking the same question of the other children produced very specific answers, however. The children were either Muslim or Sikh, which also meant that they were Pakistani, Bangladeshi or Indian. There were two main mosques in the area, one that catered for the Pakistani Muslims and one that was used by the Bangladeshi Muslims. The reason for this is that within the mosques the children learn not only to read the Qu'ran in Arabic, but also Urdu or Bengali script, and instruction is given in either Urdu or Bengali, so that the mosque is a centre for mother-tongue maintenance, as is the temple, where the main language used is Panjabi.

At school, though the dominant language was English, most of our children were very aware of the variety of languages spoken by their peers:

Mari: D'you know what the differences are between being Muslim and being a Sikh?

Mobeen: Em, all it is that Muslims they er speak like em properly and the, I know Sikh people they don't actually speak like our language, because they em do it like English and em England, and Panjabi and er they say a bit at the end where we don't say it.

Mari: Right, so that's the difference, is it?

Mobeen: And er, they go to the temple, we go to the mosque.

Mobeen appears to consider Sikhs as more English, compared with Muslims. This may be a way for her to characterise being Pakistani as significantly different from being both Indian and English. Later in this conversation it became clear that for Mobeen, being Pakistani and being Muslim were very closely linked:

Mari: Right, 'cos Azmat, she's a Muslim as well, isn't she?

Mobeen: No. She's Arabic.

Mari: She's a Muslim as well. Did you not know?

Mobeen: No.

Mobeen seems very surprised at this piece of information, which she has obviously not considered before, particularly as Azmat was the only Arabic child in class and did not attend either the Pakistani or Bangladeshi mosques in the area. It is evident from this that identity involves a complex set of characteristics for each child. Age and gender were reinforced both in school and in the wider society, positively as well as negatively. Ethnic and religious identities were reinforced more through home and local community than through school.

Friendships

What effect does identity have upon children's friendship groupings? Friendships were important aspects of our children's social worlds. They were valued for their pragmatic uses, for basic companionship, and also for their more intrinsic values, as a form of support, both emotional and physical, and support for identity and status.

Someone to play with

A number of models of the development of children's friendships have described young children's friendships as being based very much on proximity (Sullivan, 1953; Selman, 1981); children play with other children simply because they are there. The assumption of these theories is that young children's friendships lack a certain degree of commitment, are frequently transitory and self-serving. In part this assumption is made because of an adult-centric view of friendship (Davies, 1983) based on the sharing of values, opinions and views and the development of intimacy. However, if we take the child's point of view, having someone to play with and to share activities with is essential and can create strong bonds:

> To be alone in a new place without friends is potentially devastating. To find a friend is to partially allieviate the problem. By building with that friend a system of shared meanings and understanding, such that the world is a predictable place, children take the first step towards being competent people within the social setting of the school. Much of this building of shared meanings takes place through play. (Davies, 1983: 63)

Again, we see how important the ability to share play is in our children's views of what makes a 'good friend'. The following extracts are taken from the children's writing in their second year at school.

Abas: A good friend let me in his house. A good friend let me play computer. He hears me read. He plays with me. He sits with me.

Shazrin: A good friend can share every thing you could share. A good friend make me happy. A good friend help them make some thing. A good friend tells you the word that you don't know in the book. A good friend plays with you in the playground.

Fatima: A good friend plays with me. A good friend helps me. A good friend shares with me. A good friend likes me. A good friend colours with me.

Shiraz: A good friend is nice. A good friend gives me a biscuit. A good friend helps me. A good friend plays with me. A good friend gives me money.

Whilst there are other elements within the children's descriptions of what makes a 'good friend', such as help with reading, someone who is thought to be nice, someone who will support you, all of the descriptions include the essential aspect that a good friend is someone who will play with you. Play for our children is validated by having someone to play with, perhaps the reason why Taylor sought to make friends so eagerly. Play and friendships also enable children to revert back to being a child and to create their own culture. Much of their time is spent engaging in the adult worlds of their parents and teachers, where the emphasis is often on the process of growing up, learning how to be more adult-like. Within their own peer groups, children develop their own meanings, understandings, language and rituals, developed through the medium of play and friendship.

Friendship as a support mechanism

Research such as that of Galton and Willcocks (1983) and Measor and Woods (1984) indicated that one of the greatest fears of children transferring to middle or secondary schools was the loss of friendships. Measor and Woods found that social ties were perhaps even strengthened by the fact that children needed support in their first encounters of their new school to help them cope with the formal demands of their classrooms and the informal culture of the playground. Friendships were of equal importance to our children. Some parents commented on how the transfer from the nursery to the lower school had been made easier because their children already had established friendships (see Chapter 5). The view that young children's friendships are unstable (Maxwell, 1990) was not reflected by the children of our study. Certainly for a number of the girls, friendships they had formed in the nursery lasted throughout the two years of our research. For example, Mobeen commented that this was an important element of her friendship with Sabida:

Mari: Have you got a best friend?

Mobeen: Yes

Mari: Who's your best friend?

Mobeen: Sabida.

Mari: Sabida. Why is she your best friend?

Mobeen: Em, 'cos we been em, friends all through the erm classes, and em since we were in nursery we been friends.

The children's need to maintain friendships when first starting school was noticeable in Taylor's struggle to make friends when he first began. Perhaps part of the children's reticence in allowing Taylor to join in their play was that he was perceived to be a threat to their friendship, which at the time was one of the few stable elements in their move to the lower school. He was also an 'unknown' child in the class, and there was no one to vouch for his character except for his cousin in the next class. This was probably why he was able to play football with the older children in the playground.

Like Taylor, many of the children had siblings or cousins at the school, and they often played with them. For example Jameela during her second year at school played with her younger cousin Moin, Semina played with her cousin Adjmar and Selina played with her younger sister Merish. These kinds of friendship were important, particularly for the younger children, because the older siblings helped them to settle into school, as one mother observed of her own family:

> I think it helps the children a lot to know that they've got somebody else there. 'Cos when Miriam first started the school she knew that her uncle was there, and like uncles and older brothers are like, 'Gosh, I've got somebody to look out for me!' *[laughs]* She was actually very upset when he left to go to middle school, and she was like, 'Oh Mum, I've got nobody there to keep an eye on me now', and I said to her 'You'll be all right', and Shiraz was a lot happier knowing that Miriam was going to be here, and he's got cousins and friends, it makes it a lot easier.

However, having an older brother or sister could also result in children getting into trouble as Mobeen had observed:

Mobeen: [Shazrin] she fight with Rajub, but now they made friends.

Mari: D'you know what they were fighting about?

Mobeen: Em, Shazrin an', Razia's sister never liked her an' then she told her to hit her, and they started to fight, but Razia, Razia first hit her and then Razia and Shazrin hit her.

Mari: Did they get into trouble for that?

Mobeen: Yes, 'cos Razia did 'cos she hit her.

Friendship-reinforcing identities

As in formal activities, age and gender were important factors in informal relationships. There was only one boy/girl friendship at this time, that of Denesh and Adam, both Reception class children, but by the start of their second term of school both children had formed more stable same-sex friendships. It was observed that they played and sat together less frequently than when they first started school. Whilst the Year 1 girls were more likely to play with the Reception class girls in class, compared with the boys, close friendships were in general maintained with same-age girls. Both sexes, interviewed about friendship, commented that they had older and younger friends and also friends of both sexes. Yet when the children were interviewed in friendship groups (on which occasions the researcher asked them if they wanted to be interviewed with their friends), these were always single-sex and same-age groups. By holding to these groups the children were able to form opinions about other groups of children, for example on the differences between boys and girls. Mobeen for instance believed that it was the boys who most frequently got into trouble at school, though only certain groups of them:

Mari: Who gets into fights in your class?

Mobeen: All the boys.

Mari: All of the boys?

Mobeen: No. Not Shiraz, Adjmar, Peter, Ali, Harpreet, sometimes Harpreet fights, Imran and Shiraz.

Shareen similarly felt that the boys were most likely to be in trouble at school:

Mari: Do you ever get into trouble in school? Do you ever get told off?

Shareen: No ...
I don't get trouble, never ... Boys does, some boys do.

At the same time the children talked about differences in age in terms of work they would be expected to do at school.

Sabida: D'ya know, em er people, em er teachers innit, when them are little, people innit, they come to school innit, they get them light work. When some people are big innit, an' they get in the upper classes they give us *hard* work.

Shareen: Big people yeah, they, they get er big books. We don't, we get little books.

Mari: So are there some children in this class who are bigger than you, d'you mean? Or do you mean the bigger children in school?

Shareen: The bigger children in school.

Mari: Oh right, and they get the big books. And when they get the big books is that hard work, or is it easy?

Shareen: Hard.

Not only were friendships based on age and gender, but for some children there was a basis for friendship which had its roots in ethnicity. While many of the children formed mixed ethnic friendships, as was found in Denscombe *et al.*'s research (1993), there were examples of children forming friendships on the basis of a shared culture. Azmat, for example, an Iraqi girl whose best friends were Parminder and Fatima (Indian and Pakistani girls respectively), also had a friendship with Reef who was a younger Saudi Arabian girl, but there was a cultural connection between the two children:

Azmat: There's only about four children that's Arabic in this school, no five children, about three of them are in another Arabic country, because there's eight Arabic countries.

Mari: There's eight! Gosh, I didn't know that. So there's Reef, 'cos I know you play with Reef ...

Azmat: Yeah, Reef and her brother and sister, and then me and Omar.

Mari: So there's Reef and her brother and sister, and they come from, is it Saudi Arabia?

Azmat: Yeah, I think so.

Mari: So would you understand, if they were to speak Arabic would you understand them?

Azmat: Yeah, they speak a bit the same but a little bit different.

Mari: So do you sometimes speak to Reef a little bit in Arabic?

Azmat: No.

Mari: Does she sometimes speak to you in Arabic?

Azmat: 'Cos she knows better than me, I don't know that much.

Mari: But she does speak it to you?

Azmat: No, but she does speak it to my mum, and my mum does speak it to her.

In spite of the fact that Azmat is not able to communicate with Reef in what might be considered their 'mother tongue' there is a shared understanding between the girls of what it is to be Arabic. This sense of identity is something Azmat cannot share with Parminder and Fatima and she perhaps uses her friendship with Reef as a point of reference. However Azmat's friendship with Reef does not take precedence over her friendship with Parminder and Fatima, as illustrated in the following section.

Best friends and temporary allies

It appeared that there were two distinct types of friendship groups. Firstly there were primary friendship groups. These were characterised among the girls particularly as 'best friends', those friends that they would invariably choose to work or play with if they had the choice. For the boys these primary friendship groups appeared to be more transient than for the girls. For example when Peter first started school he was observed playing most frequently with Damian, though this at times seemed a very unhappy alliance, as confirmed in an interview held at the end of Year 1:

Mari: Do you like coming to school? Are you happy at school?

Peter: A little bit.

Mari: A little bit. Sometimes you're not happy?

Peter: No.

Mari: Why's, why's sometimes you're not happy?

Peter: 'Cos I don't like Damian kicking me, or punching me.

Mari: You don't like when Damian does that. I don't think I would like it either. Do you tell Mrs C. about what Damian does, or ...?

Peter: Not usually.

Mari: No. It's not very nice if he's doing that.

Peter: No.

Mari: Have you got friends though in school?

Peter: Quite a lot.

Mari: Quite a lot. Which ones? Are they all in this class?

Peter: Some are in, one's in, two's in Mrs J.'s and one's in Mrs B.'s. Mrs B.'s is David, and Mrs J.'s is Tracey and Michael.

Damian appeared to want Peter as a friend far more than Peter wanted Damian, and Peter's main friends were evidently in other classes in the school. Later Peter also became friends with Taylor. In their first year at school there had only been six boys in the class to begin with and so friendships, particularly between the boys, had seemed unsettled – certainly not as strong as those made by the girls. In Year 2 the class was merged with another group of children. It was noticeable that Peter in particular attempted to make friends with some of the new boys such as Riad and Mosem, joining them on the carpet to play with the Lego, but this proved to be a rather brief alliance, since Raid and Mosem were often in trouble for fighting; Peter did not like being associated with bad behaviour and had rarely been told off by his teachers. Peter subsequently returned to Damian and Taylor, but when both of them left the school at the end of the first term in year two he seemed quite lost without them. He again sought friendship with Riad and Mosem, but eventually became close friends with Imran, who became his 'best friend'. Imran was also one of the few boys in the class whom Peter had actually started school with.

Primary friendship groups were often small in number, and children might have up to three primary friends. Invariably these primary friendship groups were single-sex and same-age, but not ethnically exclusive, as shown by Peter's and Azmat's circle of 'best friends'. At the same time Azmat had not yet made the distinction between the Indian and the Pakistani girls, because they both wore the same kind of clothes. Parminder, on the other hand, was very aware of differences between herself and Pakistani children, and it had to do with something more than clothing, as we noted earlier (pp.40–41):

Mari: What about Parminder and Fatima, are they your best friends?

Azmat: They're my best friends, yeah.

Mari: Because Parminder speaks ...

Azmat: Indian

Mari: And Fatima speaks ...

Azmat: Pakistani.

Mari: And you, well you understand Arabic, but you say that you don't really speak it. So when you're playing together d'you just speak in English or ...?

Azmat: I sometimes speak in Arabic because they only, I tell them some stuff and but most I just speak a lot of English because they don't know that much.

Mari: Uhuh, and so does Fatima sometimes tell you words in Pakistani?

Azmat: Yeah, because Parminder knows Pakistani so they sometimes say words.

Azmat, Fatima and Parminder's friendship had begun in nursery. When the children began school Parminder was in a different class from Azmat and Fatima though they continued to play with each other in the playground. At the beginning of their second year at school Parminder and Azmat's classes joined up and an even closer friendship developed. On most occasions the three girls could be seen either playing or working together, and whenever the class was asked to sit on the carpet Parminder, Azmat and Fatima were usually sitting together at the back of the mat.

There were also secondary friendship groups. Davies (1983: 70) talks of 'contingency friends' – friends 'ready for emergency situations', for example if primary friends were absent from school, or the teacher grouped children in such a way that a child was not able to work with a primary friend, or when 'best friends' had 'fallen out'. Davies found that fighting and arguments amongst best friends was quite natural among the primary school children she studied. It was an important method of re-evaluating their friendships, understanding appropriate and inappropriate behaviour within the rules of friendship, and also related to the development of identity and status. Fighting and arguing with best friends, or even with contingency friends are important lessons in social skills for the children.

Contingency friendship groups were loose, flexible and often temporary and opportunistic alliances. During choosing time, for example, if children had finished work before their friends they would often play with other children on the mat until their friends were free. They might even make friendly overtures to other children who were playing something they wished to join in with. This was particularly noticeable with some of the boys during playtime when they wanted to play football or cricket, and they would begin by either directly asking if they could join the game or simply ally themselves with someone they knew who was already involved.

Identities Outside School

Children's cultural identities were most prominently supported outside school. Most of the children Mari talked with were involved in some form of extracurricular learning outside school. Of the only three white British children in the class Damian was in a karate class, Peter took swimming lessons and Alice for a short time took violin lessons. However, many of the Muslim and Sikh children in the class attended additional lessons at the local mosque and temple respectively. Many of the Muslim children visited the mosque six times a week, and the Sikh children visited the temple three times a week. One of the main reasons for attending mosque and temple was to learn to read the respective holy books. Part of this entailed the children learning to read their mother-tongue languages. Thus, attending mosque and temple was an important aspect of mother-tongue maintenance, as instruction was often given in the children's home language. But it was also an opportunity for the various communities to come together and exchange news and gossip about their local neighbourhood and their home countries. It was one way in which parents and children could reinforce their cultural identities by maintaining traditions through their religious practices.

Attendance at the mosque or temple served to strengthen the children's identities as Pakistani, Bangladeshi or Indian in a positive way. In an informal interview with Shiraz he indicated his sense of being Pakistani when talking about his family. He commented that, at that time, his father was in Pakistan building a house:

Shiraz: He has to build a house.

Mari: Oh, is that so when you go back for a visit or will you go back to live there?

Shiraz: He's gonna come back in the six weeks holiday then he's not gonna go back to Pakistan again. He's not gonna go back there.

Mari: Right, are you gonna go back?

Shiraz: No, I don't wanna go.

Mari: You don't?

Shiraz: I dun wanna go.

Mari: Why don't you wanna go?

Shiraz: Just, just. 'Cos I like, I dun wanna go.

Mari: D'you just wanna stay here, or d'you wanna go somewhere else?

Shiraz: Stay here.

Mari: You just wanna stay here. But are you, are you Pakistani or are you English?

Shiraz: Pakistani.

Although Shiraz clearly wants to remain in Britain for reasons that at this stage he is unable to articulate, his cultural identity remains first and foremost Pakistani. This may be due in part to his attendance at the mosque, but also his parents' beliefs. His mother particularly had strong beliefs about her identity as a Muslim (see Chapter 8) and as a Pakistani. When asked how she felt about the term 'British Asian' she commented:

> Well personally, I find that a bit silly. OK, you're British because you live in the country, but you're not though. D'you see what I mean? You take a person by what you see, and if somebody sees me I'm sure they're going to say I'm Paki-

stani, or I'm an Asian, and *then* I'm British, but that's just like a personal point of view. Most people will say they're British Asians, or British Muslims or whatever, but em, I would say I'm an Asian, and I'm from Britain, which makes me British I suppose ... And I think you need to hang on to that identity as well ... because no matter how hard you try, I can't become white. I can dress that way, I could cut my hair that way, I could be that way, but I won't be white. I'll still be who I am, I'll still be an Asian, and just the same as if a white person went to Pakistan and you dressed up wearing kameez and that way, but you'd still be white. You'd still be British, or Catholic or whatever you are. The way you dress or whatever doesn't make you any different from what you are ... and it all starts at home. If I was to say to my children, because we live in Britain then OK we're British because we live here, but we still have, you can live together in a community, but still have your own identity. That doesn't mean you can't mix, that you can't live together, but there are times when you are what you are, it's as simple as that.

We will see in Chapter 8 that many of the parents had strong views about their cultural and religious identities and felt it important that their children should be brought up with this sense of belonging to a culture other than British. Many of the children in class also had the advantage of sharing their culture with their peers. For Azmat however, because she and her brother were the only Iraqi children in the school, her cultural identity was perhaps less secure. At the beginning of her first term in Year 2 Mari had an informal conversation with Azmat and Parminder. They had been talking about why children would get into trouble at school, and Azmat commented that ridiculing somebody because they spoke a different language would be a serious offence. Mari asked her if anyone had ever treated her like that:

Azmat: No because nobody knows what language am I. Everybody thinks I'm English.

Mari: Everybody thinks you're English. Because you speak Arabic, don't you?

Parminder: She looks, really white innit, she's really white, she looks like a white girl. I've got a photo with you in the nursery.

Azmat: *[to Parminder]* I thought you were Pakistani.

Parminder: No. Well I do wear these [shalwar kameez]. Well Indian people do wear them.

Mari: You wear the shalwar kameez. *[To Azmat]* Now you don't, do you ?

Azmat: I don't know what we wear!

Parminder: Fatima's lot [the Pakistani children] do, so do we.

Azmat and Parminder are clearly marking identities, both their own and those of other children in their class. Cultural identity is linked with language and appearance. Because Azmat has no one to speak Arabic with at school and she has pale colouring and wears Western-style clothing, other children have assumed she is English. At the same time Azmat has not yet made the distinction between the Indian and Pakistani girls because they both wear the same kind of clothes. Parminder, on the other hand, is very aware of differences between herself and Pakistani children, and it has to do with something more than clothing. Later conversations with Azmat in her second year at school, detailed in earlier sections of this chapter, show her as able to distinguish between her friends' cultural identities, partially on the basis of language. She is also aware of religious identity, as shown in this interview from the end of her second year at school:

Mari: Parminder is a Sikh, isn't she?

Azmat: Yeah.

Mari: Right, and Fatima is a Muslim.

Azmat: And I'm a Muslim.

Mari: And you're a Muslim. So that's something you've got in common, the same as Fatima.

Azmat: Yeah.

Mari: And do you go to the mosque?

Azmat: Er, no I don't go to the mosque, there's only one mosque in England, that's in London, but that's too far away, we only go to that mosque when we go to visit, but we always forget the em scarf, so we never go.

Mari: So does it, is it because in that mosque they speak Arabic, or …

Azmat: Yeah, that's an Arabic mosque, and the Pakistani mosque, they do read Arabic, but they don't speak our Arabic.

Mari: So d'you know what happens at the, does Fatima go to the mosque school?

Azmat: After school she does, and she, in the holidays she has to go in the evening.

Mari: Oh, and what does she learn?

Azmat: She reads the Qu'ran, and she reads the Qu'ran in Arabic and Pakistani together, but we don't know if Arabic or Pakistan are both the same, it's like the same thing but different.

While Azmat observes the link between herself and Fatima in that they are both Muslim, she similarly notes that there are still differences due to language. Her Iraqi identity was most notably reinforced by trips to London, which her family visited regularly, staying with other Iraqi families in the city (see also Chapter 8).

Mari: So, when you go down to London do you meet a lot of families from Iraq or ...?

Azmat: Yeah we do ...

Mari: And so how does that, does that make you feel good, d'you like meeting people from Iraq?

Azmat: Yeah.

Mari: Do they tell you things about Iraq?

Azmat: Yeah.

Mari: Would you like to go back?

Azmat: Yeah. I'd love to live in London, 'cos there's Iraqis, but it's still a very dangerous place, don't fink I'd like that, but I would like to live in it. I visit where there is a dangerous place there, but Iraqi, Iraq is really dangerous so, so em, that's why there's no aeroplanes there to go to Iraq, so it's really dangerous there, and in London.

Azmat's growing awareness of her cultural and religious identity was indicated by the fact that during interviews she frequently talked about the situation in Iraq, and how her family were not able to return because of the war there. On occasion she actively sought out knowledge about Iraq. For example, during an art lesson in her second year at school the children were making pictures of wild animals. Azmat asked the teacher if she could draw an animal from Iraq and the teacher said yes. Unfortunately she did not know what kinds of animal there were in Iraq, so together with the researcher they went to the school library to find some information, but the sources were scarce and eventually Azmat decided to draw something else. The following week when Mari returned to the class Azmat informed her that she had asked her mother about Iraqi animals and that she remembered two, a desert hare and the 'kissing birds'.

Azmat was becoming increasingly conscious of her cultural identity as she grew older. It may be that until a certain point she had been unaware that her cultural identity was different from any other. Other elements of her identity had been more obvious before she began school, for example her identity as a girl. Age, too, was an important factor when she first started school. In an interview during Azmat's first year at school her mother commented:

Her brother start the nursery at the same, and she thinks she's big girl, she going to school. And not the nursery. And she want to learn reading and writing quickly, because she saw her sisters reading stories or something, she's very keen ... I think she always want to be like her sisters, now she thinks maybe when her brother come to her school she already gone to middle school, because she's big *[laugh]*. But just one year, but she think that she big now.

As she has matured and begun to notice other differences between herself and her friends, such as dress, language and religion, Azmat has constantly had to re-evaluate her own identity on the basis of these new observations and also new knowledge that she receives at home. The example of Azmat illustrates how social identities evolve, change with time and can be reassessed as individuals start to relate to and compare themselves with others.

Conclusion

Identity is constructed in part by the way other people construct us. Labelling, particularly in a school environment, is unavoidable. Children are categorised by age, sex, ethnicity, religion and ability. We have illustrated here how young children use these labels, too, both in talking about themselves and in discussing others. Writers such as Lawrence (1988) and Siraj-Blatchford (1996) consider that positive self-esteem and identity in young children are dependent upon the reactions of those around them. 'The way children feel about themselves is learned and every child should have the right to feel good about him/her self' (Siraj-Blatchford, 1996b: 63). It has been well documented that unequal treatment of children based on particular characteristics can have detrimental effects on their academic performance (see, for example, King, 1978; DES, 1985; Bernstein, 1990; Lloyd & Duveen, 1992).

The data presented here shows how complex identity formation is, and that it is a perpetually ongoing process. The children rely on many different sources for the development of self-identities both positive and negative, from home, from the wider society and within school. While there is evidence that the teachers attempt to promote positive images regarding gender and culture, there is less indication that the school seeks to challenge stereotypes within these areas. For example, in adopting a multicultural policy which concentrates more on the similarities between the variety of ethnicities of the children at the school than on examining some of the differences, the teachers ignore a significant part of each child's uniqueness. This approach is in opposition to the teachers' expressed belief, discussed in Chapter 2, in child-centred education, a substantial element of which must be to help each child develop an 'individual personal identity' (Lloyd & Duveen, 1992: 12). In order for teachers to achieve this, they must first be able to examine their own views and understandings of gender, ethnicity and other formative categories. We have shown in Chapter 2 how our teachers were concerned primarily with the children's social disadvantage, and how this in effect promoted a deficit model of teaching and learning. The danger in this approach is to make teacher expectations of children unjustifiably low. Additionally, concentrating on only one aspect of the children's social environment can put issues such as gender, culture and class at risk of being marginalised within the curriculum. Children such as Azmat who clearly wanted to explore their own cultural identity were not able to because of the lack of resources. A more relevant curriculum is likely to promote more positive self-images. Siraj-Blatchford (1996b: 64) comments: 'If those who work with young children are able to undermine children's self-esteem and identity through negative responses and behaviour then we have to evaluate our actions very carefully.'

Suggestions

(1) We have discussed children's perceptions of themselves and their progress in school. Perhaps an occasional personal meeting or conversation with you would enable them to talk about their assessment of their own achievements in their studies. In a number of schools children are invited to write an assessment of their own progress as part of their school report. An example on a more regular basis could be a reading conference between yourself and each child individually, in which they talk about their reading and their perceptions of their own progress and plan with you the next stages in their work.

(2) The development of friendships features highly in this chapter. The example of Taylor illustrates the difficulties that some children have in being accepted by their peers. Taylor's example ended happily, but for some children this can be a stressful time and they may need your personal support. Do you have a system for monitoring new children's friendships in class? As with the suggestion above, do children have opportunities to discuss their feelings with you as a class, in a group, individually? See Deegan (1996) for an interesting discussion of the educational and social significance of children's friendships in multicultural classrooms and how they might be fostered.

(3) Have you as a teacher examined your own role in either addressing or reinforcing gender stereotypes? Have you monitored your own attitudes to girls and boys; for example, how you address them? Perhaps you could use a tape recorder on a few occasions and record yourself as you work and speak with children. You might be surprised!

(4) As a contribution to an appreciation of cultural diversity, do you as a teacher know about the different religions represented by the children in your class? The following ideas might enable you to introduce work on religions, possibly

integrating it into a topic that could represent an important contribution to your work in the National Curriculum in Religious Education:

- You could give the children opportunities to tell you about their own religions and share their knowledge with the class.

- You could invite local community and religious leaders to come into school and talk with the children about their respective religions.

- Visits for the children could be arranged to the local mosque and gurdwara.

- Those children who attend out-of-school language classes at the local mosque or gurdwara could share their experiences with other members of the class.

- Children who go on extended visits to relatives in the family's country of origin could be invited to spend time talking with the class about their experiences. Even if they cannot tell you a great deal, the fact that a child has made such a visit could form the basis for some work on the cultural, religious and social aspects of that country.

Chapter 8
The Parents' Perspectives

Introduction

In previous chapters we have argued the importance of drawing on knowledge and understanding of children's languages and cultures as a means of planning relevant experiences in their formal education. We have also argued that an awareness of bilingual children's linguistic and cultural identities, together with the attachment of due status to these identities in the relationship between adult and child, is necessary for the fully effective employment of the children's 'prior knowledge' (Woods & Jeffrey, 1996: 118). As Gravelle (1996: 74) notes:

> Like all children, bilingual learners arrive in school, at whatever stage in their education, with a range of abilities and experiences to build on. They come with an identity and personality, a personal history and experiences, a culture including language(s) and an education, whether formal or informal.

Prior knowledge arises to a substantial degree from the familial and community experiences that have formed children's early learning. Parents' perspectives, therefore, are crucial in any consideration of child-meaningful learning. Parents are educators of the 'whole child' and have much to contribute to the relevance of their children's schoolwork. They are also learners themselves, developing in tandem with their children, undergoing transitions with them, learning from them as they encounter new experiences and new knowledge.

We have emphasised in Chapter 5 the importance of parental knowledge being sought in the school's profiling as a basis for a successful induction of children into the school. Later in this chapter we argue for a relationship between parents and schools that moves beyond the mere provision of information to a more genuine partnership between parents, communities and schools. In the first instance this might include the extension of a process of 'partnership teaching' (Bourne & McPake, 1991, in Gravelle, 1996: 129), in which teachers work together to provide a relevant curriculum and attendant resourcing for their pupils:

> In a school which is developing its links with the community, Partnership Teaching will involve not only teachers and teaching assistants, but will draw on wider Partnerships by involving parents, other adults and community groups; and it will bring in primary-secondary and home-school liaison partnerships.

We shall return to these ideas later. First, we examine parents' views and understanding of their children's development before and during their early experiences in school. These will demonstrate the central role they have to play in the formal education of their children.

Nick interviewed 12 sets of parents of children on the point of starting at the nurseries. In the case of the four families of Indian origin, both parents had been born and educated in this country. In the case of the eight Muslim families the situation was more varied. Of the two families originally from Bangladesh, for example, only one mother was born and educated in this country. A number of languages were spoken among the parents, including Bengali, Panjabi and Urdu, some parents speaking both Panjabi and Urdu. All parents spoke English with varying degrees of confidence and fluency. There was often a diversity of languages spoken by parents within the same home. For example, in one home (that of Iqbal Ali) the mother, who had been born and educated in Pakistan, normally made a point of speaking to her children in Urdu, although she also had a knowledge of Panjabi and English. By contrast her husband, who had been born and brought up in the area in which the lower school was situated, tended to speak English to his children, but also some Panjabi.

In addition, Mari interviewed four mothers of children from the lower school, one Pakistani Muslim, one Indian Sikh, one Indian Hindu and one Iraqi Muslim. As with the parents of the nursery children the languages spoken at home were diverse, and parents had come to this country at different times.

Parental Transitions

Just as their children underwent transitions as they started and changed schools, so did the parents. They developed in their role as mentors and educators, and in these roles they manifested a wide variety of skills as parents and informal teachers. They also developed their own personal identities. On the negative side, some experienced a loss of influence and status.

Parents as educators

All the parents had a positive attitude towards their children's education, and took a keen interest. However, they differed in their aspirations for their children. Mr and Mrs Islam wanted theirs to enter professions, such as medicine or teaching; Mr and Mrs Ali wanted their son Iqbal to be an engineer; Mr and Mrs Jain merely wanted Naveen to be happy in life:

> Me and my husband we just feel as long as they're happy, we're not really that ambitious for them, we don't want a child to be backward, you know, be achieving well, but we just want them to be happy ... At the end of the day it's what

they want, we can't really say what we would like for them ... If he decides that 'No, sorry Mum, don't want to do that', not going to push him.

From the school they expected a variety of things, ranging from good discipline (Mr Sarwar, Jabidul's father) to the provision of a centre for a community of cultures. Mrs Mousaf (Rushan's mother), for example, was keen 'not to isolate the school but make it a community school', and Mr Sarwar had chosen the school because he judged it culturally the most suitable one for Jabidul.

Some of the nursery parents voiced concern about the more long-term use of play in the nursery. Aleena (Amar's mother) favoured a more structured approach during the children's last term, so that they would be better prepared for lower school. Iqbal's father Mr Ali (Mrs Ali nodding in agreement) felt teachers should 'let them play first from three to four, then from four they should slowly start breaking them in to having some experience of school.'

The lower school parents were pleased with the progress their children were making and held high opinions of the teachers. Shiraz's mother, for example, was delighted with her daughter's first report:

> It's actually nice for them to be able to bring it home and say 'Look Mum, this is what the teacher said about me' ... The first time I got a report it was my youngest daughter's and I sat there and I started crying because you don't realise it's this little six- or seven-year-old who's doing so much at school and everything and coming home with so much stuff and that was really good and that's something I'll remember.

Azmat's mother also was 'very proud' of her daughter:

> ... because when we first came here, others [the two elder daughters] didn't think it very exciting to go to school, because they don't know the language, and that's why they didn't like, but I saw her very, very exciting, she want to go.

Shiraz's mother was:

> ... pleased with his progress at school actually, because it does surprise me sometimes the things they come home with ... because it's so long since I left school and you don't realise that they're actually doing so much at this age, because he's not even six and half yet, and he comes home and tells me about the glass for instance and I was like sat there! 'What do they do in school these days? I don't remember doing that!'

Parents were astute observers of their children. Mrs Hussein, for example, found that with her son, Tariq:

> when we were walking in the road, even sitting in the pushchair, he was asking

me questions all the time, 'What colour is this car?' Even if it was cars, car colours and we were talking and I think that's how his vocabulary, his knowledge of the colours [developed]. If he was going to toilet and we had an upstairs toilet he used to count the stairs all the time, so that's how his numbers came about, so he was doing things and learning things at the same time.

The level of direct involvement of parents in their child's formal education was related to their own self-confidence. Iqbal's mother, a qualified teacher in Pakistan, worked with Iqbal on specific activities. For example she had taught him his early numbers, teaching him also to draw the correct amount of objects for a specific number. She had also tried to teach him the initial letters of the English alphabet and how to write his name. On several occasions in the nursery he would come to Nick and 'write' his name in the air, with some accuracy. Rushan's mother had already taught her son his initial sounds so that he could play with his talking-word computer that consisted of a screen with a keyboard attached. Mrs Mousaf would tell him which word to key in to the computer and, although he might not be able to spell the word, he usually knew its initial sound. Balkis, on the other hand, was deeply concerned about what she saw as Aisha's lack of academic progress, but felt she needed advice on how to help her daughter:

> Sometime when I'm cooking she likes to get a chair and see what I'm doing like cutting onion or sometime she'll peel the skin off garlic. No, she's been interested in what I've been doing, not that she wasn't before. Before she's been playing with her own stuff, I've been trying to teach her to write, like her name but no, she doesn't want to know ... Well my friend goes, 'Start rough like, writing out a letter and then letting her colour it in just to introduce her to the letters and she'll start solving it that way.'

Help could come in other ways. Azmat's mother, for example, noticed her daughter

> ... always playing something with the post office and the letters and something and she use her father typewriting, and sometimes she go and do work on the computer, and he allowed her. She does this more than playing with a doll ... because she see [her sisters] studying maybe yeah, em she always copy them.

The whole family helped with priority activities like reading. Azmat's mother told us:

> She read sometimes with me but most with her father, because I always busy, but her father he's really do the reading with all the daughters, and do the study with the oldest one, but after she reading with her father she start reading to her younger brother, because she's always reading bedtime story for her brother *[laugh]*. But sometimes me sometimes to her father. [Her sisters] read to her,

sometimes when she wants them, sometimes when she has difficult story they read to her, but not always. They always doing their thing *[laugh]*.

Guvinder's mother illustrated the importance to the child of parental appreciation:

He chose his dad to read his books with, yeah, he'll read 'em to him and his dad will say 'I'm going to sleep, I have to go to work', 'Not yet!', and then he goes 'Dad listen', then he will read it, then he will say 'Very good, Guvi', and then he gets happy. But that's what he's waiting for, just to hear that word *[laugh]*.

To Shiraz's mother encouragement of her son's reading development was particularly important, as he had encountered difficulty at school:

When I noticed that his reading wasn't quite so good, and then the teachers mentioned it as well, and they said, 'It's not that he can't read, it's just that he needs a bit of help getting there'. So since then I try to give him at least 10–15 minutes every day, him on his own, nobody else is allowed to interrupt, and it really has helped a hell of a lot ... I try very hard not to criticise, very hard, it's hard at times *[laughing]*, but it's paid off.

Of the nursery parents, Mr and Mrs Mousaf made a point of setting time aside to talk with their child, usually on his return home. On these occasions they spoke to him in English, asking him about his day at the nursery and correcting his language if necessary. At other times the family would speak in Bengali.

The development of parental identities

When their children began at nursery, parents formed new relationships. Balkis, for example, moved beyond her isolation as a mother at home and took an active part in the mothers' and toddlers' group at Bridge. She had also newly found access to friends and mutual support systems beyond her immediate family and cultural community:

I just like getting involved. At the beginning when I first went to the nursery Aleena kept saying, 'Come around, come around', but then after a couple of weeks I went and I've enjoyed it. We do fund raising as well. I go in half an hour early and I just have a look around, look at what the children are doing, which Rosalind doesn't mind. I like making new friends as well. Since I went to the toddler group I had Pat Mattu living round the corner. When I was pregnant with him again I had a very difficult time so she went to pick up the children from school, dropping them off which was really helpful.

Aleena was encouraged by the school to fulfil her own aspirations. Ever since Amar began at the nursery she had visited regularly and had also been active in the mothers' and toddlers' group. Eventually she decided on a career as a trainee nursery nurse:

Now the children have grown up I want to do something to be independent a little bit, to be able to go out to work and really contribute to the family income, to be able to go out with the children without a worry about the mother-in-law because she's homebound, literally. I think this is something I wanted to do, well I had to do, not only for myself but for the children as well.

Mrs Ali (Iqbal's mother) similarly combined familial obligations with the desire to use her teaching qualifications to give herself a personal sense of purpose. She began working as a care assistant as well as attending professional courses, while in her role as a qualified teacher she was actively participating in the education of her two sons using methods she hoped would be reflected in the work of the nursery. As her husband told Nick:

She makes little patterns of numbers, she's getting him ready, make him learn like one, two, three, four, he knows how to count and stuff like that, slowly, slowly, she's doing it anyway so they won't lose out in that way. My wife says that she hopes that ... they start these kinds of things at the nursery.

Some parents with similar desires were not so fortunate. Azmat's mother, for example, felt the need to work outside the home because her youngest child, Omar, had already started nursery and would be at school the following year:

However it's very difficult for me to find job here because there's a lot of people also looking for jobs *[laugh]*. I have a degree in statistics and I used to work in a company ... and I used to work for eight or nine years before I came here ... I miss my job, I miss my life, I miss my friends. Difficult to just stay at home and looking after children, you know? *[Laughs.]*

The experience of Azmat's mother emphasises the difficulties that parents recently arrived in this country can have in finding employment, particularly since their qualifications are often not recognised here.

The loss of parental influence and status

Some mothers experienced feelings of personal inadequacy or loss as they attempted to adjust for the first time to a pattern of care controlled by others. 'This step marks a change in their relationship with their child and a fresh relationship with a group of adults, the pre-school staff' (Hutt *et al.*, 1989: 153). Gita, for example, owing to her full-time job and also to a developing physical illness, was unable to give Aditya as much attention as she would have liked. The nursery's apparent success with Aditya added to Gita's sense of her own shortcomings as a mother:

I've never stopped them from doing things or deprived them of things, they've always had paints and things, but because I haven't got the time to sit with them, I wish I had, and I just haven't got the patience either, I just feel that someone who knows what they're doing and can sit them down. This is what amazes me, when I go to collect her Rosalind says, 'She's been fine, she's all right', but when I take her out shopping she's all over the place, I can't keep up with her.

A sense of personal inadequacy could lead to a heightened sense of personal responsibility. Balkis also was worried that she was not helping Aisha enough:

> I've seen her at nursery, she's always playing with bangles in the corner, like she plays with the telephone, she'll do painting, drawing, they'll tell her a story as well. In a way I feel I should be teaching her to write and ABC 'cos they have enough work in the nursery.

The transition from home to nursery could result in a sense of loss. Mrs Jain, for example, had never left Naveen before. As she watched him on his first day at nursery:

> ... my heart was like, he was wandering around and playing, I was the one with the tears in my eyes, not him ... I didn't want no negativity to rub off on him and I was trying make him all enthusiastic, encourage him. In no way would I say to him, 'Oh Naveen I feel', it's like, 'Mummy's really happy for you darling', and all the rest of it. Even though inside it's a different story.

The parents of the lower school children were, on the whole, less affected in this way. These parents had already been through the experience of their children starting at nursery school, and in general now saw their move to the lower school as a further indication that the children were developing in positive ways. They saw institutional preparation for the lower school as vital. Shiraz's mother, for example, considered it important that the children had the opportunity of spending their last term full-time in the nursery unit:

> It does help them to prepare from going to nursery ... He used to come in in the mornings earlier, and then he started all day, and I'm sure that made it easier for him to go into the school and then be there all day as well, because to go from plenty of children in nursery and then to a whole school full and then you've got a whole day as well, I should think that would have been a bit much.

The fact that the children were moved as a group was also thought to have eased their transition from the nursery to the lower school:

> It wasn't just him [starting school], there was some of his mates as well went in together, 'cos, obviously that's how they do it don't they? and he was quite happy to have his friends at the same time with him. Not like he was leaving them behind or they were going before him. (Guvinder's mother)

There was reassurance in further signs of the children's progress, as Guvinder's mother indicated:

He's getting a good report. I always used to think sometimes when he used to be in school, 'Is that boy learning anything?' And then I used to say, 'He should know that.' And, the report, when I was walking (to the school) I was saying to Guvi, 'If you've hitted anyone, you know what I'm gonna do to you' *[laugh]*. He just walked, and I said he's thinking, you know, what I've said to him. Then I said, 'Guvi are you all right?' He wouldn't talk to me until we got to school, then he said, 'Mum, I've got to go and watch the video', so I said, 'You go on then.' Then I said, 'D'you remember what I said?' He just walked off. And then when I sat down Mrs B. was there, and she said that she's really pleased.

The Cultural Divide

As children moved into the new environments, the cultural influences of the schools became stronger (see Chapter 5). Parents experienced considerable tensions over how far this alternative culture should be encouraged, and how far resisted. Many of these tensions centred on language. We examine some of those here, and go on to consider how parents reaffirm their community languages and identities, concluding with their views on multicultural education.

Language tensions

The children's use of English began to take on a greater influence at the expense of their community languages. For some parents, especially in the lower school, their children's increasing use of English was viewed positively because of its importance as a route to success in English society. For example, Guvinder's mother actively encouraged her son to learn English at home:

> [Guvinder speaks] English even at home. Some words, he won't know how to say the words, like, I can't say for instance this word and that word, but some words he'll say in Panjabi more quickly, and then I'll have to say it to him, 'Say it this way, say the word, say the word', then he will say it a couple of times and then he forgets, and I will say 'All right, he's just a little kid', and I'll say 'It's all right, he's put a lot of courage in it learning the language'. It's not very easy for him.

Azmat's mother felt that her daughter had not had enough English language input when she had been at the nursery,'because there's a lot of non-English-speaking this nursery. Maybe it's better if she go to another nursery, all English-speaking is better.' Mr Dhariwal (Zeeshad's father) was adamant that he wanted all his children, including Zeeshad, to learn English at school to the exclusion of all other languages. In this case both he and his wife lacked confidence with their own English, and Mr Dhariwal had been unemployed since 1992. He was attending English classes locally and it is possible he saw his own lack of English as a stumbling block to employment in the period since he had been made redundant.

However, the growing predominance of English also induced a sense of loss of cultural identity, which led to some ambivalence. Aisha's mother Balkis said:

> I've been speaking with them in my own language. They've been answering back, now they're speaking more English which I prefer, you know they'll pick up our own language later on as well. I'd like her to have a conversation with me sometime in our language, but it's always in English.

Both Reena and Gita also noted the increase that had taken place in their children's use of English at home. Reena noticed that Sonny's English was improving and that he tended to answer her in that language rather than Panjabi, despite the fact that she still made a conscious effort to translate stories into Panjabi when she read to him. Gita, anxious about Aditya's academic progress, felt positively about the fact that Aditya's English was improving:

> She's quite fluent at Panjabi, she's very good actually but just recently since she's been going to full-time nursery she's really improved her English which I'm really shocked. I'd rather she got a lot more English at school than she has. She's Asian, I feel she needs to be taught early-stage English.

At the same time:

> They're at school all the time and they're learning English there, so I like them to switch off a bit when they're at home so they can relate to their own speech and start speaking to me in Panjabi so they don't lose it.

Mrs Ali (Iqbal's mother) affirmed that 'in this country we need English,' and she told her son stories in English, but 'when he doesn't understand I tell him in my own language and then he understands.' However, as Iqbal developed his confidence in English at nursery and used it more and more, she experienced that feeling of her own culture slipping away from her control:

> At home I don't like English because I want they speak Urdu at home and at school English. Saturday I always remind them, 'Today we are not going school so please talk Urdu today.' Sometime they speak little bit then again they start speaking English.

Mrs Ali expressed her concern that Iqbal was speaking English almost exclusively at nursery and she would have liked him to have the opportunity there to be able to speak more in Urdu and Panjabi. Mr Ali also noticed the changing balance between English and community languages:

> At home probably what me and my wife would tend to do is speak to him more and more in Panjabi. They do understand what everybody says to them in Panjabi. It's just that when they're at school they talk a lot more than what they do at home with their friends and everything, so the reply they give you is in English.

Aleena spoke to her children in Panjabi, 'but they won't answer me back because they don't know how to use it. Unfortunately, it's something I didn't want to happen. When I used to see it in somebody else's children, I used to think that's wrong.'

Some parents, like Azmat's mother, experienced problems when their own proficiency in the second language was not equal to their children's (see Gregory, 1994a):

> A lot of children, my friends from Arabic, the parents, the mother she didn't speak English, and they speak no English at all at home, and they have to teach the child, it's difficult. It's different when school, when already the mother and father education they speak good English ... Sometime [Azmat], she telling me, sometime you know she can pick a little bit of the word, sometime she correct me, 'Don't say that one please' ... she's very bossy.

Azmat's behaviour illustrated the developing predominance of English.

> She speak a little bit Arabic ... but usually she speak with her sisters English, and she plays and she reads and she writes English, and you know the TV and things. But she speak Arabic only to her father, but she usually play with the children English only.

Guvinder's mother describes other sources of tension:

> My husband's got a different accent from what I have. I'm pure British, my husband isn't. He's from abroad, so his language, the way he will talk will be a bit different from me, the way they pronounce the words and write varies as well. I mean we even sometimes start arguing *[laugh]*, because it's not spelt properly, and it's not written how it's supposed to be written, like say if I want to go shopping, I would write 'I am going shopping', but he will say 'I'm going to shopping', and I will say 'That's not how you say it, so if you say that, that's how these two [children] will say it, and then when they go to school they're gonna get told off, 'cos you saying the wrong thing' *[laugh]*. I say 'If you don't know it, talk Panjabi to them' *[laugh]*. But it's all right when you go to the shop, and you've got to do your own translating, that's different, but with the kids you have to tell them which is right and which is wrong.

As time goes on it is likely that the experience of Azmat's family will become the norm, as newer generations adopt English as their first language rather than, as in these cases, Arabic and Panjabi. It was noted that one particular Indian boy in Shiraz's and Azmat's class, Harpall, commented that he and his family spoke only English and that he did not know any other language. Where bilingual children are not encouraged to use their mother tongue there is a danger of their becoming monolingual in their adopted language, and thus losing a significant element of their cultural identity.

The affirmation of community languages

For some parents the resolution of inevitable tensions between their two cultures meant viewing each language as having a different purpose to, and being linguistically unconnected with, the other. This attitude is not endorsed by contemporary research, which suggests that the development of children's first language has a direct bearing on the success with which they will develop a second or a third (Siraj-Blatchford, 1994: 46; Wiles, 1985: 91). However, for such parents the languages did not move in parallel, but instead developed separately depending on their function, as Aleena exemplified:

> First comes Panjabi, then your English because the English is going to be around you all your life and you'll pick it up just like that. The Panjabi aspect of it doesn't come into it till you're at home, and unless you've got a non-English speaker.

To Mrs Mousaf (Rushan's mother) this separation of languages avoided the danger of confusion:

> The first word he learned is our language, so I don't think he would be confused because we made it clear to him, 'You're not speaking one minute English at home', and next minute when he's mature enough starts speaking his own lingo. That's when the kids get confused.

This sharing of language as a communicative necessity could lead to an awareness of how the knowledge of different languages could be applied appropriately, depending on the audience. Mrs Hussein described how Tariq, no doubt through her and her husband's influence, had developed a natural respect for his community language. This had contributed to his identity as a bilingual learner since he had begun to understand the appropriate use of his community language and its relevance to his familial and social relationships:

> If he knew that somebody couldn't speak English he'd just talk to them in Panjabi and that's it. I don't know how he senses that or picks it up but if I told him, say, we were going somewhere once and we were in the car and we told him to speak in Panjabi but he would not do it for us because we told him to, he'll do it because he wants to. Say, my parents who can't speak much English, he'll automatically talk to them in Panjabi. Say, there was a certain word he knew in Panjabi and didn't know it in English even when he's speaking in English he'll use that Panjabi word in it.

The power and validity of community languages were asserted in different ways. They represented primarily an important means of communication and meaning-making. Rushan would need to communicate with his paternal grandmother when he visited Bangladesh. Both Sonny and Amar needed to be able to speak Panjabi in order to understand their own grandmothers who lived with them, and Jatinder and his brother similarly needed to be able to speak Panjabi to talk with their paternal grandfather who also lived with the family. Shiraz's mother was concerned that Shiraz might be disadvantaged if he were to return to Pakistan and not be able to communicate in Panjabi: 'He'd have to know how to speak the language, because he'd be totally lost! It's no good being able to jabber away in English all day long if you can't speak Panjabi as well.' For Aleena this necessity emphasised her frustration at what she saw as her children's lack of skill in their community language: 'They try to speak Panjabi with [their grandmother], not very well, but they know she's the only Panjabi speaker, totally Panjabi speaker in the house and they speak Panjabi although it's not as fluent as it should be.' Mrs Mousaf described the social consequences of the failure of other families to encourage their own children to speak their community languages:

> That is one thing we decided when Rushan was born, because we're seeing the kids that parents bring them up to speak English at home and not their own lingo, these kids when they go out in the community or with relatives they can't communicate because all the kids speak our language, and the other kids will name them as dumb, but they're not dumb, it's just that they can't speak it. So it's not their fault, it's the parents' fault.

Extended trips back to home countries were a regular feature of many of the children's lives. Jatinder's parents had recently built a new house in India close to the father's relatives and were planning a visit in the autumn of that year for five weeks. During our fieldwork at the school, at least 12 of the children in the lower school classes had been on visits to their home countries.

> End of the day we all have to go back to our own countries or visit relations and I don't want them to turn round and say, 'Ah, he's British, you know.' This is what they will say if he start speaking English down there without knowing their own culture. (Mrs Mousaf)

Community languages also provide a source of identity. Reena was clear in her own mind that she wanted Sonny to be able to speak Panjabi because of its cultural significance, 'because it's our language' as she put it. Aleena also affirmed, 'We're Asians, we're Indians, we ought to be speaking our own language really.' This is why Amar's rejection of Panjabi in the face of the influence of English represented for Aleena a refusal to embrace so much of what she considered culturally significant: 'He'll laugh or he'll start hitting me and saying no. He knows it's Panjabi and he knows I want him to speak it but he won't.' Gita, despite her own anxieties about Aditya's academic progress and her recognition of the need to engage with the culture and language of the nursery, was nevertheless firm in her personal identification with her own language and its significance for her and her family:

> It's quite important that she should learn her own mother tongue as well because no matter what, she'll still be Asian and she'll still be Indian, although we might study English and we're probably in the Western world, even then you can't lose your own culture and that's the way I've been brought up.

The affirmation of cultural identity

For some of the mothers the affirmation of their cultural identity was a complex and often contradictory experience. Reena came from Birmingham to her husband's house on her marriage to live with her in-laws. Her own sister and her sister-in-law and husband were living with the family as well. Reena had a baby whom her sister looked after while she herself looked after Sonny. She viewed the family as a network through which she was gaining considerable support and in this sense her experience of it was positive. However, within this closely structured network she was at the same time isolated from her peers because she had left her own parents and friends in Birmingham. Although she was able to visit her parents she had no personal friends in the town. For Aleena the experience of forging a career for herself had created a difficult relationship with her mother-in-law and her husband's family:

> I've always had problems with my mother-in-law because she's elderly and I'm supposed to be at home looking after her and everything. If we want to go out as a family we're not able to because I've always got to have my daughter at home, and now my son's a little older so he can stay with her for a little while, and that's created problems because her daughter also lives in the town so there's interference from them, saying things like, 'Where's Mum? Where's Mum?' very politely, but you know what she's thinking. And at one point it gets so irritating sometimes I answered back to her and I said, 'Well I haven't left her on her own you know, there's somebody there with her'. So there's always that in the air.

However, despite these difficulties, Reena and Aleena both saw their community and familial cultures as strong sources of personal identity. Mrs Mousaf had no doubts about the potential strength of the family in its influence on society:

> Same as at home, if everybody sets the same rule and same standard then the street would be cleaned up as well. I mean, parents, obviously they don't mind if the kids out till 10 or 11 at night in the street, this is not right, they shouldn't be, they should be at home with their parents.

Their alternative cultures, in fact, offered an antidote to what they viewed as the failures of English society. For example, the breakdown in values which Mrs Mousaf saw around her was offset by the values which she maintained still existed in Bangladesh. Consequently, Rushan needed to develop his Bengali and to learn the standards of his own culture:

> I would take him back when he mature enough, when about eight or nine that he really know what's coming and maybe stay there year or two to pick up the culture properly like respecting the elders, how to behave because here, no offence, but there's no respect. You know, when you go to a shop if there's an elderly person waiting you let them go first, but now the youngsters will just pick the mick out of them and push them and go first.

Mrs Hussein made the same cultural comparison through the example of a mother whom she had seen at the nursery and with whom she went to school before being sent back to Pakistan for her secondary education:

> We used to live on the same road but she doesn't recognise me now, she was about Tariq's age then and I was about eight, nine. Looking at her and myself we're two different people because we've gone through different lifestyles, different education systems and that's partly the reason, so living in England is not too bad in the sense that you've got your privacy, you can manoeuvre a bit more whereas if we were in Pakistan we would stay where our parents' or our grandparents' land is and you don't manoeuvre so much so that's about all. The rest, say, women's status, I'd be free there, I'd have a lot more freedom to move, to integrate with the family. Here, you know, you're isolated in nuclear families, you're not extended families, and there I'd have the experience of the extended family.

For some mothers the strong social and familial ties could be restrictive, placing overwhelming responsibilities on them and leading to their personal isolation, but the family also gave them another kind of identity founded on a sense of a shared culture. An extension of this culture came via a shared religion. As the children moved up the lower school the influence of religion on identity became increasingly important to their parents. When they started at the school, many of the Sikh and Muslim children also attended religiously oriented classes at the local Sikh temple or mosque (see Chapter 7 for the impact of these classes on the children's lives). Religion was a considerable identifier for the parents. Shiraz's mother particularly felt that her identity as a Muslim was a strong aspect of her life.

> Some people don't agree with having so much of that, having everything that you do is toward your religion, but being Muslim it's a way of life ... if you don't have that teaching there you can have a lot of difficulties later on, because when you're expected to do things and you've not been taught to do them it's very hard.

She believed that having strong religious roots was important for her children and was somewhat dismayed at how many Muslim children were losing their faith and subsequently facing problems as they grew older:

My grandfather is very strict Muslim and my father has always been very strict, but they've done the right thing as far as I'm concerned. But then there's not a lot of Muslim children who believe that you should hang on to your religion. And they're mainly the ones who are not behaving the way they ought to be behaving. Drinking and drugs for example, no way is that allowed anywhere in the religion. And if you look at children who are on drugs, or are drinking at the age of 12 and 13, and you look at the religion, and it's not there.

Some parents were excluded to some extent because of religious differences. There were two main mosques in the area, one that served the Bengali Muslim community, and another which served the Pakistani community. For Azmat's family going to the mosque meant travelling to London, because as Iraqi Muslims they would not understand some of the instruction in the local mosques where community languages were most frequently used. Azmat's mother also noted how difficult she had found it to make friends in the area because of the complex social situations of the various groups of parents:

I have some people I talk to them but not like friends. The Asian families a lot of them just have the contact with their families and don't make friends with others, and then some Arab ladies, I think they don't like me because I not cover my hair, I didn't wear a long dress, I think Iraqi we're a lot different than what the other families. More freedom because Iraqi girls can do anything, like we used to it. Other Arabics too, so they have their traditions, that's why I didn't make friends, different traditions ... And there's no Iraqi families. I think before the war there's a lot, but not now.

Cultural affirmation for Azmat's family came from frequent trips to London where they had relatives and there was a large Iraqi community, people with whom they could share traditions and understanding.

Parents' views on multicultural education

All the parents were enthusiastic for their children to learn about other cultures. Jatinder's mother commented: 'I suppose it is better really because they're learning about all the different pasts and things. It's good for them, because they're learning about the [different religions].' Mothers noted how much school had changed since they were pupils:

They listen to you, and your points, like the Muslims ... they wear their shalwar kameez ... and in the same colour as what the school [uniform] is. I think that's quite good. That way, the kids, the Asian kids and the English kids, they all know what type of religion they are and what they wear, and how they cope with all these pressures with it. They learn it, instead of guessing it. (Guvinder's mother)

They seem to take far more notice of a child's background and their colour, or their religion or whatever, and these sorts of things are taken into a lot more consideration, than they ever did when I was at school ... I think it comes over quite well (at Westside). I think they do make an effort to cater to all the different religions or backgrounds that the children may have. (Shiraz's mother)

They thought it very important for children to have an understanding of other religions and cultures:

Any religion needs to know about other religions, because you're living in a community where you've got all sorts of people, and you need to know about each other's religions, each other's way of life to be able to live together. Some people don't like the fact that their children are Christian and their children are being taught about Muslim festivals, or Hindu festivals or Sikh festivals or whatever, but that's going to give them problems later on, because if you're living in a community where it's just you and your religion, well then that's fine, but when they move out of that community and that environment, then it'll be strange for them. As far as Islam is concerned, we Muslims have a very bad image *[laughing]*, and it's probably down to a few silly people, but it's all about tolerance, you have to accept other people. You don't have to follow their way of life or anything, but you have to accept that people are different, and this is what different religions do. (Shiraz's mother)

Similarly Guvinder's mother felt that the way in which the school itself took children to visit the local places of worship was a valuable way for them to learn about other cultures and religions. After her son's recent visit to one of the local mosques she commented:

That way a child can't say that, 'You're a Paki, I don't want to be friends with you', because he doesn't know what it actually means, and how he's coped with it, and how that person's worshipped that god ... I mean we're Hindus. I think that when they're together, they know that we're just us, or one innit, instead of apart ... they'll know when they grow up we went in that place, [Guvinder] can't say bad things to them because we went up there, and we even worshipped a bit. I think that is really good. That [the teachers] take them and let them know by their own eyes and to learn from their own heads.

The parents viewed such opportunities as a way of countering racism through understanding, showing perhaps a greater awareness of British multicultural society than might many white families living in predominantly white areas. Their 'multiculturedness' was something that was reflected in their children (see Chapter 7).

Azmat's mother also commented on the support her eldest daughter Reef had received from the school in learning English:

I like the school as whole because Reef when she first came here she didn't know any language, any word, and er, they took her and they gave her special lesson, special care, I think for all the children who are there, and she's very good now in [middle school], after five years is a long time for the child's life, but she's very good ... and after few months she's very good reading, writing, I think this was good. I think they take more care for the not English speaker.

However, whilst the parents were very complimentary about the school and its accommodation of their religious and cultural identity within its overall approach to multiculturalism, they admitted that they rarely went into school except for parents' evenings or to meet individual teachers. In Chapters 1 and 2 we examined how models of the normal pupil and the normal school curriculum made it difficult for teachers to implement a thoroughgoing multicultural policy. This was an aspect of the school that the parents had not been able to observe.

The Professional Divide

The cultural divide drove a wedge between home and school. Parents sought a solution by withdrawing into their own cultures and giving them meaning within the confines of their own immediate communities. Iqbal's father said his sons would be taught 'from the house, from the mother and father, about our culture, about our religion and everything'. Interviews, however, emphasised the potential benefits for parents, children and the schools of a close and active relationship between parents and teachers. To what degree was such a relationship encouraged by our teachers?

Teachers' views of partnership with parents

The teachers expressed a belief in building a partnership with parents, but it was one over which they retained ultimate control. At Westside Nursery Unit the written policy expressed a desire to 'establish good relationships with the children's families', but the practical role of parents was viewed as no more than an opportunity to 'make a contribution' to the work of the unit by 'making labels in mother tongue, and lending artefacts etc.' At Bridge, the written policy declared:

> Staff also aim to work in partnership with all parents valuing their special knowledge of their child and his/her learning experiences. Parents have many skills that they can share with us thus enriching the life of the school. It is important for children to see parents and teachers working together in a strong positive relationship.

Jenni echoed this view of teachers and parents working together: 'You're asking the parents really to bring [their children] to the door and go, whereas in fact it perhaps needs to be more of a combined learning thing, parents and teachers, working together.' Rosalind recognised that parents possessed special knowledge of their children, but felt it had to be deployed within the context of the teacher's professional knowledge in the school environment:

> Parents first of all know their own child far better than we can ever know them. They may not know them in the institution better but they know them far better ... I think they can be used to do a number of things under our direction, not just cutting paper, they can come in and cook with the children and read stories with the children. If I was going to ask them to do a very skilled job like the woodwork or the cookery I would want to perhaps talk it through with them first. We have a lot to learn from parents and other people who are sensitive to children. We have one view as professionals but parents have another view, and if there were things that I actually didn't want a parent to do I would discuss that with them. Like don't draw it for them or whatever it is, don't make the plan for them, talk to them about a plan; but I still think they can do a lot.

Kate also emphasised the importance of careful preparation for and direction of parents as helpers in the classroom:

> I do think it's important. I think it's hard work to achieve actually. I think it's OK to say, 'They can help', but it's more difficult than that because, say you asked a parent to come in. Some parents may be quite shy and when a parent comes in you have to be prepared for them. So I think it would be nice, otherwise you spend your whole time not working with the children but explaining to the parent, 'Maybe you'd like to go here', or, 'This is what we do here', so if you got yourself organised so you had a little booklet saying, 'This is what we do when we mix paint', or if we got some information for them so that they would know what was expected of them or what they could do to help, because you can't say it every time they come in and you're taking for granted that they know things and they don't. So there's all that side of it, but I do think it's important, but I think it's important to organise for them otherwise it won't work properly.

Jenni had doubts about the role of some parents in the daily life of the nursery, from both a social and educational viewpoint:

> Sometimes it's a good idea if parents come in and play with their children, sometimes it's not a good idea. I mean some people you wouldn't want to be in with the children. I'm very wary about the parents who come in and say, 'Can I have some worksheets to do the alphabet at home?', or, 'We're going on holiday, can they have the next maths book and things?'

However, practical co-operation with parents was viewed as a way of supporting them, whether it was in the mothers' and toddlers' group at Bridge or through the kind of personal support Jenni described at Westside:

Quite a lot of them do come. We have one mother who's having trouble with her husband and she climbs out of the kitchen window because he's locked her in and she came in and we said, 'Oh come in, have a cup of tea, have a play.' Really, when you've got parents involved anyway, counselling becomes one of the skills, doesn't it?

The teachers expressed some support, therefore, for co-operation with parents, but it was a relationship over which, in the context of the schools, they felt they should retain control.

Parents' experiences of relationships with teachers

Although there was no substantial level of involvement by parents in the work of the classrooms or the schools, there was a welcoming atmosphere in the settings. For example, parents at the lower school found:

They all welcome you really nicely, and even help you with things. You walk in the school, first thing they'll ask you, 'Would you like a cup of tea and a sit down?' I think that is nice. You won't get that from some schools. They just don't want to know you. Standing there for hours, and leave you there *[laugh]*. I think this is a nice school and the teachers as well. (Guvinder's mother)

The caring nature of the school was something that had particularly impressed Azmat's mother, especially as shortly after her family's arrival in England the Iraqi war broke out:

[The teachers] they're very good. We always, me and my husband we come down of an evening or something, because came to school for my other daughter to speak to the teacher, because when she start here my second daughter, very difficult thing, the war in Iraq, me and my husband very bad time because we had no news from our families for a year, and financially it was not very good and my other daughter came, and we usually had a good life, but when we came here and all the trouble, and I feel very scared for them because I think the general idea about Iraq is like any for all the peoples, and I very scared for my daughters, and she feel that and she has trouble in school ... and she crying and she scared, that's why I had to come a lot to school to see the teacher. That's why I know [the headteacher] Mrs M.'s very good and the teacher's very caring, and they understand ... they deal with [the problem], they took very good care for her ... but first year very hard.

Shiraz's and Jatinder's mothers similarly had found that any time they had needed to come to the school for any reason they had always been pleased with the reception by the teachers and also any subsequent action taken by the school. As Shiraz's mother said:

It's easier to go in and talk to the teachers than it was when I was at school. But then that's maybe because I can speak the language myself, and I know I can come in if I've got a problem, and I'll speak to somebody whether they like it or not *[laughing]*.

The school had, in fact, attempted to meet the language problem through making Hardip, the bilingual teaching assistant, available for translation. Parents approved; Guvinder's mother said: 'A parent who doesn't know English, they've got a teacher ... she can translate, so that woman won't go without getting any translation.' It was also the policy of the school to translate letters home to parents into the various community languages.

There had been various attempts within the school to encourage parents to take a greater part in the life of the school, for example the setting up of parent and child reading sessions once a week; inviting parents of new starters to special meetings before their children started school, in order to explain school policies; regular home-school liaison, particularly with new parents, which was frequently carried out by Chris and Jenni. Chris often paid visits to parents whose children seemed to be experiencing difficulty at school, or when the school was concerned about attendance. It was noticeable that at Eid and Diwali parents and children themselves often invited Chris and other members of the staff to visit their homes and join in their celebrations.

In many respects, therefore, social relations between parents and the staff of the lower school appeared to be very good, but as with the nurseries parents were rarely seen in classrooms working alongside teachers. In part this was perhaps due to staff reluctance to have parents in the classroom, but there was also an element of parents not taking up opportunities that were available to them. Jatinder's mother, for example, had not attended the meeting for parents of children just starting school because 'Well I did that for Harkirtan [his elder brother] ... I already sort of knew what they were doing, I knew the books and everything, like Mrs M. [the headteacher] she's very good, you can go and talk to her any time.' Jatinder's mother felt that having already had Harkirtan going through the system she had enough knowledge to judge what Jatinder would be doing. Shiraz's mother also felt disinclined to attend school meetings:

I don't actually ever turn up for any of the meetings, to be honest. I always make sure I'm here for parents evenings or sports days, but really meetings I just think they're going to go ahead and do what they're gonna do anyway so *[laughing]*, but if there's anything I'm not happy about, then I'll try and make a point of it, and come on in.

This kind of attitude among parents was particularly noticeable after OFSTED had inspected the school. As part of the dissemination of the findings of the report Chris and the deputy head chaired a parents' meeting to discuss the outcome of the inspection. In all five parents turned up. Chris commented on the lack of interest parents had shown in the written report they had each been sent. It wasn't until the school's report was mentioned in the local newspaper, in a very favourable light, that parents appeared to take notice.

Conclusion: Towards a Learning Community

Teachers in both schools expressed the desire for a successful relationship with parents, particularly as a source of mutual support. This was exemplified by initiatives such as the mothers' and toddlers' group in one of the nurseries and a general welcoming of parents both as 'assistants to teachers' and to events being held in the schools. However, the system was based on a traditional model of teacher-parent relationships. The insights provided by the parents recorded here reveal the potential that lies in a more far-reaching collaborative approach, one that promises the creation of a curriculum with relevance for all children within school settings; the enhancement of pupil learning; the acquisition of a valuable resource for teachers; and a positive move toward the resolution of the tensions experienced by bilingual parents over their children's education. How might such a partnership be begun?

Wolfendale and Topping (1996: 2) argue that there has been a general change in home-school links over the past decade:

> The conception of 'parents as educators' has broadened beyond the original narrow pedagogical focus (helping parents to help their child with reading) towards the notion of a home-school alliance that promotes the wider interests of children as learners in the community.

This takes into account the needs of parents as well as those of children, and embraces within formal education the cultural and linguistic heritage of the child (see also Griffith & Schechter, 1998). Vincent (1996) recommends increasing democratic control of the school, since this has greater potential to affect relationships. It also assumes more input into the school from parents and other citizens within the community. It is a short step from here to the idea of a 'learning community'.

The 'learning community' is particularly appealing in the context of bilingual learners and their parents as portrayed in this chapter, and indeed throughout this book. First, the school moves outwards to its community in order to create a collaborative culture in which all participants act as teachers and learners:

> No longer is learning solely the domain of those vested with power in a hierarchy of knowledge relationships, but requires the interactive involvement of families and children, as well as principals, teachers and administrators. (Cocklin *et al.*, 1996: 3)

This concept involves whole communities joining in a relationship of 'working together' and 'working with', both as teachers and as learners, exchanging social and educational information and ideas. For parents and children the active participation through a partnership with the school provides them with a sense of belonging and ownership, reflecting itself in the children's learning situation (Cocklin *et al.*, 1996: 5). Teachers in the learning community possess a dual role (p. 4), in that they 'take more responsibility as learning *leaders* for the children and the school community. They are also leading *learners* as they find themselves learning with and from the children and community.'

The notion of participation has the ability to move beyond the traditional concept of parent-teacher co-operation as merely a relationship in which parents act as 'assistants for teachers' (Little & Meighan, 1995: 18), to become instead what Torkington (1986: 14) describes as a parent-centred approach to parental involvement in school:

> The rationale for the parent-centred approach is that parents' knowledge of their individual children is far greater than that of a teacher and that the teacher's knowledge and skills about children and learning in general should merely complement and build on the specific knowledge that parents hold – both these aspects are equal and essential for learning to take place.

Rennie (1996: 193) suggests that a parent-centred approach to involvement in school provides a way in which practical help can be combined with a sharing of knowledge and expertise between teacher and parent for the benefit of the child at home as well as at school:

> Teachers and parents must recognise their own strengths. Teachers know how to work with groups, to organise learning materials, to create a learning environment. They need to use those skills to help bring the far greater knowledge parents have of their own children to bear and to encourage the parents to use such knowledge and experience as well as other skills which collectively parents are bound to have, with their children at home.

The active parent-centred approach to involvement in school can be viewed as particularly relevant in the case of bilingual children and their families. The cultural knowledge of bilingual parents actively involved in the work of the classroom is capable of providing cultural and language expertise which will contribute not only to the children's understanding but to that of the teachers as well. Teachers will be able to use this same expertise to develop culturally relevant experiences within the classroom setting. As Athey (1990: 66) argues, 'perhaps the greatest benefit to teachers in working with parents is the spur towards making their own pedagogy more conscious and explicit'.This type of partnership possesses the potential for enabling educators to share their early years expertise with parents within the context of developing the kind of skills which can be applied in a multilingual home environment. In this way the relationship can be transformative in the sense of each party to the relationship being developed and changed by the other.

It may not be easy for many parents to participate. Despite some changes in the patterns of childcare and employment in the last few years (Little & Meighan, 1995: 26), it is in the main mothers who are more likely to be found taking an active part in nursery settings than fathers (David, 1990: 130; Keating & Taylerson, 1996: 32). Many mothers will, however, be in full-time employment and will find it difficult to attend school during session times. There may also be parents who wish to support the nursery but lack the confidence to do so (David, 1990: 126). Ethnic minority parents may find it difficult to enter the culture of the school and establish common ground either culturally or educationally with the teachers. Schools need to be sensitive to these problems; to, for example, the educational experiences of ethnic minority parents, if these have been gained in another country (Siraj-Blatchford, 1994: 103).

In what ways could such a programme of parental involvement be introduced into a school? Rennie (1996) suggests a five-stage model:

(1) A process of confidence-building, in which both teachers and parents get to know each other on a more social basis. These more social occasions can consist of parents being invited to the school to have a cup of tea during a session to meet one another and the teacher. This could also be organised to take place towards the end of sessions when parents come to collect their children (p. 198). Other activities directed at parents can include open days and an occasional newsletter to keep them informed of events in the school. When parents bring their children into school for the first time they possess very little immediate knowledge of the setting, apart from information they have obtained from the school's brochure, or from an initial home visit, or an introductory visit. What the new parents do possess, however, is a natural affinity with other new parents (p. 195), and these groups could be encouraged to become a normal feature of the life of both school and nursery by providing a place for them to meet which they can regard as 'theirs'.

(2) A process of awareness-raising for parents within the school. This might include parents' evenings at which teachers show parents aspects of their provision and work; helping with outings and fundraising; and organising aspects of the school's provision, such as a toy library (p. 198).

(3) The 'real involvement' stage in which the relationship between teacher and parent becomes more educationally direct. This stage can include parents organising social activities within the school and the organisation by teachers of workshops showing parents aspects of the children's education within the setting.

(4) Co-operation moves directly into the classroom where parents begin to help educators in planning activities and making materials (p. 197).

(5) Genuine partnership occurs (p. 199) when the parents, to some extent, become co-educators. This stage would include teachers providing guidance for parents in the preparation of materials for use by them in the classroom, or parents working with children as teachers under the leadership of the teacher. This level of partnership also enables parents to develop specific educational skills which they can then use with their own children at home (p. 197).

Suggestions

(1) Think about Rennie's ideas for parental involvement. How could these be introduced into the school? For example:

- How could a new parents' affinity group be set up? Are there any parents who could help, or parent-governors or bilingual educators? How often could the headteacher or other educators or parent-governors be available during sessions to meet and talk with these parents?

- Would there be anywhere for the affinity group to meet in the school?

- Open days or evenings could be used to invite parents into the school to look at children's work. This could also be used to invite parents in on a more regular basis.

- Subject co-ordinators could organise workshops to which parents could be invited.

(2) A parents' room (if there is space) could be set up which parents and their families could use as a meeting-place during the day.

(3) A home visiting policy could be established, beginning with pre-school visits to those families whose children would shortly be entering school. How could this be organised? Who would be available to carry out visits? Would a bilingual educator or other adult be available to accompany visits to families?

(4) Representatives from the community could be invited into the school to talk about community matters with educators and children at assemblies, in the classrooms, and at staff meetings (see Hamilton, 1993, for further ideas on employing the bilingual and multicultural strengths of a variety of adults within the community).

(5) Groups of children could be taken on visits to places in the local community, for example, shops, churches, the mosque, the gurdwara. This may well result in

teachers being invited to speak to community groups about the work of the school.

(6) The composition of the governing body could be reviewed. When vacancies arise members of the local community, including parent-governors, could be invited to become governors.

(7) The Parent-Teacher Association could play an active role in the building of links between the school and the community. The PTA could help in setting up meetings and events. Parents in the community with children at the school could be encouraged to take an active part in the PTA.

(8) The school's governing body could be invited to play an active role in setting up partnerships with parents and the community. For example, they could begin by organising a social evening to which educators, parents, the PTA and representatives of the community could be invited.

(9) A subcommittee of the governing body could be established to begin the process of building links with the community.

(10) The local education authority could be invited to provide help and advice in setting up links with the community.

Some good practical advice on working with parents in early years settings is given in:

Whalley, M. (1997) *Working with Parents*. London: Hodder and Stoughton.
Vincent, C. (1995) Schools, community and ethnic minority parents. In S. Tomlinson and M. Craft (eds) *Ethnic Relations and Schooling: Policy and Practice in the 1990s*. London: Athlone Press.
Open University (1996) *Confident Parents, Confident Children: A Community Education Study Pack*. Milton Keynes: Open University Press.
Hamilton, S. (1993) A community project. In R.W. Mills and J. Mills (eds) *Bilingualism in the Primary School: A Handbook for Teachers*. London: Routledge.
Edwards, V. and Redfern, A. (1988) *At Home in School: Parent Participation in Primary Education*. London: Routledge.

References

Abbott, L. (1994) 'Play is Ace!': Developing play in schools and classrooms. In J. Moyles (ed.) *The Excellence of Play* (pp. 76–87). Buckingham: Open University Press.

Acker, S (1995) Carry on caring: The work of women teachers. *British Journal of Sociology of Education* 16 (1), 21–35.

Alexander, R. (1992) *Policy and Practice in Primary Education*. London: Routledge.

Alexander, R. (1997) *Policy and Practice in Primary Education: Local Initiative, National Agenda* (2nd edn). London: Routledge.

Alexander, R.J., Rose, J. and Woodhead, C. (1992) *Curriculum Organisation and Classroom Practice in Primary Schools: A Discussion Paper*. London: Department of Education and Science (DES), HMSO.

Allan, G. (1989) *Friendship: Developing a Sociological Perspective*. London: Harvester Wheatsheaf.

Anning, A. (1995) A National Curriculum for Key Stage 1. In A. Anning (ed.) *A National Curriculum for the Early Years*. Buckingham: Open University Press.

Apple, M.W. (1986) *Teachers and Texts: A Political Economy of Class and Gender Relations in Education*. New York: Routledge.

Athey, C. (1990) *Extending Thought in Young Children: A Parent–Teacher Partnership*. London: Paul Chapman.

Austen, S. (1992) Storytelling and culture. *TALK* 5 Autumn, 10–11.

Aylwin, T. (1992) Retelling stories in school. In P. Pinsent (ed.) *Language, Culture and Young Children*. London: David Fulton.

Baker, C. (1996) *Foundations of Bilingual Education and Bilingualism* (2nd edn). Clevedon: Multilingual Matters.

Baker, C. and Perrott, C. (1988) The news session in infants and primary school classrooms. *British Journal of Sociology of Education* 9 (1), 19–38.

Barrs, M. (1990) Children's theories of narrative. *English in Education* 24 (1), 32–39.

Bennett, N. (1976) *Teaching Styles and Pupil Progress*. London: Open Books.

Bennett, N., Wood, L. and Rogers, S. (1997) *Teaching through Play*. Buckingham: Open University Press.

Berger, P.L. and Luckmann, T. (1967) *The Social Construction of Reality: A Treatise in the Sociology of Knowledge*. Harmondsworth: Penguin.

Bernstein, B. (1977) Vol. 3 of *Class, Codes and Control: Towards a Theory of Educational Transmissions* (2nd edn). London: Routledge.

Bernstein, B. (1990) *The Structuring of Pedagogical Discourse*. London: Routledge.

Best, D. (1991) Creativity: Education in the spirit of enquiry. *British Jounal of Educational Studies* 34 (3), 260–278.

Beynon, J. (1985) *Initial Encounters in the Secondary School*. Lewes: Falmer Press.

Biott, C. and Nias, J. (eds) (1992) *Working and Learning Together for Change*. Buckingham: Open University Press

Blackledge, A. (1994), 'We can't tell our stories in English': Language, story and culture in the primary school. In A. Blackledge (ed.) *Teaching Bilingual Children*. Stoke-on-Trent: Trentham Books.

Blenkin, G. and Kelly, V. (1994) The death of infancy. *Education 3 to 13*, October, 3–9.

Bourne, J. and Mclake, J. (1991) *Partnership Teaching*. London: NFER/DES.

Boyle, M. (1999) Exploring the worlds of childhood: The dilemmas and problems of the adult researcher. In G. Walford and A. Massey (eds) *Studies in Educational Ethnography* 2. JAI Press.

Boyle, M. and Woods, P. (1996) The composite head: Coping with changes in the primary headteacher's role. *British Educational Research Journal* 22 (5), 549–568.

Brehony, K. (1992) What's left of progressive primary education. In A. Rattansi and D. Reeder (eds) *Rethinking Radical Education: Essays in Honour of Brian Simon*. London: Lawrence and Wishart.

Bruce, T. (1987) *Early Childhood Education*. Sevenoaks: Hodder and Stoughton.

Bruce, T. (1991) *Time to Play in Early Childhood Education*. Sevenoaks: Hodder and Stoughton.

Bruce, T. (1997) Adults and children developing play together. *European Early Childhood Education Research Journal* 5 (1), 89–99.

Bruner, J. (1980) *Under Five in Britain: The Oxford Pre-school Research Project*. London: Grant McIntyre.

Bruner, J. (1983) *Child's Talk: Learning to Use Language*. Oxford: Oxford University Press.

Bruner, J. (1985) Vygotsky: A historical and conceptual perspective. In J.V. Wertsch (ed.) *Culture, Communication and Cognition: Vygotskian Perspectives*. Cambridge: Cambridge University Press.

Bruner, J. (1986) *Actual Minds, Possible Worlds*. London: Harvard University Press.

Burns, R. (1982) *Self-Concept, Development and Education*. New York: Holt, Reinhart and Winston.

Burns, T. (1992) *Erving Goffman*. London: Routledge.

Byrne, D. (1971) *The Attraction Paradigm*. New York: Academic Press.

Campbell, R.J. and Neill, S.R.StJ. (1990) *Thirteen Hundred and Thirty Days*. Final report of a pilot study of teacher time in Key Stage 1, commissioned by the Assistant Masters' and Mistresses' Association.

Campbell, R. J. and Neill, S.R.StJ. (1994a) *Primary Teachers at Work*. London: Routledge.

Campbell, R.J. and Neill, S.R.StJ. (1994b) *Curriculum Reform at Key Stage 1: Teacher Commitment and Policy Failure*. Harlow: Longman.

Carr, W. and Kemmis, S. (1986) *Becoming Critical*. Lewes: Falmer Press.

Chinoy, E. (1967) *Society: An Introduction to Society*. New York: Random House.

Clarricoates, K. (1987) Child cultures at school: A clash between gendered worlds. In A. Pollard (ed.) *Children and their Primary Schools*. Lewes: Falmer Press.

Cocklin, B. (1996) Learning communities and creative teachers: Some explorations of the concepts derived from a case study. Open University, School of Education: Research Seminars.

Cocklin, B., Coombe, K. and Retallick, J. (1996) Learning communities in education: Directions for professional development. Paper presented at annual conference of British Educational Research Association, Lancaster, 12–15 September.

Collier, V.P. (1995) Acquiring a second language for school: Directions in language and education. *National Clearinghouse for Bilingual Education* 1 (4): 1–8.

Cooper, P. and McIntyre, D. (1996) *Effective Teaching and Learning: Teachers' and Students' Perspectives*. Buckingham: Open University Press.

Cummins, J. (1976) The influence of bilingualism on cognitive growth. *Working Papers on Bilingualism* 9, April.

Cummins, J. (1984) *Bilingualism and Special Education: Issues in Assessment and Pedagogy.* Clevedon: Multilingual Matters.

David, T. (1990) *Under Five – Under-educated?* Buckingham: Open University Press.

David, T. (1992) Curriculum in the early years. In G. Pugh (ed.) *Contemporary Issues in the Early Years.* London: Paul Chapman.

David, T. (1996) Their right to play. In C. Nutbrown (ed.) *Children's Rights and Early Education* (pp. 90–98). London: Paul Chapman.

David, T., Curtis, A. and Siraj-Blatchford, I. (1992) *Effective Teaching in the Early Years: Fostering Children's Learning in Nurseries and in Infant Classes.* Stoke-on-Trent: Trentham Books.

Davies, B (1983) *Life in the Classroom and Playground: The Accounts of Primary School Children.* London: Routledge.

Day, C.W. (1991) Roles and relationships in qualitative research on teachers' thinking: A reconsideration. *Teaching and Teacher Education* 7 (5/6): 537–547.

Dearing, R. (1994) *Review of the National Curriculum: Final Report.* London: School Curriculum and Assessment Authority (SCAA) Publications.

Deegan, J.G. (1996) *Children's Friendships in Culturally Diverse Classrooms.* London: Falmer Press.

Denscombe, M., Szulc, H., Patrick, C. and Wood, A. (1993), Ethnicity and friendship. In P. Woods and M. Hammersley (eds) *Gender and Ethnicity in Schools.* London: Routledge.

Department of Education and Science (DES) (1967) *Children and their Primary Schools* (The Plowden Report). London: HMSO.

Department of Education and Science (DES) (1985) *Education for All* (The Swann Report). Final report of the Committee of Inquiry into the Education of Children from Ethnic Minority Groups. London: HMSO.

Department of Education and Science (DES) (1988) *Education Reform Act.* London: HMSO.

Department of Education and Science (DES) (1988) *English for Ages 5–11* (The Cox Report). London: HMSO.

Department for Education (DfE) (1995) *Key Stages 1 and 2 of the National Curriculum.* London: HMSO.

Department for Education and Employment (DfEE) (1998) *The National Literacy Strategy: Framework for Teaching.* London: DfEE.

Derman-Sparks, L. (1989) *Anti-bias Curriculum.* Washington, DC: National Association for the Education of Young Children.

Drummond, M.J. (1993) *Assessing Children's Learning.* London: David Fulton.

Durkheim, E. (1956) *Education and Sociology* (translated by Sherwood D. Fox). New York: Free Press.

Dyer, M. (1982) *History in a Multicultural Society.* Historical Association.

Early Years Curriculum Group (1989) *The Early Years Curriculum and the National Curriculum.* Stoke-on-Trent: Trentham Books.

Edwards, A. and Knight, P. (1994) *Effective Early Years Education: Teaching Young Children.* Buckingham: Open University Press.

Edwards, D. and Mercer, N. (1987) *Common Knowledge: The Development of Understanding in the Classroom.* London: Methuen/Routledge.

Edwards, V. (1983) *Language in Multicultural Classrooms.* London: Batsford.

Edwards, V. (1995) *Reading in Multilingual Classrooms.* Reading and Language Information Centre: University of Reading.

Edwards, V. and Redfern, A. (1992) *The World in a Classroom: Language in Education in Britain and Canada*. Clevedon: Multilingual Matters.

Edwards, V. and Walker, S. (1995) *Building Bridges: Multilingual Resources for Children*. The Multilingual Resource for Children Project, University of Reading: Multilingual Matters.

Egan, K. (1988) *Teaching as Storytelling*. London: Routledge.

Eisner, E.W. (1979) *The Educational Imagination*. London: Collier Macmillan.

Emblem, V. (1988) Asian children in schools. In D. Pimm (ed.) *Mathematics, Teachers and Children*. London: Hodder and Stoughton.

Ervin-Tripp, S.M. (1986) Activity structure as scaffolding for children's second language learning. In J. Cook-Gumperz, W.A. Corsaro and J. Streek (eds) *Children's Worlds and Children's Language*. New York: Mouton de Gruyter.

Evans, L., Packwood, A., Neill, S.R.StJ. and Campbell, R.J. (1994) *The Meaning of Infant Teachers' Work*. London: Routledge.

Fagot, B.I. (1974) Sex differences in toddlers' behaviour and parental reaction. *Developmental Psychology* 10, 554–558.

Ferdman, B.M. (1990) Literacy and cultural identity. *Harvard Educational Review* 60, 181–204.

Fox, C. (1993) *At the Very Edge of the Forest: The Influence of Literature on Storytelling*. London: Cassell.

Galton M. and Willcocks J. (1983) (eds) *Moving from the Primary Classroom*. London: Routledge and Kegan Paul.

Gay, G. (1985) Implications of selected models of ethnic identity development for educators. *Journal of Negro Education* 54, 1.

Gillborn, D. (1995) *Racism and Antiracism in Real Schools*. Buckingham: Open University Press.

Gipps, C., Brown, M., McCallum, B. and McAllister, S. (1995) *Intuition or Evidence? Teachers and National Assessment of Seven-year-olds*. Buckingham: Open University Press.

Glauert, E. and Thorp, S. (1993) Science for all pupils: Teaching science for equality. In R. Sherrington (ed.) *Science Teachers' Handbook: Primary*. ASE/Simon and Schuster.

Goalen, P. (1988) Multiculturalism and the lower school history syllabus: Towards a practical approach. *Teaching History* 53, 8–16.

Goffman, E. (1961) *Asylums: Essays on the Social Situation of Mental Patients and Other Inmates*. Doubleday: Anchor Books. Also (1968) Harmondsworth: Penguin.

Goffman, E. (1963) *Stigma: Notes on the Management of the Spoiled Identity*. NJ: Prentice-Hall.

Gravelle, M. (1996) *Supporting Bilingual Learners in Schools*. Stoke-on-Trent: Trentham Books.

Gregory, E. (1993) 'What counts as reading in this class?' Children's views. In P. Murphy, M. Selinger, J. Bourne and M. Briggs (eds) *Subject Learning in the Primary Curriculum: Issues in English, Science and Mathematics*. London: Routledge.

Gregory, E. (1994a) Cultural assumptions and early years pedagogy: The effect of the home culture on minority children's interpretation of reading in school. *Language, Culture and Curriculum* 7 (2), 111–124.

Gregory, E. (1994b) The National Curriculum and non-native speakers of English. In G.M. Blenkin and A.V. Kelly (eds) *The National Curriculum and Early Learning: An Evaluation*. London: Paul Chapman.

Gregory, E. (1996) *Making Sense of a New World: Learning to Read in a Second Language*. London: Paul Chapman.

Gregory, E. and Mace, J. (1996) *Family Literacy History and Children's Learning Strategies at Home and at School*. Final Report of ESRC project R000221186. London: Goldsmiths' College.

Griffith, A. and Schecter, S. (eds) (1998) Mothering, educating and schooling (special issue). *Journal for a Just and Caring Education* 4 (1). Thousand Oaks, CA: Corwin Press.

Grosjean, F. (1982) *Life with Two Languages: An Introduction to Bilingualism.* Cambridge, MA: Harvard University Press.

Guba, E.G.and Lincoln, Y.S. (1981) *Effective Evaluation.* San Francisco: Jossey Bass.

Gura, P. (ed.) directed by Bruce, T. (1992) *Exploring Learning: Young Children and Blockplay.* London: Paul Chapman.

Halliday, M. (1975) *Learning How to Mean.* London: Edward Arnold.

Halpin, D. (1990) The sociology of education and the National Curriculum. *British Journal of Sociology of Education* 11 (1), 21–36.

Hammersley, M. (1977) School learning: The cultural resources required by pupils to answer a teacher's question. In P. Woods and M. Hammersley (eds) *School Experience.* London: Croom Helm.

Hamilton, S. (1993) A community project. In R.W. Mills and J. Mills (eds) *Bilingualism in the Primary School* (pp. 145–159). London: Routledge.

Hardy, B. (1977) Towards a poetics of fiction: An approach through narrative. In M. Meek, A. Warlow and G. Barton (eds) *The Cool Web, The Patterns of Children's Reading* (pp. 12–23). London: Bodley Head.

Hargreaves, A. (1994a) *Changing Teachers, Changing Times: Teachers' Work and Culture in the Postmodern Age.* London: Cassell.

Hargreaves, A. (1994b) Restructuring restructuring: Postmodernity and the prospects for educational change. In P.P. Grimmett and J. Neufeld (eds) *Teacher Development and the Struggle for Authenticity.* New York: Teachers College Press.

Hargreaves, A. and Tucker, E. (1991) Teaching and guilt: Exploring the feelings of teaching. *Teaching and Teacher Education* 7 (5/6), 491–505.

Heath, S.B. (1983) *Ways with Words: Language, Life and Work in Communities and Classrooms.* Cambridge: Cambridge University Press.

Hoffman, L.W. (1987) The value of children to parents and child-rearing patterns. In C. Kagitcibasi (ed.) *Growth and Progress in Cross-cultural Psychology.* Berwyne: Swets North America Inc.

Holt, J. (1969) *How Children Fail.* Harmondsworth: Penguin.

Hughes, P. (1993) Double delivery. *Language and Learning,* September, 19–23.

Hutchinson, D. (1994) The 'three wise men' and after. In A. Pollard and J. Bourne (eds) *Teaching and Learning in the Primary School.* London: Routledge and Open University Press.

Hutt, S., Tyler, S., Hutt, C. and Christopherson, H. (1989) *Play, Exploration and Learning: A Natural History of the Pre-school.* London: Routledge.

Jeffrey, B. and Woods, P. (1997) The relevance of creative teaching: Pupils' views. In A. Pollard, D. Thiessen and A. Filer (eds) *Children and their Curriculum: The Perspectives of Primary and Elementary School Children.* London: Falmer Press.

Jeffrey, B. and Woods, P. (1998) *Testing Teachers: The Effect of School Inspections on Primary Teachers.* London: Falmer Press.

Jenner, H. (1988) Mathematics for a multicultural society. In D. Pimm (ed.) *Mathematics, Teachers and Children.* London: Hodder and Stoughton.

Kearney, C. (1990) Open windows: A personal view of the issues involved in bilingualism, identity, narrative and schooling. *English in Education* 24 (3), 3–13.

Keating, I. and Taylerson, D. (1996) The other Mums' Army: Issues of parental involvement in early education. *Early Years* 17 (1), 32–35.

Khela, A. and Deb, M. (1993) Storybox. In H. Claire, J. Maybin and J. Swann (eds) *Equality Matters: Case Studies from the Primary School* (pp.77–90). Clevedon: Multilingual Matters.

Kelly-Byrne, D. (1989) *A Child's Play Life: An Ethnographic Study*. New York: Teachers' College Press.

Khun, D., Nash, S.C. and Brucken, L. (1978) Sex role concepts of two- and three-year-olds. *Child Development* 49, 495–497.

King, R. (1978) *All Things Bright and Beautiful*. Chichester: Wiley.

Kook, H. and Vedder, P. (1995) The importance of parental book-reading: Tensions between theory and practice. *International Journal of Early Years Education* 3 (3), 5–15.

Kress, G. and Knapp, P. (1992) Genre in a social theory of language. *English in Education* 26 (2), 4–15.

Kress, G. (1982) *Learning to Write*. London: Routledge.

Kress, G. (1995) *Writing the Future: English and the Making of a Culture of Innovation*. Sheffield: National Association for the Teaching of English.

Kress, G. (1997) *Before Writing: Rethinking the Paths to Literacy*. London: Routledge.

Kumar, R. (1989) Sharing stories: Writing in two languages. *English Magazine* 20, 36–37.

Langer, S. (1953) *Feeling and Form*. London: Routledge.

Lawn, M. and Grace, G. (1987) (eds.) *Teachers: The Culture and Politics of Work*. Lewes: Falmer Press.

Lawrence, D. (1988) *Enhancing Self-esteem in the Classroom*. London: Paul Chapman.

Levine, J. (1996) *Developing Pedagogies in the Multilingual Classroom: The Writings of Josie Levine* (edited by M. Meek). Stoke-on-Trent: Trentham Books.

Little, J. and Meighan, J. (1995) Developing appropriate home-school partnerships. In P. Gammage and J. Meighan (eds) *Early Childhood Education: The Way Ahead* (pp. 18–35). Derby: Education Now Books.

Lloyd, B. and Duveen, G. (1992) *Gender Identities and Education: The Impact of Starting School*. London: Harvester Wheatsheaf.

MacFall, A. (1993) Talking story: What children know and feel about literature. *Reading* April, 20–25

Mandell, N. (1988) The least-adult role in studying children. *Journal of Contemporary Ethnography* 16 (4), 433–467.

Martin, D. and Stuart-Smith, J. (1998) Exploring bilingual children's perceptions of being bilingual and biliterate: Implications for educational provision. *British Journal of Sociology of Education* 19 (2), 237–254.

Martin-Jones, M. and Saxena, M. (1996) Turn-taking, power asymmetries, and the positioning of bilingual participants in classrom discourse. *Linguistics and Education* 8(1), 105–23.

Maxwell, J. (1988) Hidden Messages. In D. Pimm (ed.) *Mathematics, Teachers and Children*. London: Hodder and Stoughton.

Maxwell, W. (1990) The nature of friendship in the primary school. In C. Rogers and P. Kutnick (eds) *The Social Psychology of the Primary School*. London: Routledge.

May, S. (1994a) *Making Multicultural Education Work*. Clevedon: Multilingual Matters.

May, S. (1994b) School-based language policy reform: A New Zealand example. In A. Blackledge (ed.) *Teaching Bilingual Children*. Stoke-on-Trent: Trentham Books.

Mayor, B.M. (1987), *Unit 13: Bilingualism and Second Language Learning*. Milton Keynes: Open University Press.

Mayor, B.M. (1994) What does it mean to be bilingual? In B. Stierer and J. Maybin (eds) *Language, Literacy and Learning in Educational Practice*. Buckingham: Open University Press.

Measor, L. and Woods, P. (1984) *Changing Schools: Pupil Perspectives on Transfer to a Comprehensive*. Milton Keynes: Open University Press.

Meek, M. (ed.) (1977) *The Cool Web*. Oxford: Bodley Head.

Meek, M. (1985) Play and paradoxes: Some considerations of imagination and language. In G. Wells and J. Nicholls (eds) *Language and Learning: An Interactional Perspective* (pp. 41–57). London: Falmer Press.

Meek, M. (1987) Symbolic outlining: The academic study of children's literature. *Signal* 53, 97–115.

Meek, M. (1991) *On Being Literate*. London: Bodley Head.

Mercer, N. (1995) *The Guided Construction of Knowledge: Talk amongst Teachers and Learners*. Clevedon: Multilingual Matters.

Mills, J. (1993) Language activities in a multilingual school. In R.W. Mills and J. Mills (eds) *Bilingualism in the Primary School: A Handbook for Teachers*. London: Routledge.

Minns, M. (1990) *Read It to Me Now*. London: Virago Press.

Moore, A. (1993) Genre, ethnocentricity and bilingualism in the English classroom. In P. Woods and M. Hammersley (eds) *Gender and Ethnicity in Schools: Ethnographic Accounts*. London: Routledge.

Moorhouse, J. (1989) Sharing stories: Talking in two languages. *English Magazine* 21, Winter, 32–35.

Mortimore, P.(1992) Trends in education and society in the 1990s. Paper to the Institute of Education Society, London University Institute of Education, 16 March 1992.

Moyles, J. (1989) *Just Playing?* Buckingham: Open University Press.

Moyles, J. (ed.) (1994) *The Excellence of Play*. Buckingham: Open University Press.

Musgrove, F. (1983) *Education and Anthropology: Other Cultures and the Teacher*. London: John Wiley.

National Curriculum Council (NCC) (1989) *The National Curriculum and Whole Curriculum Planning*. Preliminary Guidance 6, October. York: NCC.

National Curriculum Council (NCC) (1990) *The Whole Curriculum*. Curriculum Guidance 3. York: NCC

Nias, J. (1989) *Primary Teachers Talking: A Study of Teaching as Work*. London: Routledge.

Noddings, N. (1992) *The Challenge to Care in Schools: An Alternative Approach to Education*. New York: Teachers College Press.

Nutbrown, C. (1994) *Threads of Thinking: Young Children Learning and the Role of Early Education*. London: Paul Chapman.

Osborn, M. (1995) Not a seamless robe: A tale of two teachers' responses to policy change. Paper presented to European Conference on Educational Research, Bath, September.

Paley, V.G. (1984) *Boys and Girls: Superheroes in the Doll Corner*. Chicago: University of Chicago Press.

Paley, V.G. (1995) Akemi. In A. Pollard and J. Bourne (eds) *Teaching and Learning in the Primary School*. London: Routledge.

Parker-Rees, R. (1997) The tale of a task: Learning beyond the map. In A. Pollard, D. Thiessen and A. Filer (eds) *Children and their Curriculum: The Perspectives of Primary and Elementary School Children*. London: Falmer Press.

Pinsent, P. (1992) (ed.) *Language, Culture and Young Children*. London: David Fulton.

Pollard, A., Broadfoot, P., Croll, P., Osborn, M. and Abbott, D. (1994) *Changing English Primary Schools? The Impact of the Education Reform Act at Key Stage 1*. London: Cassell.

Purkey, W. (1970) *Self Concept and School Achievement*. London: Paul Chapman.

Pyke, N. (1997) British pride cures racism, Tate argues. In *Times Educational Supplement*, 23 May, 3.

Reid, D. (1992) Linguistic diversity and equality. In P. Pinsent (ed.) *Language, Culture and Young Children*. London: David Fulton.

Rennie, J. (1996) Working with parents. In G. Pugh (ed.) *Contemporary Issues in the Early Years: Working Collaboratively for Children* (pp. 189–208). London: Paul Chapman.

Rex, J. (1986) Equality of opportunity and the ethnic minority child in British schools. In S. Mogdil, S.K. Verma, K. Mallick and C. Mogdil (eds) *Multicultural Education: The Interminable Debate*. Lewes: Falmer Press.

Riley, J. (1996) *The Teaching of Reading: The Development of Literacy in the Early Years of School*. London: Paul Chapman.

Rivers, W.M. (1969) From skill aquisition to language control. *TESOL Quarterly* 3(1), 3–12.

Rix, C. and Boyle, M. (1995) 'I think I know what you mean'. *Primary Science Review* 37, 19–21.

Romaine, S. (1989) *Bilingualism*. Oxford: Basil Blackwell.

Rosen, B. (1988) *And None of It was Nonsense: The Power of Storytelling in Schools*. England: Mary Glasgow.

Rosen, H. (1982) *Stories and Meanings*. Northamptonshire: NATE.

Said, E. (1994) *Culture and Imperialism*. London: Vintage.

Savva, H. (1994) Bilingual by rights. In A. Pollard and J. Bourne (eds) *Teaching and Learning in the Primary School*. London: Routledge.

Sawar, A. (1994) *British Muslims and Schools*. Muslim Educational Trust, 130 Stroud Green Road, London N4 3RZ.

Schön, D.A. (1983) *The Reflective Practitioner: How Professionals Think in Action*. London: Temple Smith.

School Curriculum and Assessment Authority (SCAA) (1996) *A Guide to the National Curriculum*. Middlesex: SCAA Publications.

School Curriculum and Assessment Authority (SCAA) (1997) *Looking at Children's Learning: Desirable Outcomes for Children's Learning on Entering Compulsory Education*. Middlesex: SCAA Publications.

Schutz, A. (1971) The stranger. In B.R. Cosin, I.R. Dale, G.H. Esland and D.F. Swift (eds) *School and Society: A Sociological Reader* (2nd edn). London: Routledge.

Selman, R.L. (1981) The child as a friendship philosopher. In S.R. Asher and J.M. Gottman (eds) *The Development of Children's Friendships*. Cambridge: Cambridge University Press.

Sharp, R. and Green, A. (1975) *Education and Social Control: A Study in Progressive Primary Education*. London: Routledge and Kegan Paul.

Short, G. and Carrington, B. (1996) Anti-racist education, multiculturalism and the new racism. *Educational Review* 48 (1), 65–77.

Singh, G. (1993) *Equality and Education*. Derby: Albrighton Publications.

Siraj-Blatchford, I. (1992) Why understanding cultural differences is not enough. In G. Pugh (ed.) *Contemporary Issues in the Early Years*. London: Paul Chapman.

Siraj-Blatchford, I. (1994) *The Early Years: Laying the Foundation for Racial Equality*. Stoke-on-Trent: Trentham Books.

Siraj-Blatchford, I. (1996a) Language, culture and difference: Challenging inequality and promoting respect. In C. Nutbrown (ed.) *Children's Rights and Early Education* (pp. 23–33). London: Paul Chapman.

Siraj-Blatchford, I. (1996b) Values, culture and identity in early childhood education. *International Journal of Early Years Education* 4 (2), 63–69.

Skutnabb-Kangas, T. (1981) *Bilingualism or Not: The Education of Minorities*. Clevedon: Multilingual Matters.

Sofer, A. (1996) Beyond the shock horror headlines. *Times Educational Supplement* 10, May 19.

Steedman, C. (1988) The mother made conscious: The historical development of a primary school pedagogy. In M. Woodhead and A. McGrath (eds) *Family, School and Society*. London: Hodder and Stoughton.

Stevenson, C. (1992) Language and learning in the multicultural nursery. In P. Pinsent (ed.) *Language, Culture and Young Children* (pp. 26–36). London: David Fulton.

Stone, G.P. (1962) Appearance and the self. In A.M. Rose (ed.) *Human Behaviour and Social Processes*. London: Routledge.

Sullivan, H.S. (1953) *The Interpersonal Theory of Psychiatry*. New York: Norton.

Sutton-Smith, B. (1975) quoted in Gura, P. (ed.) directed by Bruce, T. (1992) *Exploring Learning: Young Children and Blockplay*. London: Paul Chapman.

Sylva, K., Roy, C. and Painter, M. (1980) *Childwatching at Playgroup and Nursery*. London: Grant McIntyre.

Tajfel, H. (1981) *Human Groups and Social Categories: Studies in Social Categories*. Cambridge: Cambridge University Press.

Taylor, C. (1992) The politics of recognition. In A. Gutmann (ed.) *Multiculturalism and the 'Politics of Recognition'*. Princeton: Princeton University Press.

Thomas, G. (1986) 'Hallo, Miss Scatterbrain; hallo, Mr Strong': Assessing nursery attitudes and behaviour. In N.Browne and P. France (eds) *Untying the Apron Strings*. Milton Keynes: Open University Press.

Tizard, B. and Hughes, M. (1984) *Young Children Learning: Talking and Thinking, at Home and at School*. London: Fontana Press.

Tomlinson, S. (1993) The multicultural task group: The group that never was. In A. King and M. Reiss (eds) *The Multicultural Dimension of the National Curriculum*. London: Falmer Press.

Tomlinson, S. (1995) Education for All in the 1990s. In S. Tomlinson and M. Craft (eds) *Ethnic Relations and Schooling*. London: Athlone Press.

Torkington, K. (1986) Involving parents in the primary curriculum. In P. Preece (ed.) *Involving Parents in the Primary Curriculum: Perspectives 24*. Exeter: School of Education, University of Exeter.

Troyna, B. (1991) Underachievers or under-rated? The experience of pupils of South Asian origin in a secondary school. *British Educational Research Journal* 17 (4), 361–376.

Troyna, B. (1995) The local management of schools and racial equality. In S. Tomlinson and M. Craft (eds) *Ethnic Relations and Schooling*. London: Athlone Press.

Tuckwell, P. (1982) Pleasing teacher. In T. Booth and J. Statham (eds) *The Nature of Special Education*. London: Croom Helm.

Tyler, E.B. (1871) quoted by E. Chinoy (1967) in *Society: An Introduction to Society*. New York: Random House.

Verma, G.K. (1984) Multicultural education: Prelude to practice. In G.K. Verma and C. Bagley (eds) *Race Relations and Cultural Differences*. Beckenham: Croom Helm.

Vincent, C. (1995) School, community and ethnic minority parents. In S. Tomlinson and M. Craft (eds) *Ethnic Relations and Schooling*. London: Athlone Press.

Vincent, C. (1996) *Parents and Teachers, Power and Participation*. London: Falmer Press.

Vygotsky, L. (1978) *Mind in Society: The Development of Higher Psychological Processes*. London: Harvard University Press.

Wagner, D.A. (1993) *Literacy, Culture and Development: Becoming Literate in Morocco*. Cambridge: Cambridge University Press.

Walkerdine, V. (1981) Sex, power and pedagogy. *Screen Education* 38, 1–24.

Waterhouse, S.R. (1991) *First Episodes: Pupil Careers in the Early Years of School*. London: Falmer Press.

Watson, A. (1993) Parents and equal opportunities. In H. Claire, J. Maybin and J. Swann (eds) *Equality Matters: Case Studies from the Primary School* (pp. 176–186). Clevedon: Multilingual Matters.

Wells, G. (1987) *The Meaning-makers: Children Learning Language and Using Language to Learn.* Sevenoaks: Hodder and Stoughton.

Wiles, S. (1985) Language and learning in multi-ethnic classrooms: Strategies for supporting bilingual students. In G. Wells and J. Nicholls (eds) *Language and Learning: An Interactional Perspective* (pp. 83–93). Lewes: Falmer Press.

Wilkins, D.A. (1986) cited in Sawar, G. (1994) *British Muslims and Schools.* Muslim Educational Trust, 130 Stroud Green Road, London N4 3RZ.

Wolfendale, S. and Topping, K. (1996) *Family Involvement in Literacy: Effective Partnerships in Education.* London: Cassell.

Woodhead, C. (1995) *Chief Inspector's Annual Report.* London: OFSTED.

Woodhead, C. (1996) *Chief Inspector's Annual Report.* London: OFSTED.

Woodhead, M. (1990) Psychology and the cultural construction of children's needs. In A. James and A. Prout (eds) *Constructing and Reconstructing Childhood: Contemporary Issues in the Sociological Study of Childhood.* London: Falmer Press.

Woods, P. (1979) *The Divided School.* London: Routledge.

Woods, P. (1983) *Sociology and the School.* London: Routledge.

Woods, P. (1986) *Inside Schools: Ethnography in Educational Research.* London: Routledge.

Woods, P. (1990) *The Happiest Days? How Pupils Cope with School.* London: Falmer Press.

Woods, P. (1993) *Critical Events in Teaching and Learning.* London: Falmer Press.

Woods, P. (1994) Adaptation and self-determination in English primary schools. *Oxford Review of Education* 20 (4), 387–410.

Woods, P. (1995) *Creative Teachers in Primary Schools.* Buckingham: Open University Press.

Woods, P. (1996a) *Researching the Art of Teaching.* London: Routledge.

Woods, P. (1996b) *The Social World of the Pupil, Unit 11 of Course EU208, Exploring Educational Issues.* Milton Keynes: Open University Press.

Woods, P. and Jeffrey, R.J. (1996) *Teachable Moments: The Art of Teaching in Primary Schools.* Buckingham: Open University Press.

Woods, P., Boyle, M. and Hubbard, N. (1997) *Child-meaningful Learning: The Experiences of Bilingual Children in the Early Years.* Final Report to the ESRC.

Woods, P., Jeffrey, B., Troman, G. and Boyle, M. (1997) *Restructuring Schools, Reconstructing Teachers.* Buckingham: Open University Press.

Woods, P. and Pollard, A. (eds) (1988) *Sociology and Teaching.* London: Croom Helm.

Wright, C. (1993) Early education: Multiracial primary school classrooms. In R. Gomm and P. Woods (eds) *Educational Research in Action.* London: Paul Chapman.

Index

Author Index

Abbott, L. 24
Acker, S. 18
Alexander, R. 2, 4, 18, 30
Allan, G. 161
Apple, M.W. 2, 84
Athey, C. 206
Austen, S. 113

Baker, C. 76, 112
Barrs, M. 89, 112
Bennett, N. 67, 137
Berger, P.L. 118
Bernstein, B. 120, 182
Best, D. 3
Biott, C. 9
Blackledge, A. 112-3
Blenkin, G. 118
Bourne, J. 185
Boyle, M. 8, 18, 24, 28-9, 75, 129
Brehony, K. 13, 71
Bruce, T. 24, 66-7, 87, 137, 150
Bruner, J. 16, 17, 38, 95, 147
Burns, T. 117
Byrne, D. 168

Campbell, R.J. 1, 2
Carr, W. 9
Carrington, B. 168
Chinoy, E. 32, 118
Clarricoates, K. 164
Cocklin, B. 205-6
Cooper, P. 2
Craft, M. 2
Cummins, J. 21, 38
Curtis, A. 2

David, T. 2, 3, 13, 24, 38, 68, 150, 207
Davies, B. 170, 177
Day, C.W. 9
Dearing, R. vii, x, 33, 45, 59

Deb, M. 114
Deegan, J.G. 183
Denscombe, M. 174
Derman-Sparks, L. 28
Drummond, M.J. 60
Durkheim E. 32, 118
Duveen, G. 157, 166-7, 182
Dyer, M. 48

Edwards, A. 117
Edwards, D. 3, 16, 65, 147
Edwards, V. 37, 63, 108, 209
Eisner, E.W. 136
Emblem, V. 39, 62
Ervin-Tripp, S.M. 146
Evans, L. 1, 2

Fagot, B. I. 164
Ferdman, B.M. 65
Fox, C. 98, 111, 112-3, 130

Galton M. 171
Garcha, J. 43
Gay, G. 167
Gillborn, D. x, 60
Gipps, C. 2
Glauert, E. 49
Goalen, P. 49
Goffman, E. 117, 126, 157
Grace, G. 2
Gravelle, M. 155-6, 185
Green, A. 2
Gregory, E. 42-3, 90, 102, 110, 114, 124, 156
Griffith, A. 205
Grosjean, F. 5, 44
Guba, E.G. 8
Gura, P. 66

Halliday, M. 5
Halpin, D. 4

Subject Index